Praise for
How, Then, Shall We Live?

"In his wonderful new book, Wayne Muller asks the most important questions of life—not to provide pat answers, but as a guide to the clarity, openness and freedom in the asking. Through this book we can gratefully touch what it really means to be alive."

—Sharon Salzberg, founder of the
Insight Meditation Society and author of
Loving-Kindness: The Revolutionary Art of Happiness

"In this wise and comforting book, Muller, by delving beyond jargon and theory, offers a glimpse into the heart of living well."
—*Publishers Weekly*

"A wonderful exploration of the weight, the breadth, and the possible answers to our ultimate queries. This one should be read slowly and savored, with many pauses for reflection on one's own answers."

—*NAPRA ReView*

"With tenderness and compassion, clarity and insight, [Muller] guides us on a journey of awakening and healing. . . . A wonderful, enchanting book."

—Editor's Choice, *Bodhi Tree Book Review*

"In more than twenty years of practice as a therapist and spiritual counselor, Wayne Muller has enabled people to tap the divine source within and to make use of the wisdom learned from pain. *How, Then, Shall We Live?* vividly and compellingly describes what a path with heart really means."

—*Body Mind Spirit*

"This fine book speaks in a gentle voice that penetrates a reader's whole being."

—Natalie Goldberg, author of
Writing Down the Bones and *Wild Mind*

four
simple questions
that reveal the
beauty and meaning
of our lives

HOW, THEN, SHALL WE LIVE?

Wayne Muller

BANTAM BOOKS

New York   Toronto   London
Sydney   Auckland

HOW, THEN, SHALL WE LIVE?
A Bantam Book

PUBLISHING HISTORY
Bantam hardcover edition published July 1996
Bantam trade paperback edition / June 1997

Copyright © 1996 by Wayne Muller
Cover design copyright © 1996 by E. Nagele/FPG
Library of Congress Catalog Card Number: 96-825

ISBN 0-553-37505-9

Published simultaneously in the United States and Canada

Bantam Books are published by Bantam Books, a division of
Random House, Inc. Its trademark, consisting of the words "Bantam
Books" and the portrayal of a rooster, is Registered in U.S. Patent
and Trademark Office and in other countries. Marca Registrada.
Bantam Books, 1540 Broadway, New York, New York 10036.

PRINTED IN THE UNITED STATES OF AMERICA

20 19 18 17 16 15 14 13 12 11

I dedicate this book to my children,
Sherah and Maxwell.

May they be happy, wise, and kind.

Acknowledgments

I WANT TO THANK all those who invited me to be a part of their healing, especially those whose stories appear within these pages. I am grateful for their loving company on this challenging and fruitful journey.

I also thank everyone who, through their lives, their companionship, and their suggestions, taught me to listen carefully to the meaning of these questions and helped me write with more precision and accuracy: Dottie Montoya, Max Cordova, Jone and Cullen Hallmark, Julie Daniel, Katherine Shelton, Owen Lopez, Henrietta Calderon, Paul Glick, Kenneth Siciliano, Peter Djordjevich, Dr. Fred Ey, Peter Guardino, Ed Broderick, Herbie Mann, Sharon Salzberg, Steve Chambers, Marcy Grace, Ben and Carolyn Whitehill, S. J. Sanchez, Henri Nouwen, Dr. Richard Heckler, Stephen and Ondrea Levine, Jack Kornfield, and many others who have given so much. And it would be impossible to express the fullness of my gratitude to my dear friend Dr. Trevor Hawkins, a man who has cared for the lives of so many, and who also happened to literally save mine as well, just as I was completing this book.

I am grateful for all those individuals who have supported the work of Bread for the Journey, through their time and generous donations of critically needed funds. I also want to especially thank the McCune Foundation for their faith in us, and for their innumerable gifts to the people of northern New Mexico.

Thanks also to Jennifer and Jeffrey for generously allowing me to use their home to finish this manuscript.

As always, I am grateful for my friend and agent Loretta Barrett, a loving and ethical beacon by which many of us guide our way. And I am deeply indebted to Toni Burbank, a consummate editor and artist, and a delightful colleague. Her infallible ear and persistent companionship have helped make this book come alive.

And finally, of course, for Christine Tiernan, my best friend and dharma sister. Her beauty, her wisdom, and her company are blessings beyond measure.

Contents

Prelude·
The Four Questions

FOUR SIMPLE QUESTIONS have shaped the spiritual journeys of pilgrims and seekers for thousands of years. They call forth the very nature of who we are and how we live our brief time on the earth.

Many of us, distracted by the rush and pressure of our days, manage to suppress or ignore these fundamental questions—until we are confronted with something that wakes us up, and we begin to listen to how things really are in our life. Perhaps we face a divorce, a change of employment, a move, some inexplicable spiritual experience, a grave illness, the birth of a child, or the death of a loved one. Or perhaps something that used to feed or satisfy us now seems strangely over or complete. We feel pulled in a new direction; one phase of our life journey has ended, and a new one is beginning—but we do not know where it will lead us. Where do we find the map for this new path?

When we meditate upon these four questions, they reveal the true nature of our love and our strength, our courage, and our wisdom. They allow us to break free, to grow beyond what we already know. And through them we glimpse that relentless spark of spiritual magic that burns within each of us, a spark that can light our way as we venture forth.

In this book I offer these questions as contemplations, something to hold in the hand as we walk, something to feel in the heart as we live our daily lives. They enable us to gently awaken the four fundamental realms of the inner life: **Identity, Love, Daily Practice,** and **Kindness.**

Who am I?

Beneath all the stories of our past, beneath our joys and sorrows, we have within us an essential nature that is whole and unbroken. What is this true nature, and how do we find it? If we can take nourishment from this inner strength and wisdom, we will find great peace and courage.

What do I love?

By what star do we navigate our journey on the earth? What we love will shape our days and provide the texture for our inner and outer life. How can we plant what we love in the garden of this life?

How shall I live, knowing I will die?

Every moment in this life is a precious gift. In our brief time here, what qualities do we wish to cultivate? If we are aware of our mortality, we can live less by accident and live instead with clarity and purpose.

What is my gift to the family of the earth?

Each of us has a gift to bring to the table, and the family of the earth yearns to receive it. How do we uncover our true gift? How do we balance giving and receiving? And where can we find the confidence to offer our gift freely and happily?

These are the questions that shape our lives, and they have no final answers. They remain with us, companions in our spiritual unfolding. *"Live* the questions now," wrote Rilke to his young poet friend. "Perhaps you will then gradually, without noticing it, live along some distant day into the answer."

I have included in this book stories of ordinary people who confronted crucial moments in their lives and listened carefully to the questions that arose within them. In most cases, I have changed their names for privacy, but I have tried to faithfully convey how each responded to this call to a life of greater meaning and beauty. I invariably felt privileged to be a part of their lives, and I feel equally blessed to be able to share them with you.

the
first
part

❖

WHO AM I?

❖

A Hidden Wholeness

> There is in all visible things . . .
> a hidden wholeness.
>
> —THOMAS MERTON

MANY SPIRITUAL TRADITIONS and practices begin with a single question: Who am I? The question is a persistent and intimate companion. The search for our essence, our identity, is fundamental; it is as necessary for individuals as for nations, tribes, races, and spiritual communities. Who am I? Am I spirit or flesh? Am I sacred or secular? Am I irrevocably shaped by the circumstances of my personal history, or am I still free to move and grow, to uncover a new and brighter path? Am I fragile or am I strong, am I broken or am I whole? When I listen deeply to my inner life, what do I hear? What is the substance of my soul, the core of my being? What is my true nature?

Jesus said, "You are the light of the world." What does this mean, to be the light of the world? In the same manner the Buddha, in his parting words of comfort and advice to his disciples, insisted: "Be lamps unto yourselves; be your own confidence. Hold to the truth within yourselves as the only truth." We are, he said, all Buddhas, filled with divine nature.

How do we find this nature? The instant we begin to look deep inside ourselves, we often discover what we perceive as imperfections in our character and personality, and we confront any lingering doubts we may have about our spiritual worthiness. Perhaps we begin our spiritual journey by trying to rid ourselves of everything that is wrong with us, to cleanse ourselves of our negative qualities, to purify ourselves of our defects—in short, to become like the saints. But perhaps the more gentle and ultimately more accurate path is the one that leads us directly into the fertile garden of our own spirit, into what Merton calls our "hidden wholeness." Our most fruitful practice is the one that most gently leads us into ourselves just as we are, into the innate perfection of our true nature.

When the time came for Jesus to be baptized, he went to John the Baptist, a prophet preaching in the wilderness. When John baptized Jesus, the heavens opened, and the spirit of God descended like a dove and alighted upon Jesus. Then a voice from heaven spoke clearly and with great authority: "This is my Son, with whom I am well pleased." At this point in the gospel story, at his baptism in the river, we find out who Jesus really is: He is the son of God. For Jesus, this baptism marks the beginning of a long journey that will fully reveal his true identity.

Immediately after he is baptized, Jesus is led into the wilderness. He must prove to himself and to God that he understands his divine nature. There he is tempted by Satan, who tries to entice Jesus to bargain away his spiritual power for worldly comforts and powers. He tries to induce Jesus to do things that would dishonor the truth of who he is, to settle for less than his spiritual destiny. With courageous resolve Jesus refuses again and again to bargain away his allegiance to his divine birthright. Jesus finally sends Satan away, and the angels flock to minister to Jesus. Now, more clearly than ever before, Jesus can feel with absolute certainty who he is. He is a child of God.

The story of the Buddha's awakening is not unlike the Jesus story. Young Siddhartha was raised in a palace. When he grew older and discovered the inevitability of illness, old age, and death, he resolved to undertake austere ascetic practices to cleanse his mind and body, thereby attaining freedom from suffering. But his asceticism seemed to bring him only weakness and more suffering. In his most extreme moment of self-mortification, he recalled the first time he had sat in meditation, when he was nine years old, in the cool shade of a rose-apple tree. He remembered how the refreshing ease of that sitting had brought him a sense of clarity and calm. At that moment Siddhartha decided to seek a middle path, to cultivate a more gentle practice of mindful attention to the quality of his experience.

Siddhartha sat under a tree and resolved to meditate until all was revealed to him. Finally, at the rising of the morning star, he saw clearly the nature of joy and sorrow, birth and death. He saw into the nature of all things, perceiving his own true nature as well. Freed at last from the prison of ignorance and illusion, Siddhartha was now the Buddha—meaning, simply, "the one who is awake."

In the Hebrew tradition, the prophet Jeremiah was a passionate defender of the spiritual path. Jeremiah spoke eloquently and often to the people of Jerusalem, urging them to remember their relationship with their God. In one exquisite Old Testament passage, Jeremiah has awakened from a dream in which God offers to renew the intimate covenant with the people of Jerusalem, promising to remain within and among them forever: "Behold, I will put my law within them, and I will write it upon their hearts, and I will be their God, and they will be my people."

In everyday life this recognition of our fundamental identity may not be quite so dramatic as it was for Jesus, the Buddha, or Jeremiah, but our acknowledgment of who we are is no less precious or necessary. Whether we call ourselves father or mother, lover or friend, weak or strong, Democrat or Republican, the naming of who we are will set the course of our life, determine what we love, how we live, and what gifts we will bring to the family of the earth.

If we are unsure of who we are, we will live tentatively, always guessing at where we should go and what we should do. But when we know who we are and feel comfortable with ourselves, we can live clearly and courageously. Bolstered by a strong sense of our own nature, assisted by reliable inner voices, we are guided toward what is necessary and right.

Jack Kornfield, a friend and respected teacher of Buddhism in the West, relates the following story:

There is a tribe in Africa where the birth date of a child is counted—not from when they're born, nor from when they are conceived—but from the day that the child was a thought in its mother's mind.

And when a woman decides that she will have a child, she goes off and sits under a tree, by herself, and she listens until she can hear the song of the child that wants to come. And after she's heard the song of this child, she comes back to the man who will be the child's father, and she teaches it to him. And then, when they make love to physically conceive the child, some of that time they sing the song of the child, as a way to invite it.

And then, when the mother is pregnant, the mother teaches that child's song to the midwives and the old women of the village, so that when the child is born, the old women and the people around her sing the child's song to welcome it. And then, as the child grows up, the other villagers are taught the child's song. If the child falls, or hurts its knee, someone picks it up and sings its song to it. Or perhaps the child does something wonderful, or goes through the rites of puberty—then as a way of honoring this person, the people of the village sing his or her song.

And it goes this way through their life—in marriage, the songs are sung, together. And finally, when this child is lying in bed, ready to die, all the villagers know his or her song, and they sing—for the last time—the song to that person.

What is our song? How do we name ourselves? Which word, when we speak it, reveals what is most deeply true about this inner voice, our deepest heart, our fundamental nature?

Every time I ask myself this question, it drives me a little deeper—and each time the answer reveals a little more about the complexion of my life. When I am "child of an alcoholic," I feel small and afraid. When I am "therapist," I feel caring, sometimes grateful, sometimes grandiose, sometimes overwhelmed. When I am "father," I feel responsible, watchful. When I am "minister," I feel peaceful, although at times self-important or pretentious. Each name brings a way of seeing and responding to the world; I walk differently, with a different gait, a different balance.

The more time I spend on the earth, the more I yearn to go deeper, to find the place that lies beneath these names. For the last ten years, I have practiced various forms of meditation. Meditation helps me feel the shape, the texture of my inner life. Here, in the quiet, I can begin to taste what Buddhists would call my true nature, what Jews call the still, small voice, what Christians call the holy spirit.

When I am able to listen carefully, I find that in meditation I discover that even my inner identity is always changing. In those moments when I sit quietly, I gradually become aware of particular sensations as they arise and fall away in the body and mind. The more I listen, the clearer these sensations become. I may feel the sensation of "tired," for example, or "stiff," or "hungry." These are simply sensations arising. Similarly, I feel the rising and falling of the breath as it seems to breathe itself in rhythm. Likewise I may feel sadness, joy, fear, or peace, one following another. None of the sensations remains the same. So is it not possible that we ourselves are changing all the while? With every breath, the possibility of a new aspect of self arises.

Can it then be that what we call the "self" is fluid and elastic? It evolves, strikes a different balance with every new breath. Our "self," like all living things, expands and contracts: the heart opens and closes, the lungs and abdomen rise and fall, the earth itself as it moves through space expands and contracts through the seasons—winter, spring, summer, fall, winter. When we cease to move in this way, we die. In fact, this is the very definition of death: a cessation of expansion and contraction in the organism.

In Zen monasteries, there are certain roles that must be filled if the monastery is to work efficiently. There is the cook, the gardener, the keeper of discipline, the housekeeper, the caregiver of the zendo, the one who chops wood, and so on. Students are assigned one of these roles for a period of time, a year or two, so that they come to know themselves in this role. One student may be assigned cooking, another the keeping of discipline. The cook may come to know him or herself as an important hub of the community, nourishing everyone, taking care to prepare the food with reverence, receiving everyone's gratitude. The keeper of discipline may be forced to use the stick to keep sleepy students awake and to correct those who are lazy in their practice.

Then, the following year, the cook may be assigned to clean toilets. Now the teachings are about cleanliness, service, and humility. Similarly, the disciplinarian may now become the caregiver of the temple, providing cushions for the monks, tending to the sick, and attending to a host of needs. Again, the shift from disciplinarian to caregiver allows the sense of self to remain flexible. We cannot hold for too long to an idea of self; it is all in flux. Who we are changes with every moment, every breath. The roles we play can remind us that we are always changing. There is nothing solid.

DENISE'S BROTHER MARK was dying of AIDS. He had come to live with her, to ready himself for his death. Denise came to see me because she was confused and frightened. She loved her brother very much, and she did not know how she could watch him die. She worried she would not be strong enough. She didn't want him to go.

Mark had recently been experiencing transient ischemic attacks, or small strokes, common to people with certain neurological conditions. These strokes are relatively minor and in themselves not completely debilitating, but cumulatively they take away portions of brain function. Over time they can result in significant mental deterioration.

Denise told me that watching Mark have these strokes was particularly difficult because when she was a child she had watched her father go through the same thing; a similar series of strokes. Then she told me something fascinating. "My father was a confirmed, relentless smoker. Even when he was sick, he continued to smoke. My mother hated it and kept telling him to quit, but he would have none of it.

"Then one morning, after one of these small strokes, when my dad woke up he forgot he was a smoker! He just forgot to smoke! I guess the part of his brain that believed himself to be a smoker was simply erased. Gone. From that moment, he never smoked again. Cold turkey. He never had any withdrawal symptoms, no aftereffects, no problems. He no longer craved a cigarette, didn't even think about it."

I thought this was an amazing story. I asked Denise to repeat it so I could be sure that I understood what had happened. The implications were delightful: What if our personality, our "self," is so thoroughly elastic that we can simply "forget" to be one kind of person and "remember" to be another kind of person?

Occasionally, when we find ourselves trapped in a single facet of our life, we feel smothered by the smallness of who we have become. We feel we are only this or that—only child of divorce, only manager, mother, cancer patient. We walk on the earth compressed by a certain narrowness of life. What if—like the man who forgot he was a smoker—we can recall the flexibility we carry within us always, moving more easily through the roles and responsibilities of our lives?

Buddhists use the example of the Big Dipper to describe the self. If we look at the constellation from our vantage point here on the earth, this particular group of stars looks a great deal like a big dipper. It looks as if it could actually hold water. But if we leave the earth and travel closer to this group of stars, we soon see the pattern break up, and eventually the image of the dipper disintegrates altogether. There is no dipper, big or little—it is merely a collection of perceptions. What we call "dipper" is an illusion. So it is with our experience of our psychological identity. The collection of emotions, feelings, and sensations merely looks and feels like something solid, when in fact it is a constantly shifting aggregate of perceptions, with nothing solid there at all.

Who do we believe ourselves to be? Do we believe we are a solid entity, something that does not change? Does the "I" inside feel self-contained, complete in itself, defined by clear, reliable boundaries? What if we are more fluid and elastic than we imagine? Can we imagine how flexible our identity must be? If our personality is supposed to be set in stone, a firm and necessary outgrowth of our childhood trauma, we cease to believe we can move and change. But we are more elastic than we imagine. Our true nature can take shape in a million forms, all unique and useful in their own way. Perhaps we are infinitely malleable in the way we walk on the earth. Perhaps we are not prisoners of our history.

YEARS AGO, during my first week-long silent meditation retreat, one of the first things I uncovered in my body was deep sorrow. Where was this sadness coming from? Was it from my childhood? Was it the hurt I had absorbed from all those who had suffered? Was it something larger—was I feeling the pain of the whole world? Perhaps it was all these, what Buddhists call *bodhicitta,* "the tender heart of awakening." But after a while the source of the sorrow became less and less interesting, less important. I needed only to acknowledge the deep ache in my chest and belly. Sometimes it would fill me up to overflowing, this sadness, I thought I would drown in it. Then it would spill out of my eyes as warm tears, turning cool as they fell from my chin. Still, I kept silence.

Then it got quiet, quieter than ever. And I began to sense something beneath even the sorrow. I could feel a place inside, below all my names, my stories, my injuries, my sadness—a place that lived in my breath. I did not know what to call it, but it had a voice, a way of speaking to me about what was true, what was right. And along with this voice came a presence, an indescribable sense of well-being that reminded me that whatever pain or sorrow I would be given, there was something inside strong enough to bear the weight of it. It would rise to meet whatever I was given. It would teach me what to do.

All my life I have felt this presence; but at that moment I could feel its fundamental integrity. As I think back upon my life to the times when I have been lost or confused, I realize that whenever I have ignored this voice I have quickly found myself in even more confusion. There is something inside me that has—for as long as I can remember, since I was very small—always guided me toward what was right and true. I also realize that when I am too busy, rushed, or preoccupied, I rarely take the time to listen. It is this unconsciousness—this desperate unwillingness to be quiet enough to hear what I essentially know to be true—that has been the cause of much of my suffering in this life.

Unfortunately, I can recall many times when—out of fear, pride, or simple stubbornness—I did not heed these intuitive rumblings in my soul. When I was twelve, I fell in with a group of tough boys in the neighborhood and quickly found myself involved in a ring of shoplifting and vandalism. It took me almost a year to extricate myself from these hard-drinking and smoking delinquents. I had known that what I was doing was wrong, but I felt compelled to ignore my inner guide in order to keep their companionship at any price—something I desperately needed at a very lonely time in my young life.

Later, striking out on my own, I recall taking on a difficult roommate simply because the person asked to stay in my house—even though my inner voice insisted from the start that it would be a bad mix. When it inevitably ended months later in a terrible fight, I resolved to pay closer attention to whom I could honestly befriend and whom I could not. Similarly, I remember taking a job with a governmental organization, with a supervisor whom I knew I did not respect. She was a troubled and spiteful person and habitually hurt those who worked for her. My inner voice told me it could never work between us, and I should have left immediately and sought other employment. But, ignoring any wisdom I might have had, I constantly sought ways to please her, redoubling my efforts each day, though no amount of effort on my part would dissuade her from demeaning me and her staff at every turn. Again, when I finally left that painfully uncomfortable position, I resolved to honor the usefulness of this reliable inner guide.

Neither my pain nor my confusion can stop the relentless companionship of this true and faithful voice. Something more vital, strong, and true lies embedded deep within me. Sometimes I barely see it, can't quite touch it. Then I will experience a starry night, a forest after the rain, a loving embrace, a strain of sweet and perfect melody—and that is all it takes to remind me who I am: a spirit, alive, and whole. It helps me remember my nature, hear my name.

IN THE LAST CENTURY—since the writings of Freud indelibly transformed the landscape of human thought about our interior life—we have learned to use the language of psychology to categorize ourselves. We have been reluctant to say, "I am the light of the world," and more likely to confess, "I am neurotic; a child of an alcoholic; a manic-depressive; a codependent; an adult child of family dysfunction; an overachiever; an incest survivor; an addict," and so forth. While these names may be accurate in some particular way, tracing the legacy of early trauma, they are limiting and inadequate in the largest sense. They cannot describe our true and deepest nature.

I am often asked to lead spiritual retreats for people who want to heal their emotional wounds and at the same time hope to deepen and enrich their spiritual life. When we gather, we quickly discover that we all share some measure of human sorrow and that there is much nourishment and succor to be found in the spiritual teachings and practices that are available to us. Through discussion, prayer, quiet meditation, and creative exercises, we try to uncover the natural wisdom and courage we need to live our lives fully and well.

At one of these retreats there was a woman named Angela. She took me aside during a break and told me she felt separate from the others, set apart from the group. Our group felt so close, intimate, and loving—yet Angela still felt removed, isolated. She wanted to be a part of us. She had, she said, been sexually abused as a child. When she was small, she had been touched. Touched by hands with no kindness in them. This had made her always wary of intimate contact with others. She desperately wanted to belong but did not know how, or if it could ever be safe. I asked her if she wanted to explore this with me in front of the rest of the group. She hesitated and then said yes. She was frightened and nervous, but the pain of being separate was too much to bear for the rest of her life. She wanted to see if this could be healed.

When we all returned, I asked Angela to sit next to me, in the front of the room. *Tell me what happened,* I asked.

She wanted to speak, but her throat was closed, her breath labored. "I was hurt. I was abused." Quiet, thin, painful words.

Tell me about the abuse.

"There was anger, and emotional abuse."

Tell me what else.

"There was sexual abuse, and my mother didn't protect me. I think I am more angry at my mother for not protecting me than at my stepfather for abusing me." Her lip trembled ever so slightly. Perhaps only I could see it, for I was sitting very close to her. I held her eye with my own. Her eyes were wary, like a deer.

Tell me about the abuse. My voice was soft. I felt soft inside.

"I was abused sexually," she said.

Part of her wanted to end there and wanted me to begin my work—tinkering, repairing, healing. Others in the room wanted her to stop. It was too private, tender, intimate. They ached for her, and for their own anguish, whatever lay unspoken and unnamed within them. Some silently urged her deeper, yearning for the truth to be spoken aloud—for her, for all who have suffered. We all waited in that breath.

Tell me what happened, I said.

"I would wake up in the morning, and he would be touching me." Her eyes were moist now, her breathing difficult.

Touching you where, I asked gently, breathing in rhythm with her breath.

"All over," she replied. And wept.

I asked her if there was someone else in the room she trusted. She chose Mary, a friend who had come with her, someone who loved her very much, someone who knew her sorrow. I asked Mary to stand behind her, touch her shoulders, speak softly of her care, her devotion. To stand with her, in the deepest way.

I then asked a man, Thomas, to sit in front of her. To stand for the one who hurt, the one who betrayed, the one who violated. Angela continued to weep quietly.

Tell me where you feel the pain, I asked.

"In my chest, right here," she explained, pointing to her heart.

I asked her to place her hand over the place where the hurt was strongest. *What does it say? What words does this pain need to speak?*

She fell silent, going inside, listening. "I don't belong to you," she said finally. "I will not be hurt by you."

Please say this to Thomas, to this man, to the one who brought you this suffering.

"I don't belong to you. I will not let you hurt me." Her voice was thin, restrained, the words reluctant to be spoken aloud. There was a deep conflict. Should she be allowed to speak this truth, out of this darkness?

Again, I asked.

"I don't belong to you. I will not be hurt by you."

With each repetition, I urged her to feel the place deep in her body where the words were true and powerful and right. After many times, the sound became louder—a shout, then a scream, words and tears rising together. All of us in the room seemed to breathe together with her. We could taste the imminent possibility of freedom.

Then for a single breath she was quiet again. There was

no need for language; a knowing was taking form inside her. A truth was making itself clear, a certainty was being born.

"I don't belong to you." She said. Now her voice was clear, unshaking, precise. The truth of her words made dramatic emotion unnecessary. Angela simply spoke the truth, calmly, easily. "I will not let you hurt me." She repeated this a few times, finally with a giggle. It felt so easy and true in her chest. "I don't belong to you." She laughed. "I won't let you hurt me." Speaking these words, she was finished with him.

In this moment Angela was beginning to rename herself. As she felt the truth of what she said, a calm assurance took root. There were strength and courage where there had been fear. She now felt the truth of her identity. She was no longer simply a victim of her stepfather's story, but rather claimed herself as the primary subject of her *own* story. Before, she had taken her name through what he had done to her. Now, his actions were no longer able to name her.

She was not simply a child of abuse. She did not belong to her abuser. She possessed her own spirit, her own nature, something free and whole that could never, ever belong to someone else. With this confidence, she could now begin to find her place in our group, bringing her own strength to the circle—a little tentative, but a little less afraid.

There was once a man whose ax was missing, and he suspected that his neighbor's son had stolen it. The boy walked like a thief, looked like a thief, and spoke like a thief. But one day the man found his ax while digging in his valley, and the next time he saw his neighbor's son, the boy walked, looked, and spoke like any other child.

What happened in this traditional German folktale? A man lost his ax. In his confusion, he concluded that his neighbor's boy was the thief. Whenever he saw the boy, the idea of *thief* was in the man's eyes. And so the boy became, for him, more and more guilty. Then when the ax was found, the boy was transformed. Now the man had the idea of *boy* in his eyes. The very same boy had become two radically different beings. The single element that determined the boy's fundamental character was the eye of the man who was seeing him.

Who do we think we are? Erik Erikson, the gentle sage of childhood development, was one of my most beloved teachers. He said, "The sense of 'I' is one of the most obvious facts of existence—indeed, perhaps *the* most obvious—and it is, at the same time, one of the most elusive." What we call our "self" is elastic; it shifts and moves. The "who" that we are depends upon the way we see. If we believe we are a thief, we will act like a criminal. If we think we are fragile and broken, we will live a fragile, broken life. If we believe we are strong and wise, we will live with enthusiasm and courage. The way we name ourselves colors the way we live. Who we are is in our eyes. "The eye is the lamp of the body," said Jesus; "if your eye is sound, your whole body will be full of light."

To begin, we must be careful how we name ourselves. Where I live, in New Mexico, Native Americans take their name from the color of the sky, or from the power characteristics of a particular animal, the way it moves on the earth or improbably defies gravity and takes its place in the air. Thus whenever they are frightened, confused, or lost, they can, by calling on their own name, remember who they are, their strength, their wisdom.

Today, people come to me bearing their diagnosis: *I am a child of a dysfunctional family. I am an alcoholic. I am a love addict.* These names are worn like shields, psychological coats of arms. They do not move, these names. They are cold and solid, like an epitaph. I am certain these names reveal little of our true nature. Beneath the stories, beneath the diagnoses, these are all children of spirit, beings fully equipped with inner voices of strength and wisdom, intimations of grace and light. But their clinical diagnoses prevent them from believing in their own wisdom. Such names suffocate people's unfolding and limit the breadth of their spiritual evolution. I

consider it my responsibility to help these individuals uncover the resilient spirit that remains whole and true even
now, beneath all these familiar diagnoses.

Many psychological theories have persuaded us that our
childhood imprint is the single most potent factor determin-
ing our identity and destiny. If we are children of divorce or
wealth or poverty or alcoholism, then we must, according
to these theories, live our lives irrevocably molded to the
shape of our early successes and failures. We are incapable of
transcending trauma; we are bent by the gravity of our weakness.

Psychology is not alone in looking at us with limited
eyes, seeing only a small part of who we are. Neurologists
see us in terms of chemical and electrical impulses; biologists
focus on structure and function and the evolutionary processes that shaped us; politicians see us as voters; economists
look at us as producers and consumers. Of course we are all
of these, and more: electricity, chemistry, matter, energy,
consumers, citizens, patients. However, in the end, each
model is limited in its capacity to accurately render our essential identity. Is there not something deeper, something that
names more deeply and carefully the way our spirit inhabits
flesh and mind?

Jesus said, "You are the light of the world." It is instructive to note that he did not say, "You are the light of the
world—if you grew up in a loving, supportive, two-parent
biological family and had no sorrow in your life." Nor did he
say, "You are the light of the world—if you were never violated or harmed, if you never had illness or grief." No, regardless of the shape of the sorrow or victory or grief or ecstasy
we have been given, there is a potent inner luminosity that is
never extinguished and is alive in us this instant. We are the
light of the world.

When Angela learned to name both her pain and her
strength, she could taste the place in her that was deeper than
her wounding, the place that was always free, never broken.
She had never allowed herself to listen deeply enough to feel
the place that had always been there, the spirit that had
never belonged to her abuser or his wounding of her. Here

was a persistent spiritual luminosity that refused to die, even in the face of her very real and tangible suffering.

The language of psychological diagnosis may be ultimately incapable of circumscribing our fundamental, spiritual nature. For this we must look deeper, to where words do not come easily, to where essential truths are uncovered more easily with poetry and prayer, with quiet, with music and dance, with loving embrace of things beloved, with prayer and meditation. It is into this investigation that I invite you.

LAST FALL I was speaking to a national conference of social workers. We were exploring this problem of diagnosing, of naming our clients through their diseases, real or imagined. Many of the social workers took me aside after my talk, confessing to me that in the privacy of their offices, they work with their "patients" by affirming the natural strength and wholeness that grows within them. And yet in order to keep their funding, to keep their jobs, they are required by clinics and insurance companies to give every person a concrete diagnosis. Without a neurotic or pathological name, people are ineligible for help. Thus we unintentionally perpetuate the practice of naming ourselves through our illnesses.

Throughout history artists, writers, teachers, lovers, mothers, gardeners, musicians, and others have spoken eloquently of the immeasurable depth and breadth of the human spirit. Here Pablo Casals, the cellist, pointedly inquires how we see ourselves and our children:

> When will we teach our children in school what they are? We should say to each of them: Do you know what you are? You are a marvel. You are unique. In all of the world there is no other child exactly like you. In the millions of years that have passed there has never been another child like you. And look at your body—what a wonder it is! your legs, your arms, your cunning fingers, the way you

move! You may become a Shakespeare, a Michel-
angelo, a Beethoven. You have the capacity for anything. Yes, you are a marvel. And when you grow
up, can you then harm another who, like you, is a
marvel?

The Hippocratic oath, taken by physicians throughout
the world, begins with this phrase: *First, do no harm.* We must
first ensure that nothing we do (including the naming of the
disease itself) produces additional suffering. This process of
diagnosis—naming ourselves only through what is broken or
defective—can fracture our sense of self. It maligns the resilience of the human spirit, ignoring any possibility of grace
that may lie embedded within the sorrow. It creates the illusion that because we suffer, we are broken, defective, handicapped beings. This, I would argue, can be as damaging as
the original hurt.

Warren came to one of our retreats. He was very sad,
having separated from his wife, who had custody of their
children. She had moved with the children to Europe, and
Warren could see them only once a year. He told us he had
come to this retreat because he needed to "deal with his
issues." Specifically, he said, "I want to deal with my issue of
missing my children."

Can we hear how quickly we use diagnostic, psychological language to transform one of the most pure, simple
human emotions—missing our children—into a psychological "issue"? The fact that we weep, that we carry sadness in
our heart, is now a psychological "problem." Clearly this is
no "issue"; it is simple human sadness. Warren is simply a
father who aches to hold his children.

When I studied with Erik Erikson, he would lead super-
vision groups for analysts in Cambridge. At one meeting a
young analyst raised his hand and told Erik of a case he was
having some difficulty with. Apparently he was working
with a man who was terminally ill. The man had very little
time to live. The analyst was becoming increasingly frustrated, he explained to Erikson, because the man simply re-

fused to deal with his issues about death. The young therapist sought Erikson's advice.

Erik took a long, quiet breath. "My friend," he said to the analyst, with gentle compassion, "death is not an issue. Death is simply death. The end of our lives. And we all come to it as we will. There is no 'issue' here at all. Go back to your patient and try to be with him as he meets his death."

The danger is that professional therapy, medicine, and treatment clinics would have us named as a collection of symptoms, defects that need to be repaired, handicaps that burden us forever, make us heavy. Because we have this or that wound, they say, we will never fly. What a blasphemy against the spirit that lives in us! We cannot be a collection of symptoms. It is simply impossible. We are children of God, of spirit, and we inherit the grace and courage and wisdom of all who have gone before. We have been given a precious and potent gift. We must reclaim the richness of the miracle of being alive.

Linda Lancione Moyer:

> *Standing in the garden,*
> *left hand laden*
>
> *with ripe strawberries. The sun*
>
> *beams off the glassy*
> *backs of flies. Three*
> *birds in the birch tree.*
>
> *They must have been there*
> *all year.*
>
> *My mother, my grandmother,*
> *stood like this*
> *in their gardens,*
>
> *I am 43.*
> *This year I have planted my feet*
> *on this ground*

and am practicing
growing up out of my legs
like a tree.

Listen: There is a delicate truth in the names of things. *Crocus, daffodil, poppy, dew, tulip, hyacinth, lilac, rose*—each name elicits a picture, a fragrance, a sense of the morning, a way of greeting the fruits of the earth in spring. The names we bestow on the things we encounter are sacraments, holy things. A name reveals a secret covenant: *willow, clover, chokecherry, jasmine.* When we hear the name, we remember the beauty, the essence of what we have named.

Jaune Quick-to-See Smith, White Buffalo Woman, Black Elk, Brave Buffalo of Standing Rock. The name reflects the spirit. I know a man named Sky. I know a man named Littlebird. Our name can help us recall the fragrance of our deepest nature. Our name not only reflects who we are—it helps us define who we will become.

We must take great care with how we name ourselves. When we take our name, we are declaring in some subtle, indescribably potent act the most intimate, sacred truth of who we believe ourselves to be. For this reason, many traditional peoples have names they keep secret—private names they reveal to no one, or only to those most intimate. Some are shared only with the divine; others, only with family or friends. To broadcast our name, to be flippant or unconscious in the speaking of it, is to trample the holiness underfoot.

JOSEPH EPES BROWN:

> Native American languages are joined to other sacred languages of the world in the sense that words are not conceived simply as symbols assigned arbitrarily to other units of meaning, as tends to be the case with our own English language. Rather, words in themselves are experienced in an immediate manner as units of power. Thus, to name a being or any element of creation is actually to make manifest the power or quality, soul or spirit, of that

which is named. For this reason words and personal sacred names tend to be used carefully in Native American Languages; one avoids using one's own or another person's sacred name, and especially, out of both respect and awe, the name of the deceased person. It is due to such a concept of language that N. Scott Momaday has titled his recent autobiography *The Names;* he tells us, "A man's life proceeds from his name, in the way that a river proceeds from its source."

The more deeply we probe our true nature, the more quickly we come to feel that there are things in us so powerful, so deep, they cannot really be named at all. In the Hebrew Torah it is told that Moses was tending the sheep of his father-in-law, Jethro. Moses led the flock into the wilderness near the holy mountain of Horeb. There an angel of the Lord appeared to Moses in the form of a burning bush—the bush was enveloped in flame but was not consumed. God called out: "Moses, I have seen the affliction of my people who are in Egypt, and have heard their cry because of their taskmasters; I know their sorrow, and I have come down to deliver them out of the hand of the Egyptians, and to bring them up out of that land to a good and broad land, a land flowing with milk and honey. . . . Come, I will send you to Pharaoh that you may bring forth my people, the sons of Israel, out of Egypt."

But Moses, uncertain of his own power and authority, said to God, "If I come to the people of Israel and say to them, 'The God of your fathers has sent me to you,' and they ask me, 'What is his name?' what shall I say to them?" And God answered Moses, "*I am who I am.* Say this to the people of Israel: '*I am* has sent me to you.'"

The nature of the divine is so rich and broad it cannot be contained in a name, however magnificent the name may be. Of all the glorious names for the divine—King of Kings, Lord of Lords, Almighty God—the simple phrase "I am who I am" seems to be the simplest, the most honest. The divine is the great unnamable. The Hebrews, wisely recognizing

this, prohibited anyone from speaking the divine name
aloud.

KABIR:

> You know that the seed is inside the horse-chestnut
>   tree;
> and inside the seed there are the blossoms of the tree,
>   and the chestnuts, and the shade.
> So inside the human body there is the seed, and
>   inside the seed there is the human body again. . . .
>
> Thinkers, listen, tell me what you know of that is not
>   inside the soul?
> Take a pitcher full of water and set it down on the
>   water—
> now it has water inside and water outside.
> We mustn't give it a name,
> lest silly people start talking again about the body and
>   the soul.
>
> If you want the truth, I'll tell you the truth:
> Listen to the secret sound, the real sound, which is
>   inside you . . .

❖

PRACTICE: WHO AM I?

During the course of one day, as you do your work, travel, speak with friends and co-workers, spend time with your family, cook, clean, get ready for bed—with every change of situation—allow the following question to arise gently: Who am I? As you are driving to work, ask: Who am I? Ask the question silently, and try to be aware of any ideas, words, feelings, or images that come forth in response. As you meet someone and speak with them, reflect on this question: Who am I in this conversation? Am I the leader, the learner, the teacher, the inquisitor, the failure, the collaborator, the light of the world? Who am I? Then when you move to another interaction, repeat the question: Who am I in this task? An expert? A performer? A child of spirit? A child in the sandbox? Who am I in this moment?

The point is to explore the breadth of who we are, and who we think we are, in our ordinary life. Watch how your sense of self changes. With each change, what do you notice? How do your words, hopes, dreams, or postures change when your identity shifts? Who, in each moment, do you think you are?

Notice which words or descriptions seem most accurate, which seem to reflect more precisely your sense of your deepest nature.

❖

Sorrow and the Self

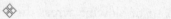

WHILE IT IS TRUE that sorrow alone is incapable of defining our essential spiritual nature, we must acknowledge that our sorrows invariably give shape and texture to our existence. I grew up in an alcoholic family. At an early age, I was addicted to drugs. I received a head injury, an accident that forced me to accept a constant level of pain in my body: a headache every day, despite the ministrations of a rich and generous host of healers.

I have spent my life intimately involved with those in pain. Many of my friends and family have died. When I was twenty-nine, I watched my best friend die of cancer, sitting with him as his body convulsed in pain, listening as his final breath on this earth sighed out of his tumor-ridden body. I have lost countless friends and patients to AIDS. I realize that some of my dreams have not come true, and I know now that others may never come true. I also see that despite my best efforts, many people still suffer, and that their sorrow comes to live in their eyes.

Whenever I become aware of another's suffering, I invariably feel myself in the presence of something both sacred and deeply human, something fundamental and true that offers a glimpse into the nature of all things. Ironically, perhaps, it is in those who have suffered, in their journeys of healing and courage, that I have perceived most clearly the miraculous, breathtaking resilience of the human spirit.

In the housing projects of Boston, children have taken me by the hand and led me into their homes, where I was always fed simple meals with great love. In the often squalid barrios of Lima, I was taught by a group of teenagers to play songs in praise of God on the *cana,* the Peruvian flute. They took tremendous delight in my fumbling attempts to master the art of blowing across the holes, laughing with joyful encouragement whenever I made a sound that came close to getting it right.

Sitting in prisons with gang members and criminals, I have shared both the heartbreak and the hope of people raised with violence and poverty. I have been privileged to work with people who were abused, neglected, or forced to suffer incest by alcoholic or abusive parents and yet, from somewhere within their pain, cultivated lives of tremendous caring and generosity. I have shared laughter, deep and long, with people who have AIDS, marveling with them at the unpredictable twists and turns that life bestows on us all. I have cried tears of gratitude for the blessings of life with those dying from cancer.

This is what I have learned: Within the sorrow, there is grace. When we come close to those things that break us down, we touch those things that also break us open. And in that breaking open, we uncover our true nature. Within the story, there is the person in the story. The word *person* comes from the Latin *per-sonare,* which means "sounding through." There is an emptiness, a hollowness through which our experiences may pass without ultimately defining us. Our life, our experiences, our joys, and our sorrows can sound through us without naming us. This is the point of healing: When we have told the story, we can leave the story behind. What remains is a hidden wholeness, alive, and unbroken.

In the Christian New Testament, the phrase "Be not afraid" is used more than any other. It is useful to recall that the people writing the gospels were being persecuted, arrested, tortured, and murdered. Clearly they could not possibly have meant, "Be not afraid—because nothing harmful will ever come to you." Rather, they counseled us to remember always that whatever sorrow or grief, illness or harm is given us, there is within us a tangible presence, a spirit of God that will bear us up, hold us, and keep us strong. Regardless of how we are hurt, our divine nature will help us bear the weight of it.

Our sorrow does not necessarily break us. Our pain is rarely strong enough to quench the fire of the soul, the resilience of the spirit, the essence of our true nature. Even in the midst of the most horrible anguish, the most unimaginable loss and suffering, the light shines, the spirit remains. Not only are we strong enough to bear the pain we are given, but our sorrow can actually become a bridge to a deeper and richer life. My drug addiction in my younger years drove me to the seminary, and to ordination, and to meditation. My childhood sorrow opened the door to great healing and taught me to listen, to watch my life carefully, to place great value on love and kindness. Sorrow alone need not permanently disfigure our life.

For the past two years an enthusiastic, committed group of volunteers has sponsored a nationwide conference on sexual abuse, called "To Tell the Truth." The people who organized the event are all themselves victims of incest. Each year thousands of people gather together, people who were wounded sexually. Part of the beauty of the event is simply in the gathering itself, to have so many people together in a large hall, all of whom have shared, albeit secretly and privately, a common invasion, a deep and intimate violation. When they first gathered in this way, everyone marveled at the feeling of safety, which naturally intermingled with sadness, regret, and relief. Many wept at the opportunity to be together.

I was asked to be the keynote speaker, to name those things that, in spite of abuse, remained strong: the wisdom born of pain, the watchfulness born of hurt, the intuition desperately cultivated in an atmosphere of dishonesty, the generosity born of knowing the true power of kindness, the healing born of attention to sorrow. Sexual abuse is a mixture of excruciating violation accompanied by the rich possibility of grace. It was good for everyone to come together to name who they really were, to see the shape of their story reflected in the hearts and eyes and hands of those around them. And at the same time we could all remember that we are larger than even this hurt.

The Place of Truth

I HAVE KNOWN JEFF FOR MANY YEARS. He is a quiet man. But when he does speak, he is a remarkable storyteller. He travels all over the country telling stories of the West, Hispanic and Indian tales that delight the listener. Children love him. He is easy, soft-spoken, and gentle, with a subtle twinkle in his eye.

When Jeff came to see me, I had not seen him for a long time. He seemed beaten down. He had been feeling tired, unable to get out of bed in the morning. Some mornings he awoke with a pressure in his chest, a tightness around the heart. Frequently the pressure turned to sadness. Often, in the mornings, he would find himself in tears.

He told me that he had been seeing a psychiatrist, who had diagnosed him as "depressed" and had recommended medication to relieve his symptoms. Jeff came to me because although he sometimes did feel sad and depressed, he felt uncomfortable taking medication. He wanted to know if there were other ways he could deal with his feelings. He also wanted, as he put it, "a different perspective," which he thought I could offer.

I asked him when this "depression" had begun. He said he had been at a party, and while many people there knew who he was, he had still felt awkward and uncomfortable. He hadn't really known how to make the kind of small talk expected at a party, and by the end of the evening he felt he was a social failure.

This had often happened to Jeff before. His natural tendency was to stay home and be alone. He enjoyed the quiet; it suited his nature. As a storyteller, part of his craft is listening. Good storytellers are often good listeners. Jeff enjoyed being alone, where he could be quiet and listen to things, to the wind, to the birds, to his own natural rhythms.

But at an early age Jeff had been taught—by his family and by the world around him—that people who were quiet and alone were fundamentally weird. Our culture expects people to be out in the world, engaged in the marketplace of work, parties, organizations, and activities. People who stay by themselves and do not join in the business of being busy are considered antisocial, defective personalities. Jeff certainly didn't want to be a defective personality. So he spent much of his life forcing himself to join things he didn't really want to join, and to go to parties and functions he really did not want to attend, just to prove to himself and others that he was not defective or handicapped.

However, when he is not performing, it is Jeff's nature to be quiet. He enjoys his time alone, the silence, the unfettered atmosphere of solitude. So when he wakes up in the morning, he feels torn between his natural tendency to be quiet and alone and the pressure to get out and join in, always having to try to be someone he is not. He feels forced to go out there and perform, when all the while he would rather simply be quiet, read, walk, write, and listen.

Our psychology, filtered through our culture, sees Jeff as depressed. He is tired, he feels paralyzed, he cannot get up in the morning. Obviously depressive symptoms. A little Prozac, and the problem is solved.

But what if there is no problem? What if we give permission for Jeff to simply live a quiet life? Each morning Jeff encounters a war of expectations. He knows what he wants and who he is: He wishes to be quiet, to be alone, to savor what he draws from solitude. However, there is an expectation that he must be more social, more outgoing, more gregarious—in short, to be someone other than who he is. This expectation hangs over his head like a sword.

When Jeff was alone, he felt he was hiding out. So we explored how he could find a more positive context for his time alone. We examined how the mystics of the world's spiritual traditions remind us that solitude can be a precious practice indeed. Solitude can be beautiful and rich; in quiet, we reap the fruits of wisdom, beauty, and grace. Placed in this context, Jeff's desire to listen to the silence is not neurotic at all. It is, in fact, his fundamental nature. As such, it must be allowed to flourish, to become the heart of his spiritual practice.

Jeff left our session feeling greatly relieved. He did not need to medicate his personality defects. He could spend as much time as he wanted in solitude, and he could begin to use it as a time of meditation, prayer, and creativity.

Months later I saw Jeff again. He was happy, easy in his walk and his words. "I feel so much lighter," he said. "I love my own time, time in the quiet with myself. And even better, when I do decide to spend time with people, I enjoy their company much more."

We are so quick to use diagnosis as our first line of defense against listening to our true nature. Depression is a particularly popular diagnosis. Now that we have chemicals to treat it, it is very convenient if we can come up with a diagnosis that fits the tools we have to fix things. So if we have a drug for depression, it is very convenient for me to diagnose you as depressed. Then I can give you the necessary pharmaceuticals and send you on your way. You are happy; I am successful.

We have learned to see our lives as a random collection of symptoms. We put them in a pattern, correlate a diagnosis, and feel we have named who we are. But this is not who we are; rather, it is simply one manifestation—and, I would argue, a rather superficial and transitory one—of who we are beneath those symptoms.

ELLEN, TOO, was feeling depressed. She was afraid she was losing it; she felt burned out. It frightened her, she told me.

I asked her to describe what she was calling "depression." What did it feel like?

"I feel tired all the time," she said. "It's not like me. I usually have so much energy. And I also feel very sad most of the time. I cry at night. It's getting harder to get up in the morning. I am usually so positive, I believe I can do anything. This depression is really scary."

Ellen works with people with AIDS. She began this work very early in the epidemic and has been serving dying people for many years. She keeps people company, arranges for nursing care, advocates for social services, and helps provide housecleaning, cooking, and a host of other things helpful and necessary for those who are sick. She also fights for funding for AIDS services in the community, battling the procedural molasses that saturates any government bureaucracy.

I asked her to speak more precisely about her depression. She thought a moment, and then she began to weep. "I am so tired of caring for people who get so sick. I am tired of seeing healthy young people succumb to this virus and die. I am tired of caring for people, only to have them all go away. And now," she continued, "David is dying, too." David was her best friend. He had been like a member of her family, often living with Ellen and her husband and children when he got sick. "I can't imagine David dying, too. I just can't face it."

Again, this did not sound like clinical depression. "Could it be that you are simply tired?" I asked her. "It seems to me, Ellen, that your heart aches, that you are frightened and sad. And very tired. If you do this work, you will sometimes be very sad and tired. This is not pathology. This is your heart speaking to you, letting you know it needs some care. What if you are simply in need of rest? Wanting care, wanting kindness, wanting rest, wanting things not to die."

Her tears flowed more gently now. "Yes," she said quietly, "yes."

When people tell me of their life, I listen for some quiet voice, some pattern that lies embedded within the words they use. I listen less to the words themselves and more for the strain or yearning ache that accompanies their language. Perhaps I see something in their body, or I listen for what they are unable to say. Inevitably some fragment of awareness peeks out, some piece of truth that we can use. I tell them what I see, what I feel, what I am beginning to notice.

I may say something like, *It sounds like you are frightened,* or *Perhaps you feel angry.* I am trying to hear what is true. I am casting about for information, and they will tell me, "No, that's not really it." Then they go on, telling me more, filling in more of the colors, more of the lines in the picture they have brought me. As a result, I can see more accurately what is happening. I may say, "It feels like you are lost and don't know what to do," or something like that. This time, they say, "Well, it's close to that, but that's not exactly it."

So, with care and time, we keep listening, both of us, to the feelings, the memories, the sensations in the body, the tremor in the voice. And then at some point a very clear image arises in my mind, or I notice some precise sensation in the body, or maybe a particular word will catch slightly in their throat. Then I know that here we have the truth. I will stop them immediately and say, "Let us feel this feeling— what is it?" And they may say, "I just feel weary" or "I feel so very sad," and I will say, "Ah, you feel sad. Tell me about your sadness." And they will say, "Yes. Yes, that's exactly it," and they will begin to weep.

How did they know what was inaccurate and which piece of feedback was right? If they are broken, damaged, handicapped, dysfunctional, how could they possibly know what is true? Impossible. Clearly there remains something inside that is not broken, something lucid and whole that knows what is true. It is simply waiting to be listened to, to be uncovered. When we touch that place of truth, we feel relief. This is the spirit of who we are.

THE PEOPLE of the Kalahari desert in southern Africa say, "A story is like the wind—it comes from a far-off place, and we feel it." Stories can be the glue that holds us together as a people. As Americans, we have certain common stories that are woven into our lives together—George Washington, Betsy Ross, Abraham Lincoln, Geronimo, Susan B. Anthony,

John F. Kennedy, Martin Luther King, Jr. The stories hold the myths of who we are as a nation.

Religious communities have stories that hold the shape of what is sacred. Christians have stories of Christmas and Easter. Jews gather to tell the story of Passover, of their liberation from slavery in Egypt. Hindus recite the Ramayana, the story of the path of devotion. Buddhists tell the story of the Buddha's enlightenment under the canopy of the Bodhi tree. There are also teaching stories, Sufi tales, Hasidic tales, Native American coyote characters, Zen koans. Stories are maps of the geography of a human life, showing us where to find the important things. Stories remind us what to look for when we are frightened or lost.

Sometimes the stories of our lives are less enlightening, perhaps more painful. The stories of our lives are filled with moments of joy and sorrow that shaped the way we have grown. Jack tells me the story of his alcoholic father, the rages, the fights, the places he would go to hide. Michelle tells me the story of her mother, the one who left her alone in a New York apartment building for hours at a time when she was eight years old, and talks to me about the fear she carries inside always. Hannah tells me about the time she ran to her stepfather, arms open for love, and he turned away without a word; she always feels alone. Joseph grew up in a Jewish ghetto, always having to fight, never safe, learning to make alliances he didn't want, just to get protection. Brenda lost her father when she was three; she aches for care.

LYNN EMANUEL:

Silence. She Is Six Years Old

She sleeps on the cot in the living room.
This is her father's mother's house.
And in the kitchen the men run their knife blades
across the oilcloth with roses on the table
and grandmother cooks them steak and eggs.
She is pretending to be asleep but she is listening
to the men talking about their friends

and grandmother in her white dress
walks back and forth past the door
and a hand reaches for salt and water.
Her father talks about divorce.
Now it is quiet.
Grandmother has left, her tight stockings
showed rainbows
and someone's upstairs undressing,
his dog tags making faint noise.
Her father walks into the room.
He is naked and there are certain
parts of him that are shadows.
And he pulls the blankets to the floor
and then the sheet—as if not to wake her—
and he lifts her up and whispers his wife's name—
Rachel, Rachel
and he takes her hand, small with its clean nails,
and he puts it to the dark:
Oh Rae, Oh Rachel he says
and over his shoulder she can see
the long hall mirror framed in black wood
and she smells lavender in her father's hair
when he gets up, first only his hands
and knees like someone playing horse,
and puts her on the chair
and she sits and rocks like a deaf woman.

Sadly, many of us have stories like this. Our stories speak about how it was in our remembered smallness, how every day we were held, hurt, loved, ignored, honored, beaten, cared for, alone, frightened, strong, watching, listening—each day adding up to a story of our life. Our story holds us as a cup holds water.

It is vital and true and deeply required that we tell our story. We must trace the shape of it, speak of the place in our body where it still lives, weep the tears of it, allow it to be seen and known. To have someone know the story of how we came to be here, how we came to be this way.

Yet there inevitably comes a point when no single story

is ever large enough to hold us. After we have told our story once, or twice, or ten times, a hundred times, a thousand times, it ceases to be a practice of awakening; it becomes a performance. While it may elicit certain levels of sympathy and support, it does not move us along the path of healing, and it does not open our eyes. In fact, it closes our eyes to anything that does not fit into our story.

When someone tells their story at a retreat or workshop, I can feel when they have told it many times before. They want me to hear their story, but more important, *they want me to hear who they are within the story.* They want me to listen, but they also want to break open, to become awake. They want to be free, free even from the story.

When we allow Angela's story of her stepfather's abuse to be told, it melts away. When we allow Jeff's diagnosis to fall away, he feels peace. When we invite Ellen's story to become more accepting, she feels relief. Allowing the story to soften a little, our deeper self reveals its secret. This is the point of healing: not just to tell our story, but to let the story fade away, revealing our true nature. When we have told the story, we can leave the story behind.

The Buddha told his disciples this parable:

A man is on a journey. He comes to a vast stretch of water. On this side the shore is dangerous, but on the other side it is safe and without danger. No boat goes to the other shore which is safe and without danger, nor is there any bridge for crossing over. It would be good therefore if I would gather grass, wood, branches and leaves to make a raft, and with the help of that raft cross over safely to the other side.

Then that man, O disciples, gathers grass, wood, branches and leaves and makes a raft, and with the help of that raft crosses over safely to the other side, exerting himself with his hands and feet. Having crossed over and got to the other side, he thinks: "This raft was of great help to me. With its aid I have crossed safely over to this side. It would be good if I carry this raft on my head or on my back wherever I go."

The Buddha then asked his disciples what this man should do with the raft. Would it not be better to say, "The raft has been a great help to me. Now I can beach it on the shore or let it float away, so I can be on my way"? In this way, explained the Buddha, his own teachings are to be used for crossing over and are not to be carried. They are practical teachings meant to bring peace and happiness. While the lessons may seem beautiful, even they are to be let go when the lesson has been learned.

So it is with our family story. Our childhood, our family identity, our diagnosis can carry us part of the way into adulthood, but its value is limited. Once our story has helped us pay attention to our history, named it, and mourned it, it is time for us to let it go. We have crossed the river. We need not carry our story on our back forever.

Poem

The spirit
 likes to dress up like this:
  ten fingers,
   ten toes,

shoulders, and all the rest
 at night
  in the black branches,
   in the morning

in the blue branches
 of the world.
  It could float, of course,
   but would rather

plumb rough matter.
 Airy and shapeless thing,
  it needs
   the metaphor of the body,

lime and appetite,
 the oceanic fluids;
  it needs the body's world
   instinct

and imagination
 and the dark hug of time,
  sweetness
   and tangibility,

to be understood,
 to be more than pure light
  that burns
   where no one is—

so it enters us—
*   in the morning*
*   shines from brute comfort*
*   like a stitch of lightning;*

and at night
*   lights up the deep and wondrous*
*   drownings of the body*
*   like a star.*

—MARY OLIVER

❖

EXERCISE: OUR FLEXIBLE IDENTITY

For five minutes, alone or with a partner, speak about your sense of who you are. Begin each sentence with the phrase "I am . . ." For example: I am a man. I am fragile. I am a person who loves children. I am often happy. I am sometimes frightened. I am confused about my work. I am strong . . . etc. Without censoring or judging the sentences, simply keep speaking continuously for at least five minutes. If you feel like going longer, feel free to continue.

Notice what you say. Notice what you feel when you say it. Are there certain themes, things that seem to repeat? What predominant impressions do you come away with? You may even find it useful to tape-record yourself as you reflect on these sentences. What do you notice as you listen to yourself? Which sentences seem most troubling? Which seem most accurate?

When you are finished, try to name the single phrase that seemed most potent. Take a few moments to speak about and reflect on this single element, the one that felt most powerful when you spoke of it. Be aware of what it may want to reveal about your current sense of yourself.

❖

Self and Community

WINE TAKES ITS CHARACTER from the grape used to make it. And the grape takes its character from the soil in which it is planted.

The sun, the location, the qualities and nutrients of the soil, the particular insects, species of fungus, and diseases that are indigenous to the ecosystem, the way each plant is tended by the vintner, the amount of water and pruning, the time of harvest, the heat or cool of the season—these all combine to give the wine its signature fragrance and bouquet.

Yet while each wine is different, there is still something that does not change—the essence of grape. Regardless where it is planted and how it is tended, the grape will always remain grape. So it is with us in community. Just as we are shaped by the soil of our lives, we also carry a deeper, fundamental identity, something unique and unchanging, our own particular spiritual essence.

Clearly our sense of who we are is powerfully influenced by the community from which we come. Our families, our neighbors, our government, our friends, our lovers—even our enemies—exert tremendous influence over the way we come to see ourselves. Every being we encounter carries their own peculiar expectations, desires, and demands, which alter the texture of our lives. Sometimes these expectations are subtle and gently shape the outline of our personality, as a river, over time, can smooth the surface of a stone. The stone comes to fit easily and gently in the current of the river, and both slightly alter their course through intimate contact with the other.

At other times the effects of community are more dramatic. Victims of war, poverty, crime, oppression, or famine all carry deep remembrance of the intrusion of pain into their lives. These experiences are more like a chisel or a hammer—smashing our sense of self, creating fissures in our identity.

Rose was a young, attractive Hispanic woman. At one of our retreats, I asked everyone to look through the large pile of magazines I had brought and to pick out any pictures that reminded them of their sorrow, pain, or loss—while also seeking out images of joy, strength, and love. After each person had chosen their pictures and made them into a collage, Rose asked if she could speak.

"First of all, I had a very painful time, because there were hardly any pictures in all these magazines of people who weren't white—except in the *National Geographic*. I feel angry that I have to go to an anthropological magazine to find pictures of people that look like me. It makes me feel invisible."

None of us had seen what Rose had seen. There was violence here, in these playful, upbeat magazine advertisements. They made certain people disappear.

There was strength in Rose, in her words. Her identification with her community was clear and strong, and yet, living as a member of a people who had been constantly wounded and oppressed by the dominant culture, there was also in Rose great tenderness and hurt. She knew the deep sorrow she shared with her family and all the families in her community. These were her people. Rose's compassion and strength had combined to make her a passionate and valuable advocate for social change in our community.

Rose went on: "I remember a time when I was small. My aunts came to my house, they were excited, they told my mother they had something that would help me. They all took me into the bathroom and started rubbing my face with this chemical. It was an abrasive, it stung my face. They rubbed and rubbed. I cried, it hurt so much. After a while they stood back and looked at me. Their faces showed their disappointment. 'It didn't work,' they told me, sadness in their eyes. 'You're still dark.' With their chemicals, they had hoped to lighten my face. It was too brown; they said I would never be happy. They had tried to make me white. In their love for me, they taught me to be ashamed of who I was. I was not white. I would never be happy."

Unfortunately, many clumsy psychotherapeutic approaches resemble these well-meaning aunts. They try to rub and rub, scraping away our humanity, trying to make us white, pure, unblemished by our lives. Their goal is to turn us into someone who is without sorrow, without blame, unburdened by the sloppy residue of being human. Rather than simply invoke the tremendous grace that lives deep within us, we try to rebuild ourselves into someone who is not tainted by suffering. I would suggest that this is impossible. I would also suggest that it is not even desirable. For it ignores the fundamental potential for the discovery of beauty, strength, and grace in our life as it unfolds, just the way it is.

THICH NHAT HANH:

> Western medicine emphasizes surgery too much. Doctors want to take out the things that are not wanted. When we have something irregular in our body, too often they advise us to have an operation. The same seems to be true in psychotherapy. Therapists want to help us throw out what is unwanted and keep only what is wanted. But what is left may not be very much. If we try to throw away what we don't want, we may throw away most of ourselves.

If we feel ashamed of who we are, we will pretend to be someone else. In unspoken collusion with those who would harm us, we strive to look like someone more desirable, someone with a better shape, a prettier face, a greater stature—a perfect specimen. In the process of trying to satisfy these demands, to become someone else, we do great harm to our natural sense of self. When we struggle to create a new persona that is less offensive and more pleasing, acting the way they want us to be, just to feel safe, acting this way over and over and over and over, each day, year after year— in time we begin to forget who we are.

At the same time, community can also become a place of awakening to a deeper sense of who we are. When I first took communion, when I stood in the circle of people who came before the altar to take in the body of Christ, I felt that I too was part of the body of God, of creation, of the holy spirit. Each time, as a child and later as an ordained minister, I would feel the same inclusion, a deep belonging, a blessing of unconditional love and acceptance. I felt loved; I felt I was all right. I invariably wept at the unspeakable relief of finally belonging somewhere.

Similarly, when I was first introduced to the practice of Buddhist meditation, I took the three *gatha*s, or refuges. I first took refuge in the Buddha, and in my own Buddha nature; I took refuge in the *dharma,* the teachings of the Buddha, the deep truth of all things that lives in us; and I took refuge in the *sangha,* the community of beings with whom I practice. When I sit for days in silence, in the company of these friends and fellow *dharma* practitioners, I slowly come to hear and feel the simple truths of who I am.

Jean Vanier began a Christian community for developmentally disabled adults in 1964. Beginning with six adults, he founded the L'Arche community in Trosly-Bruil, France. Now, thirty years later, there are dozens of L'Arche communities throughout the world, with thousands of handicapped residents as full members of these spiritual communities. Reflecting on the lessons of L'Arche, Jean Vanier describes how living in community with others can both break us down and lift us up:

Community can appear to be a marvelously welcoming and sharing place.

But in another way, community is a terrible place. It is the place where our limitations and our egoism are revealed to us. When we begin to live full-time with others, we discover our poverty and our weaknesses, our inability to get on with other people, our mental and emotional blocks, our affective or sexual disturbances, our seemingly insatiable desires, our frustrations and jealousies, our hatred and our wish to destroy. While we were alone, we believed we loved everyone. Now that we are with others, we realize how incapable we are of loving, how much we deny life to others. . . .

So community life brings a painful revelation of our limitations. . . . The unexpected discovery of the monsters within us is hard to accept. The immediate reaction is to try to destroy the monsters, or to hide them away again, pretending they don't exist, or to flee from community life and relationships with others, or to find that the monsters are theirs, not ours. But if we accept that the monsters are there, we can let them out and learn to tame them. That is growth towards liberation.

In community life we discover our own deepest wound and learn to accept it. So our rebirth can begin. It is from this very wound that we are born.

ONE NIGHT LAST WINTER, following the directions that Dottie Montoya gave me over the phone, I turned off the highway onto the dirt road across from the Conoco station in Velarde, New Mexico, an old village in the mountains surrounded by apple trees. I arrived in the dark and turned into the muddy parking lot of the Head Start center behind the small white church. They had left the lights on in the church so that I would see it as a landmark and would not get lost on my way to this sparsely populated rural village at the end of the long, serpentine dirt road.

Dottie met me at the door, anxious to know if I had seen the lights in the church, worried that I had gotten lost. She had helped to found this family support group for the people of Velarde partly with the assistance of Bread for the Journey.

Bread for the Journey is a private nonprofit charity that seeks to alleviate the tremendous poverty and hardship that afflicts so many in northern New Mexico. Second only to

Mississippi, the people of New Mexico have a lower standard of living than any other state in the United States. Bread for the Journey is based on the belief that our healing as individuals is made full and complete through attending to the healing of others, and that each one of us stands in kinship with those who experience economic, emotional, social, or physical suffering. Our work is to support the ideas, talents, and commitment of local people through projects that are simple, quick, and helpful.

The Velarde community group welcomed me as if I were family, one of their own. I was deeply moved and embarrassed by the extent of the fuss they made. Someone had baked an enormous sheet cake, garnished with flowers and decorated in the center with a large "Welcome Reverend Wayne Muller" in bright red icing. In the corner of the cake they had fashioned a drawing of a Bible, with Psalm 22, verse 22: "In the midst of the people I praise thee." They had arranged about thirty metal folding chairs in a large circle— they normally had about ten people come each week, but this was a special occasion, they explained—and they asked me to sit at the head of the circle, in a large carved wooden chair with an upholstered seat, right next to the table with the cake on it.

As Dottie spoke a few words of welcome and introduction, I looked around the room. To my right was a boy of twelve or thirteen. I hoped his mother hadn't made him come, although she probably had. Across from me was a woman who was probably eighty-five. There were mothers, fathers, grandmothers, and grandfathers. Later I would hear some of their stories. One had lost a daughter three months before in a fire. Another had lost a granddaughter a few weeks before, when the pharmacist inadvertantly substituted the wrong medicine for the croup; the child had been twenty-two months old. One woman had lost her husband; one man's wife had just been diagnosed with breast cancer.

Their families had lived there for hundreds of years, working the land, praying, struggling together and apart, worshiping, burying loved ones, giving birth to children. We spoke together about how we all suffer, how all the children of God seem to have some measure of sorrow. How we sometimes feel broken down by our sorrows, but at the same time something deep within us is broken open, helping us to become more aware of the richness of who we are. We spoke of love, and how it seems to be the precious ointment that enables our suffering to slowly and gradually emerge as healing and grace. We spoke of death, how it reminds us that our life is precious. We spoke of how we must be careful with our language and our actions, how we must pay attention to the way we walk on the earth, because our lives and our families are priceless, sacred, holy.

The woman who lost her husband said she still feels the ache in her body when she thinks of him, and she wonders if she will ever completely heal. "Will the ache ever totally be gone?" she asks. Her ache is part of her deep love for him. The day will probably never come when some ache does not remind her that he was her beloved companion.

Then Dottie's son, Roger, begins to speak. He tells the group that he is a gay man infected with HIV. This is the first time he has spoken of his HIV infection—or his sexuality—in this small, predominantly Catholic community. Until now, it has been a secret. There is a palpable hush as he speaks of losing four partners to death by AIDS, and of how he feels both blessed and challenged by his virus to become more creative, more resourceful, more generous. Three years ago Roger started a gymnastics program for children in the valley—a program that has served hundreds of children. He clearly has a gift to offer his community, and for the first time he is speaking intimately about who he really is.

When Roger finishes, his mother looks around the room, gauging the reaction of the group. With a newfound strength in her words—free at last from the burden of carrying Roger's secret—Dottie addresses her family and friends. She tells them how hard it has been to carry her son's secret. She wonders aloud if her family will support her now that it is clear what is happening to her son. In the circle, Dottie's sister and two nieces immediately rise, walk across the room, and embrace both Dottie and Roger. They all weep. Many others in the room are crying, and they come over to hold the members of the family. Dottie, through her tears, laughingly announces: "Well, I guess this is a good time to have that cake."

Later in the spring, Roger organized a public celebration in the nearby town of Española for people with HIV and AIDS. Roger called it "Accentuate the Positive," and it was the first time in this rural, conservative valley that there had been any significant public recognition of the existence of AIDS. Roger organized speakers, artists, and dancers. On the day of the event over six hundred people participated—including parents, children, and community elders. The mayor gave a welcoming speech. Everyone came out to support Roger and his work. Roger took a leap, and the community responded. He could have continued to keep the secret, as he had for almost ten years. But it was time to name who he was—because this was his home, and these were his people.

For those of us raised in family pain, surrendering into community with others is often difficult and confusing. We may harbor deep ambivalence about being seen and known by others. Is it acceptable to allow them to see who we are? If they come to know our deepest secrets, will they go away and leave us? For us, community is bittersweet. We cannot imagine surrendering into the care of others; yet to live completely alone can bring great sorrow. In separateness, said the Buddha, lies the world's greatest misery.

IT IS EASTER MORNING at Santo Domingo pueblo, the morning every year when the children do the green corn dance. In the Indian way, the children are expected to watch and learn. As soon as they learn to walk, they learn to dance. They watch the elders, their parents, the ones who have come before. As they watch, they learn. As they grow, they simply take their place in the dance.

The dances are prayers, the prayers of the whole community. This morning, as the parents and elders watch, the men drum and sing, and the children dance. They are the future of the tribe. They are the green corn. Occasionally a child drops a sprig of pine, or some clothing comes undone. An elder quietly approaches the child, picks up the sprig or rearranges the dress, and the child continues. Nothing is said. The dance continues.

To sit for hours as the children dance, all day long, is to feel the way that the children are honored as full members of the pueblo. They, too, carry the responsibility for sending the prayers of the people to mother earth, father sun. This is no Christmas pageant, no cute, condescending performance to give the children an artificial opportunity to look like the grown-ups. These children are doing the same dance that the elders do. They are responsible for the future of the people. And so they dance. Eyes clear and still, bodies precisely in rhythm, the children dance the prayers of the people.

FOR MANY YEARS in Santa Fe we have had an annual worship service for people with AIDS and their families and loved ones. We call it "Celebrating the Heart of Healing." It is a service of thanksgiving for all that has been born in our lives as a result of this virus—the love, the honesty, the compassion, the grace. During the year we go to many memorial services, but this particular gathering allows us to name not only what has died but also what has been born from within the sorrow, grief, and loss.

For the first four years of this gathering, Diana was one of our featured speakers. She had AIDS, and she was a spirited, strong, creative woman who confronted her illness with courage and resilience. She was beloved by many for her unflagging spirit and her grace under pressure. Every year at the worship service she would speak about the new things she had learned, and at the end of her talk she vowed to return again the following year. Diana came to symbolize the "Heart of Healing" for many of us in Santa Fe.

In the fourth year, a month before the service, Diana was sick and in the hospital in Colorado. She moved in and out of a coma. The doctors were not sure whether she would pull through this time. I got a message to her through a friend that we were getting ready for the annual celebration and that she was needed—she couldn't die on us now. Two days before the service I got a call from Diana. "I am coming," she told me. "I belong there, with everybody I love. I'm on my way."

Later that year Diana again became very ill, and her mother, Ruth, came to live with her. They had a stormy relationship, as both of them were emotional, vital, and stubborn. They fought passionately and often; regardless of the subject or situation, both were firmly convinced they were right. When the fight was done, they invariably returned to the comfortable ease and familiarity that comes when two old souls travel a path together for a long time.

Slowly Diana began to weaken. She could no longer recover from the infections that invaded her body, one after another. Ruth got softer; they fought less. As a mother, Ruth had every right to expect that she would grow old, and be buried by her children. And yet here she was, caring for her daughter, a daughter who would die first.

One night, toward the end, in the hospital, Diana became incontinent. She defecated in her clothing, on the bed. Ruth did not call the nurses; this was something she, Diana's mother, needed to do. She cleaned her daughter, wiped her with tremendous care and love. She had done this before, when Diana was small. Ruth was still her mother, and Diana was her daughter. She knew who she was, and she knew what she had to do.

ALICE WALKER SUGGESTS that we hold the seeds of our community within the soil of our being. Over time, these seeds come to germinate, grow, and blossom within us, even as we cultivate our own true nature:

> for two who
> slipped away
> almost
> entirely:
> my "part" Cherokee

great-grandmother
Tallulah
(Grandmama Lula)
on my mother's side
about whom
only one
agreed-upon
thing
is known:
her hair was so long
she could sit on it;

and my white (Anglo-Irish?)
great-great-grandfather
on my father's side;
nameless
(Walker, perhaps?),
whose only remembered act

is that he raped
a child:
my great-great-grandmother,
who bore his son,
my great-grandfather,
when she was eleven.

Rest in peace.
The meaning of your lives
is still
unfolding.

Rest in peace.
In me
the meaning of your lives
is still
unfolding.

For the Plains Indians, the sweat lodge is like a womb, a place where things are cleansed, prayers are spoken, deep truths are recognized, new things are born. When anyone enters the sweat lodge for purification or to offer prayers, they first speak the words *mitakuye oyasin*—"to all my relations." Thus the prayers in the lodge are offered for the healing and acknowledgment of all the beings—humans, animals, plants, the earth itself—with whom we are joined in delicate community.

Pueblo Indians descend into a kiva to pray for the whole world, because when they are in that kiva they feel the heartbeat of mother earth; they feel themselves to be a part of the whole world. In the Christian tradition, monks retire to their cells and pray for all creation, because in the quiet, in deep silent prayer, they feel the breath of the world in their bodies. And when they pray from that place, they are breathing out the *ruach,* the breath of God moving across the face of the deep; the words they pray are creating peace and healing across the earth. This too is who we are. We are the very breath of God.

Jesus said, "The kingdom of God is within you." The original Greek—*entos hymon*—can be correctly translated as either "within you" or "among you." So perhaps there is a deliberate and allowable—even desirable—ambiguity about the sense of "I" and the location of the inner kingdom. We are inside and outside. The gospel of Thomas states this even more succinctly, when Jesus proclaims, "The kingdom is within you and without you." As Meister Eckhart reminds us, there is a constant dialogue between the kingdom we hold within us and the spirit that flourishes in the world around us. Our spirit is not separate, but intertwined: "The eye with which we see God is the same eye with which God sees us."

How do we come to feel this larger sense of self, this divine "I" that moves "within us and without us"? This spring Bill, who was dying of AIDS, told me he was asked to be the godfather of Alex, the newborn son of a close friend. He asked me if I would officiate at the baptism, and I readily assented. He spoke of his deep love for baby Alex, whom he had already come to cherish. He also shared his poignant concern that he would not live very long and might not be able to provide the necessary care and guidance required of a godfather. He suggested that perhaps the child's parents should ask someone else to be the godfather—someone who would live long enough to help the child grow into a man.

When I called Patricia, the baby's mother, to arrange the details of the baptism, I shared part of the conversation I had had with Bill. I knew she was aware of Bill's medical condition. Was she sure of her choice of Bill as godfather for her son? Her reply was quiet and thoughtful. "I thought about it a lot," she began. "I know Bill may not live much longer. But he so loves Alex, and Bill just seemed so right." There was a pause, and then she continued, "I also believe there is some kind of life after this one. I don't really know what it is like exactly, but I believe that when people die, they can watch over and care for those of us who remain behind. I want Bill to do that. I asked him if he would always pray for Alex and help him any way he can, sending him love and protection from wherever he is. Bill said he would. That is all I needed."

Clearly Patricia, Alex, and Bill are honoring a deeper connection. They are courageously affirming a rich communion that is alive now and will continue to live across all boundaries of identity and time.

The Navajo have a chant that names this place of connection at the center point, intricately entwined in the community of the earth:

> *The mountains, I become part of it. . . .*
> *The herbs, the fir tree, I become part of it.*
> *The morning mists, the clouds, the gathering waters,*
> *I become part of it.*
> *The wilderness, the dew drops, the pollen. . . .*
> *I become part of it.*

If we are to make a significant contribution to the creation of peace and healing in the world, we cannot remain enmeshed in the smallness of our family story. We must allow our story to become larger—we must take our place in the rich expanse of our true nature, in deep kinship with all creation.

Healing

> Wonder of wonders! Intrinsically all living beings
> are Buddhas, endowed with wisdom and virtue, but
> because men's minds have become inverted through
> delusive thinking they fail to perceive this.
>
> —THE BUDDHA

THE PIÑON TREE outside my window stands rooted in the dry ground. Here in the high desert, the soil is devoid of moisture. Dry grasses ring the base of the trunk, and a single branch slowly shifts in the warm, gentle breeze. Other trees stand near, a community that has stood together and waited, like this, in this place, for longer than I have been alive. Their trunks have, each in their own way, accommodated their shape to the heat of the summer sun. Each has withstood winter's cold and has been shaped by driving sleet, hail, and snow. Every inch is a testimony to the relentless teachings of the successive seasons.

When I put my hand on the bark, I can feel the tree's story. I can hear the knowing of this place, a knowing that comes from years of growth, change, and time that coalesce in this singular life. Here, in this spot on the earth, time is simply one more nutrient to be digested. With my hand on the trunk of this piñon, I can feel how life can—with miraculous, deliberate concentration—adapt to the inevitable stirrings of change.

When we are molded by the events that shape us, what remains constant? What presence, what inner voice continues to hold our true nature, as the forms and textures of our life shift under the pressure of circumstance? What inner constancy remains to preserve our name, to define the outline of our unchanging spirit?

The centerpiece of Quaker theology is their fervent belief in a palpable inner light. This light, they insist, is a spark of the divine that burns brightly and surely within each and every one of us. One Quaker writer expresses it this way:

> Deep within us there is an amazing inner sanctuary of the soul, a holy place, a Divine Center, a speaking Voice, to which we may continuously return. Eternity is at our hearts, pressing upon our time-torn lives, warming us with intimations of an astounding destiny, calling us home unto Itself. Yielding to these persuasions, gladly committing ourselves in body and soul, utterly and completely, to the Light Within, is the beginning of true life. It is a dynamic center, a creative Life that presses to birth within us.

Their belief in this inner light is so certain, they have designed their organizational structure around it. Quakers make decisions by consensus; as every being holds a fragment of the divine light, no decision could ever be completely correct if all who carry that light were not in total accord. If there was dissension, part of the light could be left out—a situation they find unacceptable. And so they work, they speak, they debate, they pray, and they wait—until they can hear that place where the light of God shows itself in full agreement.

Part of healing is in this patience, waiting for the light to show itself. Sometimes our interventions and manipulations only serve to complicate or cloud an already difficult situation. Listening quietly and with faithful patience for the healing already embedded in this moment, we come to rely more surely on the fundamental resilience of our natural wisdom.

My friend Helen told me a story about her son, Jake.

Jake was hyperactive. His energy would periodically erupt in such a way that he would act out of control, disrupting his class, his family, and his own well-being. Like many parents, Helen had tried a variety of prescription drugs and other treatments, but with little success.

Finally, out of desperation, Helen decided that every time Jake became hyperactive, she would grab him and hold him tightly on her lap. She wrapped her arms around her son, holding him so that he could hear her heartbeat. She did this, she said, so that he would quiet down enough to remember who he was.

Within a few months, Jake's symptoms had subsided almost completely. This is a beautiful example of how natural healing energies emerge gently and reliably from deep within us, if only we will get quiet enough to listen. "Who is it that can make muddy water clear?" asks the Tao Te Ching. "No one," is the response. "But if left to stand, it will gradually become clear of itself."

Even in the middle of a hurricane, the bottom of the sea is calm. As the storm rages and the winds howl, the deep waters sway in gentle rhythm, a light movement of fish and plant life. Below there is no storm. And when the storm above recedes, the stillness within rises to the surface, and the sea again is calm.

Sogyal Rinpoche speaks eloquently about this place of inner resilience:

> Whatever our lives are like, our Buddha nature is always there. And it is always perfect. We say that not even the Buddhas can improve it in their infinite wisdom, nor can sentient beings spoil it in their seemingly infinite confusion. Our true nature could be compared to the sky, and the confusion of the ordinary mind to clouds. Some days the sky is completely obscured by clouds. When we are on the ground, looking up, it is very difficult to believe there is anything else up there but clouds. Yet we only have to fly in a plane to discover up above a

limitless expanse of clear blue sky. From up there the clouds we assumed were everything seem so small and so far away down below.

We should always try and remember: the clouds are not the sky, and do not "belong" to it. They only hang there and pass by in their slightly ridiculous and nondependent fashion. And they can never stain or mark the sky in any way.

LAST YEAR I WAS INVITED to consult with the treatment staff at a private psychiatric hospital. We spent two days working on the concept of healing from within, using our true nature as our wellspring and guide. We discussed the implications of this principle for the diagnosis and treatment of patients with schizophrenia, multiple personality, and other dissociative disorders. They were an open and committed staff who had worked together for many years and had grown intimately connected. They were intrigued with the premise that there is something inside each of us—including their patients—that is trustworthy, whole, and wise.

One of the staff set up a spiritual reflection group, based on the themes we had discussed in our training—belonging, stillness, faith, humility, gratefulness, and loving kindness. After the group had been going for a few months, Jim—the psychiatrist in charge of the group—called to tell me about Louise. Louise was schizophrenic and would sometimes work herself into a highly disturbed state. She would become very upset about something someone said or did—real or imagined—and she would become so agitated that she would try to run away. Jim explained to me that the only choice the staff had was to prevent her physically from escaping, using restraints and medication to calm her down.

Once when staffing was low, Louise had one of her episodes. She again became loud and angry, and she threatened to go through the window and run away. Jim took a chance. He decided that whatever was going on inside Louise was tied in some way to something deeper, and that there must be, inside her, some still, small voice that would tell her the right thing to do. And so, breaking the rules, he let Louise run away.

Jim bet on his intuition that—sitting right beside the rage, confusion, and fear that seemed to saturate Louise's actions—there was something in her that was trustworthy. In that moment he chose to believe he had made a positive alliance with the voice deep inside of Louise that knew what was best for her. Three hours later Louise returned, completely safe. She had needed to run, to get away. This was her way of allowing the terrible pain in her soul to gently heal. And when the time for running had ended, when she found what she needed, she knew it was time to return. This was her rhythm.

Until then Louise had never been able to feel her own rhythm. Instead, she had been subject to the diagnostic and treatment needs of the hospital. Now, for the first time— thanks to Jim's faith in her fundamental nature—Louise felt the natural consequence of her own inner rhythm. From that point on, Louise made rapid progress, far surpassing the treatment goals the staff had set for her. As she learned to trust her own nature, her own wisdom began to emerge.

D. T. Suzuki explains that Zen shares this fundamental trust in the "benevolent impulses inherently lying in our hearts":

> Zen, in its essence, is the art of seeing into the nature of one's being, and it points the way from bondage to freedom. . . . We can say that Zen liberates all the energies properly and naturally stored in each of us, which are in ordinary circumstances cramped and distorted so that they find no adequate channel for activity. . . . It is the object of Zen, therefore, to save us from going crazy or being crippled. This is what I mean by freedom, giving free play to all the creative and benevolent impulses inherently lying in our hearts.

How do we find this true nature? There is nothing to do, no place to go. To be quiet and listen with great mindfulness and care—this is all. The best of therapy, like the best of spiritual practice, recognizes what is basically whole, strong, and wise within each of us. It is just like good medicine, which essentially relies on the body's own resources, using treatments that gently remind the body that it is capable of healing itself. So, too, do good emotional and spiritual practices allow us to remember who we are in our strongest, deepest sense.

RUMI:

> *Let yourself be*
> *silently drawn by the*
> *stronger pull of what*
> *you really love.*

There is a principle of physics, called *sympathetic vibration,* that can be used by musicians to shape and amplify sound. When two strings are tuned to an identical pitch, striking one will instantly cause the other to vibrate in sympathy. If we place two identically tuned harps at opposite ends of a large room and pluck the note C-sharp on one string of one harp, every string tuned to C-sharp—on both harps—will suddenly come alive in a collaborative celebration of that note.

In the same way, when we are in the presence of people who precisely reflect our true nature, we feel moved. When we approach teachers or lovers or friends or children who hold in themselves the best and deepest truths we ourselves hold in us, we naturally feel a sympathetic vibration. Those people we love and respect are often those who hold more visibly the wisdom, grace, or strength that is perhaps more deeply hidden in ourselves.

Nahum is a rabbi. Before he embarked upon his formal rabbinical training, Nahum explored several spiritual paths, including Buddhism. One evening in San Francisco, Nahum went to a gathering of people practicing Buddhist meditation. There were on the stage a very respected Buddhist lama and two poets, Gary Snyder and Allen Ginsberg. They were all sitting and chanting. Onstage, Snyder and the lama were sitting in the Zen discipline, their backs straight and still "like a mountain." But Nahum noticed that as Allen Ginsberg meditated and chanted, he was rocking back and forth. As he watched Ginsberg rock and rock, Nahum suddenly realized that Ginsberg was fundamentally a Jew. "Traditionally," Nahum told me over coffee one day, "Jews rock back and forth when they pray. It is in our bodies, in our soul. When I saw Ginsberg rocking back and forth, I knew that I too would always be a Jew, whatever other practices I adopted. And so I resolved to study my heritage more deeply to discover more about who I am." This led Nahum to become a rabbi—a loving, understanding, and well-loved teacher and spiritual companion for many in our community.

Sympathetic vibration is one way we can learn the truth of who we are. Which people draw us into them? Which people seem to stir us deeply? Whom do we seek out as guides and teachers? What we see in them can help us see in ourselves those seeds that are waiting to be nourished, waiting to blossom.

IZUMI SHIKIBU:

> *Watching the moon*
> *at midnight,*
> *solitary, mid-sky,*
> *I knew myself completely,*
> *no part left out.*

MANY SPIRITUAL PRACTICES carry an invitation to deep acceptance. Sometimes, after we have struggled and fought for what we desire, we find that in spite of our most courageous efforts, we are forced to admit that our dreams did not come true. This is the heart of the serenity prayer—to accept what we cannot change, while cultivating the courage to change what we can. And, most important, to be granted the wisdom to know when to keep fighting for what we desire, and when to accept what has been given.

When, after all our efforts and struggles, it is clearly time to surrender, then acceptance becomes the heart of healing—acceptance of what has been given, of what has become of us and our lives. For many of us, the hardest thing to accept is the way our life has gone. We didn't have the family we hoped for, the childhood we longed for, the care we felt we deserved. We did not have the spouse or partner we dreamed about. We did not have the career we expected to have. There were too many unexpected turns, hardships, difficulties, decisions we might have made differently. As we grow older we find that we have not become the person we thought we would be.

David is a well-known painter who has never felt completely at home in the fast-paced glitter of the art world. "All my life my models have been Jesus, the Buddha, Matisse, Fred Astaire. People who were artistically and spiritually courageous, passionate, productive. I now realize that I will never be like them, that I have fewer paintings than Matisse, that I am not as spiritually evolved as Jesus and the Buddha, not as grand as Astaire. I realize that now, at fifty-eight, I am having to let go of my dreams. I have to accept that I will be who I am and make some peace with it. It is a little sad, and yet I also feel some relief. Those models were harsh; I had to keep my eye on that star so tightly. I could never allow myself to love anyone—or let them love me—because I couldn't allow myself to be distracted from the goal. Now I see the goal was not really mine in the first place, and I feel very sad.

"But I also feel a sense of relief that I am no longer held to that goal. I can finally allow myself to stop pretending, stop inventing myself each day, and begin allowing myself to feel who I am in this moment and make peace with it. I feel I am finally allowing who I am, here and now, to be enough."

Accepting who we are, who we have become, our lives, our jobs, our friends, our destiny as it has evolved—this is a fruitful practice. Accepting who we are is a practice of non-harming. Sadly, much self-help literature contains seeds of harm: We are urged to remake ourselves into someone who will be spiritually or psychologically acceptable, and that acceptance is conditional on our performance in the areas of therapy, growth, or meditation. We are still not accepting ourselves unconditionally, just as we are in this moment, with a full and joyful heart.

A more merciful practice begins with acceptance. It begins with the assumption that we were never broken, never defective. By surrendering into a deep acceptance of our own nature—rather than by tearing apart who we are—we actually make more room for genuine, rich, merciful, playful growth and change. If we feel our fundamental strength, creativity, and wisdom, then change is not frightening at all. Things simply fall away when they are ready, making room for the rich harvest underneath.

JACK KORNFIELD:

> In many spiritual traditions there is only one important question to answer, and that question is: Who am I? When we begin to answer it, we are filled with images and ideals—the negative images of ourselves that we wish to change and perfect and the positive images of some great spiritual potential—yet the path is not so much about changing ourselves as it is about listening to the fundamentals of our being.

FATHER JERRY IS AN OLD FRIEND. He has worked his whole life with the poor of New Mexico. One day, he told me, he was visiting a man with Alzheimer's. The man was in an advanced stage, terribly afflicted with severe loss of mental capacity. For the last five years, Jerry said, the man had been deteriorating steadily. His wife had been taking care of him the whole time, without help. This was her gift, her love for him. He does not recognize her at all. He does not know who she is.

On this day when Father Jerry goes to visit, the man is

essentially comatose. But when Jerry approaches his bedside to serve the sacraments, a tear rolls down the man's cheek. How can this be? Even from the depth of coma, after years of mental deterioration, clearly there is a conversation here, a tender, intimate exchange between the God in Jerry and the God in this man who is close to death. Even in the most debilitating circumstances, there is a light that will not die. This is what lives in us.

And what of his wife—what kind of service is this? Five years tending to the needs of the man she has loved her whole life, with whom she had spent forty years of marriage, raising their children, working to build a life together. Who is she caring for? Her husband? A stranger? Or is it simply God caring for God, the poignant and loving hand of the divine moving through each of them, a gentle dance of deep, loving kindness?

Tagore:

> *After you had*
> *taken your leave,*
> *I found God's footprints*
> *on my floor.*

Spiritual identity is not something far off, not something we need to go to Tibet to find. It is here, in the way we walk on the earth, the way we see our life, the way we care for ourselves and others. Our true nature is not something extraordinary; in fact, it is quite ordinary, an inevitable portion of our daily life.

Jacques Lusseyran lost his eyesight through an accident at the age of seven and a half. He was not a particularly spiritual child, not especially religious. But years later he would write about what he saw when he was blind, about the awareness of his inner self that began to unfold within him:

> Barely ten days after the accident blinded me, I made the basic discovery . . . [that] I could not

see the light of the world any more. Yet the light was still there. . . . I found it *in myself* and what a miracle!—it was intact. The "in myself," however, where was that? In my head, in my heart, in my imagination? . . . The light dwells where life also dwells: within ourselves.

*the
second
part*

❖

WHAT DO
I LOVE?

❖

We Become
What We Love

All that we are
arises with our thoughts.
Speak or act with a pure mind and heart
and happiness will follow you
as your shadow, unshakable.

—THE BUDDHA

Where your treasure is, there will your heart be also.

—JESUS OF NAZARETH

MY FRIENDS GAYLON AND ZENIA travel around the world. Twice a year they make a pilgrimage for several months to some corner of the earth. In their travels, they purchase a delectable variety of beautiful, interesting objects from the people and places they visit. Then, when they return home, they invite their friends to come to their house, and they sell what they have collected on their voyage. In this way, they raise enough money to make another trip.

Last Christmas my wife, Christine, and I went to Gaylon and Zenia's for their winter sale. Gaylon took me aside to show me a selection of teapots they had collected in China. The pots were made of clay and were very old, some several hundred years old. Gaylon told me the Chinese say that after a hundred years of daily use, the pot becomes thoroughly seasoned. You need only pour hot water into the pot, and the pot itself will make tea.

When we do what we love, again and again, our life comes to hold the fragrance of that thing. When we hold something in our hands day after day, our hands conform to the shape of what we have held. We become what we have cared for; our lives are shaped by what we love.

All we are, said the Buddha, is a result of what we have thought. He might also have added: All we are is a result of what we have loved. What we love draws us forward and shapes our destiny. Our love teaches us what to look for, where to aim, where to walk. With our every action, word, relationship, and commitment, we slowly and inevitably become what we love.

This past Easter, Christine, our son, Maxwell, and I spent the day at Santo Domingo pueblo with Juanita and her children and grandchildren. They were doing the green corn dance, traditionally danced after early-morning Easter services at the mission church. After the dances, about fifteen of us tumbled into cars and pickup trucks to drive to the hills for an Easter egg hunt. When we got there, we scattered across the land where Juanita had, the night before, hidden dozens of painted eggs among the cactus, piñon, juniper, and chamisa.

It was quite a sight, children combing the high desert landscape for eggs. At Santo Domingo, the land is dry and difficult to irrigate, and the dust blows hard in the spring. I was helping Maxwell—who was four years old—find his share of the treasure. We were looking everywhere—under bushes, in gopher holes, under rocks. At the top of one hill we came upon Tim, Juanita's teenage son, and we began comparing notes on how many eggs we had found. While we were talking, Tim's eyes were drawn to a pile of yellow sand under a nearby bush. He knelt down and began sifting through the sand with his fingers. "I need this sand for my pots," he exclaimed. "I've been looking for a color just like this. It will be perfect."

Like many Pueblo youth, Tim had learned to make pots from his mother and his older sister, who continue a long tradition of fine clay potters. Because of his love for the clay, Tim saw what I did not see. Tim had more than one thing on his mind. As we all searched the ground for eggs, Tim was simultaneously attuned to the peculiar colors of the hills of

Santo Domingo, his eyes alert for just the right color of sand that would put a fine touch on his pots. I, of course, had missed that small pile of yellow sand completely. Standing next to me, Tim saw the rich ochre of dry earth in a way that I simply could not.

Wherever I walked on that beautiful hillside, I carried the image of "Easter egg" in my mind's eye. Thus, whenever I saw sand of any color, I did not really see it at all. When I saw earth, it was simply a signal I had not found an egg.

Thus it is with what we choose to love. We place what we love in our mind's eye; then our eyes seek out those things we have chosen as valuable and important, and our mind discards the rest. Anything we encounter that we have not named as sacred or useful, we simply ignore. As a result, we spend a great deal of our lives asleep, oblivious to most of the universe. But when we encounter those things we truly love, we become awake, alive. We open ourselves to the gifts of wisdom and beauty of these things, because of our deep love for them.

THERE IS A WOODEN CROSS in our bedroom. It is very primitive, made by hand. In the center of the cross is a heart made of tin. I love this cross. I know the town, Chimayo, from which it comes. Chimayo is a village in northern New Mexico, very poor and remote. In the center of Chimayo is a small church, famous for miracles that take place there. The church is built over an ancient kiva—a sacred Native American prayer site— and in a small room off to the side of the sanctuary there is a hole in the ground. The hole is filled with dirt that many say is sacred. People journey from faraway places to touch this dirt. Every Good Friday thousands of pilgrims from all over New Mexico come—many on foot, from as much as three hundred miles away, walking for several days—to be healed by the spirit of this place. On the wall are dozens of crutches, left by faithful pilgrims who have hobbled in and walked out on their own. When you enter this church, you feel saturated with the intimate presence of something sacred.

Our cross comes from this village. It has been blessed

by the prayers and pilgrimages of thousands of beings who sought healing, grace, and peace.

The heart in the center is also fashioned by hand. It is a *milagro,* a devotional piece of hammered tin that is commonly found in Mexico and is also used in northern New Mexico. The *milagro* is a prayer in itself. It symbolizes the thing for which we pray—a leg-shaped *milagro* for healing a broken leg, a breast *milagro* for healing breast cancer, a heart *milagro* for a heart condition or for the healing of a broken heart. The *milagro* carries our prayers heavenward. When I lived in Latin America I often saw little children and old women on the plaza, bringing their *milagros* into the churches to pin on the hem of the Virgin Mary's garment. Such placement would ensure that their prayers received careful attention from the mother of God, who would carry them personally to the ears of the divine.

In our room is this cross and this heart *milagro.* Because we have such love for the place from which they come and for the people who made them, we know their story. Every year Christine and I go to Chimayo. We enter the church to meditate and pray. Then we gather some of the sacred dirt for friends who are ill or in need of healing. Through Bread for the Journey, we also work to help the poor of Chimayo create economic development projects, so that the people can sustain themselves in this tiny village. Drawn into this community through our love of this place, our lives become woven into the story of Chimayo.

"The center of gravity," says Sasaki Roshi, "unifies everything." In our daily lives, whatever we love becomes our center of gravity. When we love something, we feel the truth of it, we touch its deeper nature. Our love breaks it open and reveals its secrets. There are many, many things in the world that I have had neither the time nor the ability to love, and so I know little about them. But those things I love, I have come to know. What we choose to love is very important, for what we love leads our eyes, ears, and hearts on a pilgrimage that shapes the texture of our lives. As Jesus reminds us, "Where your treasure is, there will your heart be also."

What do you love? The question cannot be answered

too quickly, because first you must sift through a variety of disparate impulses. At the beginning you may encounter what you think you are *supposed* to love. You uncover what you should be able to do, or would do if only you were more perfect, more spiritual, more successful, and on and on. You may first name those things you love because of what they will do for you—impress your friends and family, earn some place of belonging, or whatever. But to discern and choose those things you truly love—this is a fruitful and nourishing practice.

A FEW MONTHS AGO I got a call from Max Cordova. I met Max through our work with Bread for the Journey, and he often calls me with ideas about what can be done to help people in northern New Mexico. We had helped Max and the people of Truchas build a new community center for a group of seven small mountain villages. Max is warm and kind, and his heart is given to helping others. I am always grateful to share a moment with him.

This time Max wanted to talk about water in Truchas. Truchas—like all of northern New Mexico—was settled by the Spanish in the sixteenth and seventeenth centuries. The Spanish irrigated these lands by climbing high into the mountains to dig a wide irrigation ditch that would bring water to the fields and villages. What the Spanish learned about irrigation from the Incas in South America, they brought to the mountains of the Southwest.

Max took me up to the mouth of the ditch, a two-hour drive in his pickup. The *acequia madre,* or mother ditch, runs for two miles at over eleven thousand feet and then feeds a smaller ditch, which runs for another twelve miles into town. Three hundred years ago, the twenty-eight families that settled Truchas worked for years to dig this ditch by hand. Like their Inca counterparts, they had only donkeys and shovels. When they found their way blocked by a large boulder, they would dig a small pit under a portion of the rock and light a fire underneath the stone. When the rock was heated, they poured cold water on it to crack it open. Then they could continue digging. Some boulders were so large it took a month of heating and cracking simply to get through them.

Max and I walked alongside the ditch. The water flowed so quietly, cradled in the earth beneath a canopy of ponderosa and aspen. Every year, in spring, the people of Truchas climb this mountain to clean the ditch, as they have for the last three hundred years. As the water poured forth from the mountain, so had the life of these people been poured into this *acequia*. This was sacred ground.

"The Army Corps of Engineers wants to tear this all out," Max finally told me. "They want to replace it with plastic pipe. They got some money from the government, and they decided to use it to fill in this ditch. They say plastic pipe will be more efficient, that we will not lose any water, and we can direct it anywhere we want." Max paused. He was clearly upset. "They say it will be better for us, and we should be happy we will not have to clean the ditch.

"But we don't think this is a good idea," Max went on, slowly, quietly. "We love this ditch. When we all climb Truchas peak in the spring and clean the ditch, it holds us together. The ditch is our life. It feeds us; it is like glue that holds the soul of Truchas together. How can they take it away from us?"

I did not know what to say. It was inconceivable anyone would want to destroy this place. I marveled again at the frequency with which people in small villages, people of color, people with little financial or political influence, must relentlessly confront powers that regularly impose their will from the outside, so often bringing unnecessary suffering and grief.

Max continued, "It is true, we have many problems. We have a lot of poverty here. We have drinking, alcoholism; sometimes there is violence. There is hardly anything for our young people. But the ditch, it is a beautiful thing. These things, they can unite us, give us hope. This ditch holds us together. Without the ditch, I am afraid we will come apart."

For the next three months Bread for the Journey worked with Max, finding lawyers fluent in the language of environmental and historical preservation. The Corps was forced to hold public hearings, open their documents to the public, and allow the people of Truchas to have a voice in the future of the ditch. There were emotional meetings, passionate encounters where people spoke of their parents and grandparents and great-grandparents and of cleaning the ditch, drawing water for their fields, tasting the sweetness of the mountain's gift to them. How could they let this die?

Finally the lawyers and representatives of the community presented the Army Corps of Engineers with a petition to keep the ditch. Of the six hundred families in Truchas, all but eight had signed the petition. Faced with such remarkably united opposition, the Corps had to back away from the project. For now, they would leave the ditch alone. Max and the people of Truchas had managed, against overwhelming odds, to save what they loved.

What do you love? You gain courage from what you love. When you know where your treasure lies, when you know what is, for you, sacred and right, then you are filled with a clarity of purpose and a breathtaking capacity to act on what you believe.

Plant What You Love
in the Garden of Your Life

Take the time to pray—
it is the sweet oil that eases the hinge into the garden
so the doorway can swing open easily.
You can always go there.

Consider yourself blessed.
These stones that break your bones
will build the altar of your love.

Your home is the garden.
Carry its odor, hidden in you, into the city.
Suddenly your enemies will buy seed packets
and fall to their knees to plant flowers
in the dirt by the road.
They'll call you Friend
and honor your passing among them.
When asked, "Who was that?" they will say,
"Oh that one has been beloved by us
since before time began."
This from people who would have trampled over you
to maintain their advantage.

Give everything away except your garden,
Your worry, your fear, your small-mindedness.
Your garden can never be taken from you.

—Lynn Park

When we plant a garden, we must first prepare the soil.
We must take great care to clear the ground of rocks, twigs,
and weeds, removing anything that will prevent healthy

growth. We work the soil, sifting the hard clumps, digging in essential nutrients. Then we might build a fence, an enclosure to keep out predatory animals—rabbits, deer, gophers—so that the garden will be safe from harm.

But what if we stop there? What if we spend all our time preparing the soil, moving rocks, pulling weeds, and building fences? At the end of our work, what will we have? Only a clear, empty patch of ground. There will be no harvest, no flowers, no nourishment from this garden.

The second, indispensable question we must answer is this: What shall we plant in this garden? What harvest, when it comes, will bring us great joy? What seeds, when they blossom, will provide us with delight? It is not enough to keep clearing, sifting, removing obstacles, securing boundaries. While it is essential that we prepare the soil, this will not in itself produce a harvest.

In the same way, our various healing methods, our psychologies and therapies, can help us clear the ground of our past and prepare us to receive a better life. But it is not enough simply to clear the debris of the past. We must plant what we love in the garden of our life. As the Tao Te Ching insists, our center will heal us. When we attend to what is loving and beautiful, we are brought forward into our most exquisite manifestation. "Correct handling of flowers," suggests Bokuyo Takeda, "redefines the personality."

This is the difference between a life repaired and a life well lived. When we spend all our time clearing the ground of our life story, we are seeking only to repair what is broken, to fix what is defective. But even when we are successful, the best we can hope for is to climb all the way up to ground level, to "recover" some imagined state of being "normal." But what if we imagine something beyond a life repaired?

Our work in therapy, telling the old stories and healing the old wounds, is necessary and important. This is the work of clearing the ground of our lives. But then there are seeds to plant.

THICH NHAT HANH:

There are many kinds of seeds in us, both good and bad. Some were planted during our lifetime, and some were transmitted by our parents, our ancestors, and our society. Our ancestors and our parents have given us seeds of joy, peace, and happiness, as well as seeds of sorrow, anger, and so on.

Every time we practice mindful living, we plant healthy seeds and strengthen the healthy seeds already in us. Healthy seeds function similarly to antibodies. When a virus enters our bloodstream, our body reacts and antibodies come and surround it, take care of it, and transform it. This is true with our psychological seeds as well. If we plant wholesome, healing, refreshing seeds, they will take care of the negative seeds, even without our asking them. To succeed, we must cultivate a good reserve of refreshing seeds.

JANET GREW UP with an alcoholic father. Now, with five children and a demanding career, she often feels overwhelmed and exhausted by her life. She is always taking care of something or someone, and she resents that she has to work so hard for so little emotional reward. Just as she did with her alcoholic father, she is always watching for what needs to be done, what tasks are required, how to make sure everything and everyone is taken care of.

Janet and I worked together for some time on her childhood and how the pain of her family alcoholism gave birth to her compulsions and her weariness. At the same time I could see that Janet was also a very playful, creative woman who rarely allowed herself to nurture her artistic spirit. "My father was the artist in the family," she reported to me one day. "It was my job to clean up the messes he left behind." We discussed the possibility of her listening more closely to her creative impulses. She said she would try, but it would be hard. Where would she find the time?

A few weeks later, Janet proudly announced she had begun taking a watercolor class two evenings a week at the community college. When she told me about her painting, her eyes were bright and her face shone. She brought me some of her paintings. They were bright and playful, rich with passionate colors. "When I'm painting, I feel something deep in my body, a joy, a happiness I didn't know I had. These may not be great paintings—I just love doing them so much. I lock myself in my room for hours, and no one is allowed to bother me. I'm just letting myself go. I'm having so much fun."

The more Janet painted, the more she shifted her awareness. She no longer watched like the child of an alcoholic. Now she saw with the eyes of a painter. Instead of always watching for responsibilities, now she also watched for colors, lines, textures, and shapes. She had shifted her inner language; she was now seeking what she loved.

Her family, her children, and her marriage were still the same. But Janet could now see with eyes that were more in balance, eyes that could also uncover what was beautiful and rich in her daily, ordinary life.

WHEN I THINK of what I love, so many things arise at once. I think first of the cool moisture in the morning air, gentle in my nose, my throat, my lungs. It is a hopeful feeling, and it nourishes me; it brings me peace.

I also remember when I first learned to meditate. I was a freshman at the University of Rochester, and I was visiting Bill Giles, my photography professor, at his farm in the country. He had asked his students to help him build a root cellar, so my friend Chuck and I hitchhiked out to his home early one Saturday morning. We set to work digging, mixing concrete, pouring, shaping. Later we picked apples, and his wife made apple pie.

At the end of a long day, Bill showed us a place to sleep

up in the loft in the barn. It was cold and smelled of hay. It felt old and safe—yet, as I was young and newly on my own, it all felt uncharted, unfamiliar, and exciting. Just before we drifted off to sleep, Bill climbed up the ladder and asked us if we wanted to meditate. Neither Chuck nor I knew exactly what that was, but the day had been so lovely that it seemed like a dangerous and perfect way to end the day. So up in the hayloft by the light of a candle, Bill—who was a practicing Buddhist—taught us how to sit, to breathe, to concentrate our minds. He had us bow and then sit for ten minutes. It was the most exhilarating ten minutes I had ever spent. At the end of the time of sitting, Bill clapped his hands, bowed, and left us to sleep. That night I first discovered my passionate love of quiet.

I recall seeing Seiji Ozawa conduct the Toronto Symphony when I was fifteen. The symphony had come to perform in a small amphitheater in my hometown, and from the moment the orchestra began under the leadership of his spirited, passionate baton, it galvanized the molecules throughout my body as I listened—and quietly wept—with confusion and deep love for this music.

I recall skipping school in the ninth grade to see Nicol Williamson perform *Hamlet* on Broadway.

I remember Mirasol, my neighbor in one of the barrios of Lima, Peru, a girl of eight who always smiled a disarming smile from deep behind her eyes—this in the midst of horrific poverty, squalor, and death.

I think of Dolores, a runaway we took in to stay at our home, and how in spite of her terrible epileptic seizures, she would always regain her composure with an inexplicably loving, generous smile.

I think of my good friend Richy, who, when he plays guitar, soft, late in the evening, coaxes such grace from wood, steel, and the breath in his belly.

And I think of my wife, Christine, at work with our daughter, Sherah, on some art project—arguing, planning, giggling, and transmitting, through the friction of their respective passions, a sense of power, creativity, and accomplishment.

These things I love—they are the things of ordinary life, miraculous threads that have been woven through the fabric of my days on the earth. These are the seeds I have planted. These are the moments I place on the altar of my life, to guide me home.

FOR MOST OF HER ADULT LIFE, Elizabeth loved her children above all other things. She willingly embraced the roles of wife and mother, dedicating herself to the care of her two boys, striving to make sure they were safe and healthy and that they received a good education.

Elizabeth came to see me because her younger boy—Elizabeth's favorite—had just had a terrible accident. Eleven-year-old Jack and a friend were mowing the lawn and began playing a game, chasing after each other with the mower. Somehow the mower tipped over and Jack fell into it, cutting off three of his fingers and mangling his right hand. Elizabeth rushed him to the hospital, where, after nine hours of surgery, they were unable to reattach his fingers.

After Jack came home from the hospital, Elizabeth crept into his room at night to watch him sleep, to reassure herself he was still breathing, still alive. Jack's accident had made her even more concerned for her children; she worried about them constantly. To make matters worse, Elizabeth had begun to fight with her older son, Mark. Their confrontations seemed to go on and on with no clear resolution, and increasingly Elizabeth felt weary and despondent. She had given so much of her life to the care of their children, and now they both seemed to be falling apart. In spite of her best efforts, she had not been able to protect Jack, nor could she make Mark happy.

"Jack is my baby," Elizabeth said to me angrily. "And I can't do anything to fix his hand. I can't ever make him whole again." She berated herself and beat herself up internally for her failures as a mother. Since Elizabeth had grown up with family pain, she was quite accomplished at judging herself harshly. "A good mother would not fight with her children," these critical voices ranted inside her. "A good mother would have been there to stop her son from being hurt." Elizabeth had tried hard to be a good mother; a good mother, she thought, should have been able to throw herself in the path of all potential harm.

Elizabeth felt something inside her was dying. She felt that her performance as a mother—something she had placed at the center of her life—was a disaster. What could she do? What could possibly make her life well again?

When we listened more carefully to these relentless internal criticisms, we came to realize that Elizabeth was facing for the first time the unsettling fact that she was not in complete control of her children's lives. Elizabeth was no failure as a mother, but she was beginning to see that, try as she might, she could neither ensure her children's safety nor direct their destiny. She had tried, with all her worrying, planning, care, and attention, to guarantee that their lives would evolve without anguish, without harm. But now, in this moment, she realized she could never give her children a perfect life. When the mower cut off Jack's fingers, Elizabeth's illusion that she could control her children's destiny was destroyed.

As we explored these feelings of powerlessness, Elizabeth recognized that some of the tears she shed were also for herself. Elizabeth, it seemed, did not have a perfect life, either. While her husband, Frank, was a good father and provider, he could also be distant and busy with his work. She was not unsatisfied with her marriage, but it was clear she needed more in her life. She was a caring, creative, intelligent woman. She felt the rumblings of a need, a need to be more than just a mother, to do more than simply try to sculpt the perfect family. The perfect family had just collapsed. It was time to build something new.

Moments like this inevitably arise in the course of our life. People or things we love change in ways we do not want or expect. Things we plant do not remain seedlings forever; they grow and change. In fear of losing them, we try to hold on, to keep things as they were. As our loved ones evolve and grow, we hold on more desperately to how they used to be, until we strangle both them and ourselves. Our love, once easy and free, can become fearful, even resentful. Why can't they be as they were? Why are they doing this to us?

Of course, Jack and Mark were not doing anything to Elizabeth; they were simply growing up, living their lives. Elizabeth's love for her children needed to change as they changed, to grow as they grew. By allowing her children to come into their own, Elizabeth too could come into her own and follow what she loved within herself.

But what would she do? How, after years of focusing her attention outside herself, on the welfare of her children, could she find her own destiny, her own inner balance? One day I suggested she try meditation. Perhaps by learning to sit quietly for a time and listen to all her inner voices—the critical voices as well as the wise, strong, and loving voices—she could begin to grant herself the same measure of attention and care she was giving her children and family. If she could listen carefully to the yearnings of her own soul, she might uncover what else, besides motherhood, nourished her heart and spirit.

As it happened, there was a ten-day meditation scheduled with my friend Jack Kornfield at the Lama Foundation, a retreat center north of Taos. For several weeks I playfully cajoled Elizabeth to become a meditator, eventually wearing her down until she finally relented. She let me know she was more than a little terrified at the prospect of ten days of silence, with only her inner voices for company. Still, she bravely signed up and went.

The retreat became a turning point for Elizabeth. She uncovered a spaciousness she had not felt in years. She softened much of her inner anger and disappointment by developing a patient kindness. She found a deep permission to love herself as well as she had been loving her family, and that love began to grow in new and exciting ways. When she returned from the retreat, she began meditating on a regular basis, at first by herself and then in the company of others. She helped start a sitting group, which now, years later, is an established meditation center in Santa Fe.

Meditation did not "cure" Elizabeth of her sadness or despair. Rather, the seeds of self-love—which had lain dormant for a long time in the soil of her daily life—simply needed to be nourished by a period of compassionate attention. In this quiet, she found the things she needed to fertilize that love, which in turn provided all the healing she required.

Elizabeth further resolved to use her passion and creativity to help others. She went back to school and earned her master's degree in art therapy. She began working with adults and children in need, offering them much of the care that her children—now grown and away from home—no longer needed.

This spring Elizabeth came to me and asked if Bread for the Journey would support a project of hers. She wanted to help organize a group of volunteer artists to teach elementary-school students throughout Santa Fe to make clay bowls. These bowls, once glazed and fired, would be filled with soup made by their parents and sold at a community-wide event. The money raised would go to serve the poor and hungry of northern New Mexico. She called her idea the Empty Bowls Project.

On the day of the event, hundreds of people came to buy these beautiful bowls and partake of the soup. With a small donation from Bread for the Journey and a tremendous investment by Elizabeth and many of her friends, her family, and volunteers, the Empty Bowls Project made a $14,000 profit for several worthy hunger projects.

Elizabeth's love had grown. She had given her love at first to her own children; then, as they needed her less, she allowed her love to expand and change, learning first to love herself, then those in need. As a result, the entire community could benefit from her kindness and care.

﷯

Ananda, the beloved disciple of the Buddha, once remarked to his master, "Half the holy life, O master, is friendship with the beautiful, association with the beautiful, communion with the beautiful." The Buddha replied, "Say not so, Ananda, say not so. It is not half the holy life. It is the whole of the holy life."

﷯

PRACTICE: ATTENDING TO WHAT WE LOVE

Attention is the physical manifestation of love. If I keep pushing my children away when they want me to play with them, they do not feel loved. I may have love in my heart; I may feel joy when I see them, and want only the best for them. But they will feel my love only when I turn around and give them my undivided attention. Through my attention, they experience my love.

Attention is a tangible measure of love. Whatever receives our time and attention becomes the center of gravity, the focus of our life. This is what we do with what we love: We allow it to become our center.

What is at the center of your life? Carefully examine where you spend your attention, your time. Look at your appointment book, your daily schedule. These things— these meetings, errands, responsibilities—this is where you dedicate your precious days, hours, and moments. This is what receives your care and attention—and, by definition, your love.

What do you notice about those people and things that get your attention? Is this what you wish to love? Are these the people and situations you hope will receive the gift of your life and your companionship? Are these the places you would intentionally choose to offer your love and devotion? Why or why not?

We become what we love. Whatever you are giving your time and attention to, day after day, this is the kind of person you will eventually become. Is this what you want?

Love and Truth

"YOU WILL KNOW THE TRUTH," said Jesus, "and the truth shall make you free." As we negotiate the multiplicity of demands, expectations, desires, and goals in our work, our family, our friendships, and our community, we may find ourselves confused about what is most deeply true. How do we know for sure what we feel, what we believe in every situation? What, in this relationship or circumstance, is the right action, the correct word, the most truthful response? We ache to know what is right and true so that we can be precise in our actions and accurate in our relationships.

Some of us came from families that rarely told the truth. Through either ignorance, fear, or denial, they were unwilling or incapable of naming accurately their feelings, thoughts, and intentions. Much of our early life was spent trying to decipher the puzzling discontinuities that permeated the words and actions of those closest to us. Did they mean what they said? If they told me something completely different yesterday, which should I believe? How can I decide?

Perhaps our parents or siblings denied the truth of something we had seen with our own eyes, or they questioned the integrity of something we inwardly knew to be true. At that point we learned either to mistrust anything others had to say or to mistrust our own intuition, to deny the truth of our own feelings. Knowing what was true came to seem painful, isolating, and confusing—even dangerous.

Following what we love can lead us to the truth. When we love something, we are granted its wisdom. If we love cooking, for example, we will learn about the fragrance of certain spices, the soil in which they grow, the way they are picked. We learn about the qualities of certain oils, where they come from, the way they change when they are heated. We learn about mixtures of herbs, the textures of flour, and the perfect season for particular vegetables. Through our love of cooking, we learn about how things grow, about soil and air and sunlight and water—truths that may escape the attention of someone without such love.

Laureen Mar, a poet, loved her mother, and so she watched her mother very closely:

My Mother, Who Came From China, Where She Never Saw Snow

In a huge, rectangular room, the ceiling
a machinery of pipes and fluorescent lights,
ten rows of women hunched over machines,
their knees pressing against pedals
and hands pushing the shiny fabric thick as tongues
through metal and thread.
My mother bends her head to one of these machines.
Her hair is coarse and wiry, black as burnt scrub.
She wears glasses to shield her intense eyes.
A cone of orange thread spins. Around her,
talk flutters harshly in Toisan wah.
Chemical stings. She pushes cloth
through pounding needle, under, around, and out,
breaks thread with a snap against fingerbone, tooth.
Sleeve after sleeve, sleeve.
It is easy. The same piece.
For eight or nine hours, sixteen bundles maybe,
250 sleeves to ski coats, all the same.
It is easy, only once she's run the needle
through her hand. She earns money
by each piece, on a good day,
thirty dollars. Twenty-four years.
It is frightening how fast she works.
She and the women who were taught sewing
terms in English as a Second Language.
Dull thunder passes through her fingers.

Politicians, economists, merchants might all look and yet miss what Laureen saw. It is Laureen's love that revealed to her the complex, poignant beauty of her mother at work.

Sam Scott is a friend and gifted artist. When I last saw him, he said, "I have decided to paint the seasons. I love being able to feel what happens as the earth changes. This year the lilacs bloomed a week later than they did last year. Most summers the first rain of the season is on the fourth of July. Some years I can smell autumn for the first time by the thirteenth of July. When I listen to the turning of the earth, there is a clock in my body; I love to feel the little shifts in the air, the sky, the temperature. I am trying to paint what I feel."

Some of us become nervous when it is time to paint what we feel. It takes courage to name and follow what we love. Indeed, the word *courage* is rooted in the Latin *cor,* "heart"; to be courageous is to follow the teachings of your heart.

EMILY WAS ABUSED by her parents as a child. She came to see me because she was now having problems with her own teenage daughter, Veronica, and she felt confused about what to do. "How can I possibly know how to be a parent, when my own parents were so violent and destructive?"

It is my practice to assume that each person who comes to see me already knows what they need to do. They feel the truth of what is necessary somewhere deep inside, but they are afraid to say it, or they are afraid of trusting what they know. I simply give them permission to name aloud what they secretly know is true. With as much gentleness and compassion as I can offer, I try to create a place of safety where they can freely admit what they already know. Sometimes it is time to end a destructive relationship, or to change careers, or to begin a deeper spiritual practice. In Emily's case, while she reported that she did not know how to parent her daughter, I assumed she knew very well what she had to do. She was simply uncomfortable trusting her own wisdom.

What if you simply trust your love for Veronica? I suggest. *Let yourself feel your care for your daughter, for her happiness, her future. What do you notice?*

"I feel a warm spot in my chest and belly. It's soft, and it hurts a little. But it's gentle, too, and strong. It's a good feeling."

If you allow the feeling to speak to you about Veronica and her needs, what does it say?

Emily began to weep. "It says it is time for her to go. She needs to leave home. I know this is true, but I can't bear to think about it." Quiet grief, silent tears.

Emily was afraid that if she let Veronica leave, her daughter would never come back. This is what Emily had done when she left home; she never returned, her parents had hurt her so much. But the feeling in Emily's body, speaking from her deep love, spoke the truth: It was time to let her daughter go. So we worked on methods that Emily could use to begin to prepare the way for Veronica to leave home, methods that would be gentle and flexible, allowing Veronica both to leave and to remain a strong and vital part of Emily's life.

In moments like these we surrender into our deep love for the people and things we hold dear. While it may at times be frightening, our love can speak to us accurately and directly about what is required of us. Our love allows us to hear the truth embedded in sorrow and confusion. As the God of the Hebrews told His people, "I have put my truth in your innermost mind, and I have written it in your heart."

DIANA'S BATTLE with HIV was legendary in our community; now, after years of successfully combating the opportunistic infections that had invaded her body, Diana was tired and close to death. She was in the hospital, in a coma, and Kathy, Diana's best friend, felt somewhere deep in her body that Diana was ready to go. Kathy knew that Diana had fought so hard to remain alive, and she felt that in order to let go, to allow the war to end, Diana would need some potent, trustworthy final permission from someone she loved.

Diana was beloved by many, and a host of family and friends came to visit and sit with her. Finally, late one night, everyone but Kathy had gone. Kathy pulled up a chair next to Diana's bed, where she could hold Diana's face in her hands. She sat in silence for a long time, listening for what to say, what was most true, most necessary. Then Kathy spoke gently and slowly to this woman who had been her devoted friend.

"Diana, I know that you have fought long and hard. I love you so much. I know you don't want to go. But I know you're tired. You don't have to fight anymore. You have been strong. You did well. There's nothing more you need to do. You can rest now. It's time to rest. I love you."

Slowly a tear rolled down Diana's cheek. In her coma, she had heard Kathy's words, heard the truth of them. A moment later, Diana passed away.

How do you know what is true? What prayers do you pray, what voices do you listen for that speak what is right? The truth is never far from your heart and your spirit. Every person you touch, every act of kindness, every gesture born of your love can uncover something deeply true within and around you. And with each act of truthfulness, you touch a deeper chord in yourself and others. As Emerson said, "Our life is an apprenticeship to truth, that around every circle another can be drawn . . . under every deep a lower deep opens."

I FIRST MET PAUL just after he had completed his second round of chemotherapy for abdominal cancer. I could tell that he had been a robust and energetic man, although he was now racked by spasms of great pain. He was frightened and frail. He was physically and emotionally depleted, a condition made worse by the severe toxicity of the chemicals in his body. I was blessed to see Paul emerge from that period and undertake a deepening of his spiritual pilgrimage. We kept one another company as he explored the nature of sorrow and grace, especially in light of the fact that they said his cancer had not been cured by the treatments.

Our work together was delicate and precious. Paul wanted very much to live, and his spirit was courageous and strong. My most distinct memory of our time together is a great deal of laughter. We laughed often as we compared notes on the ways the path of spirit had unfolded in our very different lives. We explored different healing practices, we meditated together, we spoke of the expansion and contraction of all living things. We also knew—although we rarely spoke of it, as Paul preferred to imagine a more positive outcome—that he might very well die from the cancer, and soon.

After many months, Paul had another relapse, a painful one. Back in the hospital, the doctors figured his remaining time to be only weeks. Now Paul was desperately torn between fighting and surrender. Should he redouble his efforts to find a cure, or should he simply accept the apparent inevitability of his death and peacefully spend his remaining days in meditation and intimate company with his friends?

Paul decided he would fight it with everything he had. He made a trip to Mexico, to a clinic that specialized in alternative treatments. The regimen, which lasted three weeks, left him wasted and exhausted. Even worse, it did not appear to be a cure. Upon his arrival at home, he was met by several of his closest friends, who urged him to settle in quietly and simply rest.

Still, Paul would pepper us with questions—should he continue, or should he surrender? If he kept fighting, he might live. But that would further exhaust him, and he might not enjoy the time he had left. If he surrendered, he might enjoy the time he still had, and he could surround himself with things and people that he loved. But then he would worry, could he have lived? Was he giving up too soon?

Doctors and medicine cannot answer this for us. In fact, this question often arises when medicine has already done what it can. It is a profoundly intimate, personal choice. Shall I fight or surrender? And if I fight, what am I fighting? If I surrender, what am I surrendering to?

One day Jennifer, one of Paul's closest friends, called to say Paul really needed to see me. When I arrived at his home,

Paul was frantic. He was lying on the couch talking on the phone, two lines at once, calling doctors, arranging for prescriptions, coordinating a new trip back to Mexico, discussing new chemotherapies. In his desperation he was becoming short of breath, almost hyperventilating. He had to take oxygen from the tank next to his couch just to breathe.

Jennifer and I sat down next to him, and we turned off the phone. We took his hands in ours and rubbed his chest around his heart. After a while I asked him how it was in his body. "I'm in pain, because the tumors are growing," Paul said. "There's a lot of pressure. I just have to get more information about the vitamin therapy or else I . . ." I stopped him. *Please stay with us, Paul. Don't run off into your head. Just stay with the physical sensations. Tell me what you feel in your body.*

"It hurts."

Where?

"In my abdomen, my groin. It's burning. It hurts so much."

I put my hand on his belly. *Breathe into my hand, into your belly. Just be quiet, and let the breath touch your belly, down into where the tumors are.*

He did, for a few moments. *What happens now,* I asked.

"I am afraid," he said. "I am afraid to let go of the people I love. I do not want to die. I don't want them to leave me." Paul began to weep, racking sobs. A deep moan came from his chest. He was feeling his grief, touching that place in which he knew he was going to die. For a long time he cried deep, mournful tears. He spoke about his love for his friend, Jeffrey, and especially for Ben and Casey, Jennifer and Jeffrey's two boys. Paul had been their loving "Uncle Paul," and the boys were devoted to him. They didn't want him to die. They were eleven and seven.

He told Jennifer how much he loved them and that he wanted to make sure he left them something to remember him, something that would help them. "You will always be with them," Jennifer reminded him. "You are so alive in their hearts."

As Paul spoke of the people he loved, as he wept with

his love for them, I could see his body begin to relax. *What happens in your body now,* I asked him. "It gets softer, quieter inside," he said. "I feel less pain, more peaceful. I know now it's time to let go of all this crazy running around, to let go of the world. It's time to come back inside. It's time to get ready to go."

The instant Paul allowed himself to feel the tenderness of losing what he loved, he immediately recognized what was true about his life. It was time to go. His love for Ben and Casey opened his heart. He could see clearly the truth of where he was.

SADLY, in our pain or confusion we often forget or misplace those things we truly love—especially when we feel frightened or believe we are in danger. Jim grew up in a violent family. His mother and father often fought, and there were arguments, harsh words. When Jim was small, he saw his father attack his mother with a knife. Jim remembers the men in the white coats who came in an ambulance. They wrestled his father to the ground, right in the middle of the kitchen. As they took Jim's father away he looked at his son and screamed, "Don't let them do this to me!" Jim was very small. He didn't know what to do.

Years later, sitting in my office, Jim speaks of his fear. He carries it with him always. He feels small, frightened, unable to act with courage or clarity. He is terrified of conflict, disagreement, difficult encounters of any kind. People at his work make him afraid, especially when they get mad. Jim wants me to help him heal this fear.

We investigate the fear in his body, try to learn how it works, where it lives. He feels it in his chest and deep in his belly. We do some meditation, some visualization. We make some progress, he feels a bit safer—but still the fear is a persistent companion. Finally I ask, *Is there ever a time when the fear goes away?*

"Never," he replies. "It is always there."

There must be a time, I suggest. *Think. Try to remember.*

Jim takes a few moments to scan the memories he carries deep in his body, listening for a moment of quiet, any respite from the residual terror. Something gently shifts in his face. He has remembered something. "When my daughter was born," he says. A smile takes shape. "When I saw her for the first time, I loved her instantly, completely. In that moment I don't think I felt any of the fear."

When else? I ask. "There are other times. When I'm working with my hands, building furniture. I love making things with my hands, being quiet and focused on making something beautiful. Also, when I take walks. Sometimes I go off and take walks alone. I watch the sky, the mountains. I love being outside. When I'm walking, I'm not afraid."

We began to notice that Jim's fear dissipated when he was doing what he loved. When he was with his daughter, working with his hands, taking walks in nature, the fear dissolved. The things he loved cast out the fear more reliably and perfectly than all our work on his childhood, his trauma, the history of his wound. When he was following what he truly loved, he felt at peace.

HOW DO WE BEGIN? We begin by being taught by what we love. What we love becomes the star that guides our path, lights our way. It pulls us inward, reminds us of what we know to be true. Our love uncovers the subtle truths that may otherwise be obscured by our fear or our hurt. Indeed, according to the author of the first epistle of John, "Perfect love casts out all fear."

Hoskie Nakai is a Navajo boy. His grandmother died. Afterward he speaks of her:

> My grandmother was a weaver. She knew many designs that no one knew but her children. She told me that weaving wasn't hard so I tried my best, and now I know how to weave better than I thought I could. She told me I could weave good, so now I know!

Sometimes, I see designs when I herd sheep and sometimes I don't. My grandmother told me it's a good time to look for designs when you're with the sheep because it is their wool that you weave with. You just look at things like flowers or clouds. They give you lots of designs. They're all out there by the sheep.

But sometimes, when I am lying on my back and my foster brother is asleep, I look up at the ceiling and see my grandmother's designs. My grandmother's designs come back to me and I feel her walking in the room. I feel as though she is holding me . . .

Love and Attention

> When I am working on a problem, I never think about beauty. I only think of how to solve the problem. But when I have finished, if the solution is not beautiful, I know it is wrong.

—R. Buckminster Fuller

Even if we choose to give our attention to what we love, we may soon discover that our attention is scattered and diffused. We have too many things on our plate, and we are distracted by the sheer number of commitments, appointments, relationships, and responsibilities we have accumulated. Sometimes we become so preoccupied, we actually forget what we love.

As Meister Eckhart wisely pointed out, "The spiritual life is not a process of addition, but rather of subtraction." We cannot love so many things, populating our lives with more and more, hoping to feel satisfied. This is a common complaint. The more we accomplish, the more we are expected to do. We take on more responsibility, only to feel resentful of what we have promised. The faster we go and the more we do, the sooner we forget what we love. We misplace those things that truly nourish our deepest heart.

"You don't see the stars in the daytime," said Ramakrishna, "but that doesn't mean the stars don't exist." Just because we are afraid we have misplaced what we love, that does not mean our love is gone. Eknath Easwaran, the spiritual teacher, relates a story his grandmother used to tell:

In ancient India lived a sculptor renowned for his life-sized statues of elephants. With trunks curled high, tusks thrust forward, thick legs trampling the earth, these carved beasts seemed to trumpet to the sky. One day, a king came to see these magnificent works and to commission statuary for his palace. Struck with wonder, he asked the sculptor, "What is the secret of your artistry?"

The sculptor quietly took measure of the monarch and replied, "Great king, when with the aid of many men I quarry a gigantic piece of granite from the banks of the river, I have it set here in my courtyard. For a long time, I do nothing but observe this block of stone and study it from every angle. I focus all my concentration on this task and won't allow anyone or anything to disturb me. At first, I see nothing but a huge and shapeless rock sitting there, meaningless, indifferent to my purposes, utterly out of place. It seems faintly resentful at having been dragged from its cool place by the rushing waters.

"Then slowly, very slowly, I begin to notice something in the substance of the rock. I feel a presentiment . . . an outline, scarcely discernible, shows itself to me, though others, I suspect, would perceive nothing. I watch with an open eye and a joyous, eager heart. The outline grows stronger. Oh, yes, I can see it! An elephant is stirring in there!

"Only then do I start to work. For days flowing into weeks I use my chisel and mallet, always clinging to my sense of that outline, which grows ever stronger. How the big fellow strains! How he yearns to be out! How he wants to live! It seems so clear now, for I know the one thing I must do: with an utter singleness of purpose, I must chip away every last bit of stone that is not elephant. What then remains will be, must be, elephant."

The love of our heart is the elephant in the stone. Sadly, we populate our lives with too many things that are "not elephant." When we grab things on the run, we may not choose carefully or accurately. Then, somehow, we find ourselves suffocated in a whirlwind of things that do not belong in our life. Perhaps we may begin to uncover what we love by first noticing, and then gently eliminating, those things that do not spring from the center of our heart.

What we love galvanizes our attention. It frames our life. It forms the soil in which we grow; it is the seed in the ground. We give our heart to what we love.

Traditionally, most Native Americans have spoken of their deep love for the earth. They feel her as their mother, the sky as their father. They watch the earth and the sky very carefully, because these are things they love. They have many names for the sunlight that strikes the earth: *sun that first rises over the mountain, sun that strikes the top of the trees, sun that colors the earth red and orange, sun at twilight that angles through the flowers.* Because of their love, they watch carefully.

Our own consumer society loves and respects other things. We may have only one name for sunlight, but we have many names for automobiles: *Chevrolet Caprice, Ford Mustang, Oldsmobile Cutlass, Pontiac Firebird, Toyota Corolla, Nissan Stanza.* We take the time to name what is important to us, what we place at the center.

If we love color, we will see color everywhere. In nature, in museums, on the subway, on the street, in the hair and eyes of children, our world will be saturated with color. If we love cooking, our search will lead us to foods, tastes, spices, textures to delight the palate. Where your treasure is, there will your mouth be also.

At retreats, people often come to heal their sorrows. Early on, we speak of these things, and we try, in a gentle way, to examine the nature of sorrow, and the places in sorrow from which genuine grace can be born.

Only then do I invite people to explore what they love, using the collage exercise I described earlier, I bring in a huge pile of magazines and ask them to go through the pictures without thinking, allowing the images to jump off the page, tearing out images that speak to them of people and things that bring them nourishment and delight. After a while people begin to giggle, tell stories, and laugh as they pile up pictures. They begin to play—in one retreat, everyone began singing familiar hymns and old rock-and-roll songs. Given permission to focus their energy on what they love, everyone in the room is transformed.

When I was in high school and college, I played music with a few close friends. We would get together as often as we could to play guitars and sing songs. We loved one another in ways we could not then name aloud, but our passionate harmonies wove an exhilarating intimacy. We would all stay up late, camping out together in someone's house for days. The sensual blending of our bodies and our music brought us a singular joy that I find myself missing even now.

During that time, my friend Peter got a Martin guitar. Martin guitars were the best steel-string acoustic guitars in the universe, and we watched in awe as Peter brought his out of its shiny new hard-shell case. We took turns playing it; it was like making love to music, so softly and easily did it respond to the touch of our fingers.

A few months later Peter had to take the guitar back to the Martin factory to have a few minor adjustments made to the fretboard. He asked me if I wanted to drive with him to Nazareth, Pennsylvania, where the Martin factory was located, about three hours away. I was ready to go.

When we arrived, we entered into a world many guitar players only dream about. Here were the master instrument makers, gathered together in an enormous factory with all manner of tools and presses, woods and glues, engaged in producing some of the most beautiful instruments in the world. Each guitar in the factory was made by hand, one finely tuned step at a time.

Every step had its specialists. We wandered among the craftspeople making backs, soundboards, tuning pegs, and fretboards. We watched jewelers inlay mother-of-pearl around the sound hole. They let us wander around all morning; we were in heaven.

At lunchtime the factory took a collective break. At this

moment the most delightful thing happened. As the workers finished their lunch, they began to pick up these guitars and play them. One by one, dozens of employees gathered to play on the guitars they had made—a guitar symphony orchestra. Each improvising their way into the chorus of stringed voices, there were pickers and strummers and soloists and rhythm guitarists all testing out the sounds of these fine instruments—on their time off. These people loved what they were doing. They loved the music, and they loved those guitars. Even when they could have gone elsewhere for lunch to get away from their work, they stayed to play. They were the happiest people I had ever seen at their job. They were doing what they loved; and because of their love, they lavished such delicious attention and care on wood and steel that the instruments they made were magnificent.

AT TIMES, rather than attend to those things we love, we give the bulk of our attention instead to things that bring us harm. As we try to heal what has been hurt, we focus all our care upon things that are painful. Clearly our wounds need our attention. But when we concentrate exclusively upon our hurt, we learn to see the brokenness, losses, or injuries we have been given as the most important things in our lives. We cultivate an attention to these wounds in such a way that, over time, they come to occupy the most important place in our heart. Our wound lives in the center of our thoughts. In this way, we actually come to love our suffering.

Of course, we do not actually love the pain or sorrow that came to us. Our sorrows are real indeed, and they leave us weary and hurt. But when we give so much time and attention to the process of "healing"—when we fall in love with the feeling of being healed—then sooner or later we will need to find newer, more painful things to be healed from.

If we cut our arm, and the body is essentially healthy, then the body will respond vigorously to the wound. It will mobilize immunities to protect itself from infection; it will provide the necessary nutrients and raw materials for the skin to knit together. After a time, the arm is healed. Except for a small scar, there may be no evidence the arm was ever wounded.

This is the fundamental process of healing. Once the healing work is done, the body moves on to other things.

But if, along the way, we become enamored of the process of healing itself, we must always keep our vision attuned to fresh wounds, new disappointments, and current deficiencies, so that the healing can continue. If we look for pathology, we will find pathology. And with the exuberant proliferation of new psychologies, therapies, treatment centers, and healing strategies, we have made it easier to fall in love with our own healing. This can keep us very small— imprisoned in our own healing, trapped by what we love. "Seek and ye shall find" applies equally to those things we hope for and to those things we fear the most, even those things that are painful and difficult.

"All we are," said the Buddha, "is a result of what we have thought." If we focus the lion's share of our energy on ferreting out what we believe is wrong inside us, we gradually grow into people who are good at seeing what is wrong. If we spend our lives in search of what is pathological, we will become more adept at uncovering pathology wherever we direct our eyes. Instead of creating a life of beauty and meaning, we may simply become better and better at seeing only what is broken. As Abraham Maslow once said, "If a man's only tool is a key, he will imagine every problem to be a lock."

Two women, Heidi and Ellen, came to one of our retreats. Both were victims of sexual abuse. They had come to know each other through their hurt, and they had become good friends, each supporting the other's healing work. By the end of the first day, these two women asked if they could speak with me in private. We arranged to meet before dinner.

"I feel like you don't understand us," Ellen began. "Incest is a horrible thing, horrible. It will affect me for the rest of my life. It is the most powerful thing that ever happened to me. I go to meetings four times a week, I go to my therapist, I go to workshops. I feel like I will have to do this forever. I am an incest survivor, and I will be an incest survivor for my whole life. Why would I ever want to give up calling myself an incest survivor, now that I have found out who I really am?" Heidi concurred. We discussed for a long time the many costs and benefits of taking our spiritual identity from the shape of our wound. At the end of our conversation, they seemed slightly appeased, but, I suspect, unconvinced.

For Ellen and Heidi, the process of healing from incest has been the most loving, safe, and spiritually powerful experience of their lives. And so, in a way, they have come to love even their own incest. Wherever we put all our care and attention—this is what we love. Ellen and Heidi give all their time to seeking out the wounds, the consequences, the repercussions, the teachings, and the healings that surround their own incest. For the time being, this is what they love.

This is not to say we love the pain or the excruciating violation, or that we condone the terrible injustice of one being intimately harming another. We must, of course, name what was wrong, speak the truth of it, and try to build, with an abiding passion and enthusiasm for justice, a world in which children are treated with kindness, safety, and respect.

But our fascination with what happened to us as children of divorce, abuse, or neglect can also narrow our focus. We begin to see everything in life as arising out of abuse, embedded in abuse, taught by abuse. We place abuse at the center of our life.

This is not bad. We must, to heal, do this for a while. But if we choose to make it the work of our life, we may find that it keeps us small. We must at least be conscious that we are making a choice. We should know that we are choosing this.

WHEN CHRISTINA was born prematurely, she was put in an incubator. While she was inside, the supply of oxygen failed, causing Christina to lose her hearing. At eight months of age she was declared permanently deaf.

As she grew, Christina—rather than feeling broken by her physical challenges—became a determined young girl. She worked very hard as a child, straining against her deafness to eventually learn to read lips with astounding accuracy. Now, thirty-five years later, she has come to one of my retreats. As is my custom, I lead several guided meditations. Christina keeps her eyes open, because she has to read my lips in order to "hear" me.

After a few meditations, we begin a discussion about what we love. "I love language," she says. Her speech is remarkable for one who has been deaf essentially since birth. "I love to be able to speak, to communicate. I even learned French, because it feels so good in my mouth." She pauses. "I also love to play," she adds, "because my childhood was always such hard work."

Christina is quiet, but we sense there is something more she needs to say. We all wait. "I love breathing," she said. "When I was in the incubator, I couldn't breathe; there was no oxygen. So now I love my breath. Every breath feels like a beautiful gift. I am so grateful for my breath."

How many of us have such love, such gratefulness for our breath? I have been leading meditation retreats for years. Again and again I have asked people to become aware of their breath, to feel the shape of it, to notice the texture, to use the breath as a device to become awake to our life. But in that moment, listening to Christina, I felt humbled, as one who receives a powerful teaching. After countless hours spent in concentrated meditation, how often have I felt my own breath with such love?

We can begin by loving something as simple as our breath. As we become aware of the breath, we come to appreciate how it gives us life. We become grateful for our breath, and then we naturally feel grateful for our life. And out of that gratitude may spring a renewed determination to use our life more carefully, honoring the precious gift that it is. We may then live less and less by accident, becoming mindful of how we want to walk on the earth. All this arises from a simple love of the breath.

PEOPLE WHO LOVE are naturally teachers. People who love children can show us what is beautiful and true about children.

People who love cooking can offer to unlock the succulent secrets of food. People who love hiking can take us to places we would never have gone. Lovers are useful people, they wake us up. People who love the spirit, or God, or peace, or service, inspire the rest of us to look more closely at ourselves, to feel the shape of the gift of our life.

In seventh grade I had a math teacher—Paul Cohen— who loved math. He would get so excited, it was contagious. Now everyone knows that in seventh grade, kids are crazy. We were victims of raging hormones, which erupted in snotty, uncivilized, chaotic behavior. But Mr. Cohen loved those numbers so much, he loved what they did, and because we all felt his passion for math, he managed to hold us all spellbound. We may not have understood trigonometry, but we understood passion. And his passion made trigonometry feel like a forbidden adventure.

Try to remember: Our teachers, the best ones, did they not love what they did? Our mentors, our guides, our models, was it not their love that made us feel we wanted more? Their love opened the door for us. Not simply the door of knowledge—we could always have gone to an encyclopedia for that. Their love made learning come alive.

TEN YEARS AGO I was invited to the Neem Karoli Baba Ashram for *bandhara,* the great annual feast day that commemorates the death—or liberation from the body—of the beloved Neem Karoli Baba. The ashram was built by his devotees after his death, and it is a warm and welcoming place that feeds and cares for whoever arrives to worship there.

When I arrived in midmorning, the crush of devotees who filled the small temple were singing songs to Hanuman, the deity in Hinduism that symbolizes compassion and service. There was the music of the harmonium, bells, and drums, the smells of incense and flowers, offerings of fruit and sweets. It was a thoroughly sensual experience, a festival of delight in the presence of God. They were taking care of Hanuman, dressing him in jewels and fine garments, singing praises of his life and acts, offering him *prasad.* This was breathtakingly devotional worship—these were not hymns sung with Sunday morning obligation, but songs sung for hours on end, devotional music to please God, not simply to please ourselves.

It was not a perfunctory Protestant hymn, either—four verses and it's over. Many devotees had arisen from bed in the middle of the night to begin singing at 4 A.M., and would continue singing without stopping until 2 P.M.—ten hours of continuous singing. For these people, the chanting was a gift to Hanuman, to give thanks and to celebrate the power of this loving, generous aspect of God.

To sing for ten hours is intoxicating. It melts the resistance of the mind, and it dissolves the barriers to the heart and spirit. After a few hours we begin to surrender, at first to the music, then to that place inside us from where the music comes, and finally to the strain of divine music that flows through all the beings in the room.

Hindus love to sing to God. If you worship with Hindus, there are smells, sounds, colors, food, singing—a circus of the senses. Hindus believe that God needs love—just as we do. And so they clothe statues of deities in fine garments, provide food and flowers, light incense, and sing to them, devotional songs, for hours and hours. This is truly like making love with the divine.

When we do what we love, we are performing an act of worship.

Rumi:

> Whatever you wish to marry,
> go absorb yourself in that beloved,
> assume its shape and qualities.
> If you wish for the light, prepare yourself
> to receive it; if you wish to be far from God,
> nourish your egoism and drive yourself away.
> If you wish to find a way out of this ruined prison,
> don't turn your head away from the Beloved,
> but bow in worship and draw near.

The secret of seeing is, then, the pearl of great price. If I thought he could teach me to find it and keep it forever I would stagger barefoot across a hundred deserts after any lunatic at all. But although the pearl may be found, it may not be sought. The literature of illumination reveals this above all: although it comes to those who wait for it, it is always, even to the most practiced and adept, a gift and a total surprise. I return from one walk knowing where the killdeer nests in the field by the creek and the hour the laurel blooms. I return from the same walk a day later scarcely knowing my own name. Litanies hum in my ears; my tongue flaps in my mouth, Ailinon, alleluia! I cannot cause light, the most I can do is try to put myself in the path of its beam. It is possible, in deep space, to sail on solar wind. Light, be it particle or wave, has force: you rig a giant sail and go. The secret of seeing is to sail on solar wind. Hone and spread your spirit till you yourself are a sail, whetted, trans-lucent, broadside to the merest puff.

—Annie Dillard

❖

PRACTICE: HOW TO WATCH YOURSELF BE ALIVE
(SHORT VERSION)*

What time did you wake up?
Which side were you sleeping on?
What was your first thought?
Did it make you happy?
Did you share it with anyone?
What did you do next?
Were you still in bed?
How did your feet touch the floor?
What were your eyes focused on when you got up?
Were they focused at all?
What was the first thing you did after rising from the bed?
Are you sure?
Did you remember your dreams?
Did you remember God?
Did you have any discomforts?
Where?
How did you attend to them?
How did you feel about the day?
Did you leave the room?
How many steps did it take?
What did you notice about the daylight?
What was the pace and quality of your breathing?
Were you aware of any predominant emotions?
Were you awake?

Total elapsed time: one minute

*Repeat (with variations) a thousand times every day.

❖

Love and Language

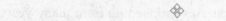

EACH OF US HAS a language that expresses most thoroughly our relationship with our life and with the hidden things of this world.

On the altar in our bedroom, my wife and I have placed a small brown clay pot. It was given to us by Maria, the Hopi woman who made it. Maria never uses a kiln. Rather, she told us, she uses a fire built with sheep dung to fire her pots. The clay is always fired in the dung, surrounded by pottery shards, which protect the pot from getting burned while it is being fired. The designs that ring the pot are painted with thin strands of yucca leaf.

"We use what we have," she tells me. "We have dung, we have shards, it all comes from the earth. We use very simple things."

Maria smiles when she speaks of the making of pots. It is something she has done since she was a little girl. She is now in her seventies. When you hold one of her pots in your hands, you feel her care warm your fingers. Clay is the language through which Maria expresses her wisdom and her love.

At a recent retreat, there was a man, Jeremy, who was blind. When it came time to do the collage of what we love— pulling out pictures from magazines—Jeremy clearly could not participate. After everyone else got involved in the exercise, I took Jeremy's hand and we went out to a porch in back of the retreat center. We sat down, and I asked him to tell me about what he loved.

"This is hard for me," he said. "It reminds me of when I was a child in school. I could never be a part of art projects, I couldn't see the blackboard, I could never join in sports. I was always like this, on the side, different, excluded." There was a weariness of old sadnesses gathered up from many years. We both sat with that weariness for several moments.

Then I repeated: *What do you love?*

Jeremy smiled. "I love music," he began. "I play guitar. I love the way it feels, the way it vibrates, the melody, the harmony." We both smiled, sharing a mutual passion for the guitar.

What else, I pressed.

"I have always loved the beach. I love the sound of the waves moving in and out, the smell of the air, the moisture, the feeling of the wave as it comes up to my feet, covers them in cool water, and then gently recedes, leaving my feet buried in the sand. It is so wonderful.

"I loved my father, times we used to have together, talking for hours. I could feel his love for me so strongly." Jeremy paused. "He's dead now. So I also feel sadness with the love.

"One time," he said excitedly, "a friend took me to a cross-country ski track. The track was so well worn into the snow that all he had to do was get my skis in the track, and off I went. I could actually ski! Completely blind, I didn't have to worry about hitting any trees or getting lost. The track let me just push and go. It was an incredible experience, finally being able to play a sport, not needing anyone's help. It was one of the happiest days of my life."

By now, people were finishing their collages, and it was time for us to go inside. I wanted Jeremy to be able to present a collage to his group. But how, without a visual language, could he construct such a collage? This is what we decided: He would make a tactile collage. For his love of music, he could put in a guitar string; for the beach, some sand. He could also include something that reminded him of his father, perhaps two small sticks to recall his ski poles and his friend. This way, when he wished to remember what he loved, he could use his hands to revitalize those moments when his love was fresh and alive.

Herbie Mann is a brilliant jazz flutist. I was fortunate to become friends with him and his wife, Janeal, when I offici-ated at their wedding. Last year Herbie and I performed together in a concert; I spoke of sorrow and grace, and Herbie accompanied and responded with beautiful flute interludes.

Later Herbie and I spoke of how well our languages seemed to interweave in the performance. "I have always had trouble with spiritual language," Herbie began. "It seems like 'spiritual' people are always after power or money, and they just use their language to get inside other people's heads, or else into their wallets. Usually whenever I hear holy men start to preach, I run in the other direction.

"But when I play music," he continued, "that is my spiritual language. It doesn't have words, nobody is trying to convince anybody of anything. It is just simple, it is what it is. Then, I feel completely comfortable. That is God to me."

ISSA:

> The man pulling radishes
> pointed the way
> with a radish

What we love becomes our language. For Anne Morrow Lindbergh, it was the sea. For Hemingway, it was the bulls; for Melville, the whale; for Matisse, color and shape. The things we love hold our experience of grace. They give voice to our heart and spirit. They provide tangible shapes for those things that, deep inside, are formless.

For as long as I can remember, I have always loved music. When I was a young boy, I sang in the choir. Those rich harmonies, bodies vibrating, the air thick with resonant magic: in them I heard God's voice. The music taught me faith and beauty. It entered me, cleansed me, fertilized something deep. Each time the music began, I felt it happen. I learned to trust the truth that music can tell about things.

When I became a teenager, I found other friends who loved music. We sang, played, practiced, wrote, harmonized. Singing together with my friends, I first learned about sex. Not physical sex—spiritual sex. We all touched, wrestled, groaned, ached inside this river of sound. It was so deep it was almost embarrassing, but not so, because we were all lost in it. Later, when I first fell in love, I loved a girl who sang.

Our love of song was passionate and unreasonable. We would sing anywhere. We sang in the subways. We sang at folk Mass on Sundays, because the church had good acoustics and they let us play every week. At night—as soon as one of us was old enough to procure a car—we would drive to Kennedy Airport, to the International Arrivals Building. Foreigners poured out of planes, and we sang for them—right in the middle of the terminal. We didn't even pass a hat, it was never about money. Singing was a miracle, and we couldn't stop doing it. It was bigger than us; the music carried us there, and we loved it.

ANY LANGUAGE—whether it be spiritual, emotional, artistic, or political—forms a paradigm that shows us where to look, teaches us what to listen for, helps us to decide what is most important. Our language affects our orientation, our alliances, and our assumptions. It directs all our senses to watch especially carefully for those things that our language holds dear. For example, people who feel comfortable with Christian language will look for evidence of sin and salvation in themselves and those around them. People who speak "psychology" are attuned to the residue of past trauma. People who speak "art" are always looking at line, shape, and color.

If we undertake a journey of spiritual unfolding, we quickly realize it is difficult to find language that will accurately reveal, portray, or reflect the intricate depth of feeling and experience at the core of our being. The sensations that arise deep within us—feelings of awe, humility, grief, bliss, and ecstasy—are often incompatible with many of the languages that have been passed on by the religious traditions of the world.

When I am sitting at the bedside of a friend who is dying, phrases such as "redemption of the holy spirit" or "forgiveness of sins" have hardly any meaning. They hold little of the truth of our experience in that poignant moment.

At times, spiritual language can soar and take our hearts to sublime places, where we feel pure and free. Other times, spiritual language can be grandiose and disconnected, removing us from the very real and precious experiences of being human and alive.

Just as we must be cautious in our use of psychological diagnoses, so must we also take great care in our use of spiritual language. Even such common and apparently simple words as *soul, spirit, sacred, holy,* and *enlightened* have many levels of meaning and can be confusing and imprecise. Who, for example, is holy and who is not? Which of our actions are holy and which merely secular? Is anything ever completely secular? How can we be sure? Do we have to work hard to become holy, or are we already sacred and whole by virtue of having been given life and spirit by our Creator? Spiritual language can quickly obfuscate rather than reveal; in our laziness, we may use these words to camouflage an absence of clear and honest naming of the way things are.

As children, we may have learned how language could mask what was true. Our families may often have used certain words to conceal their experience of pain, anger, or abuse. Perhaps parents used words to soothe or deny a painful family reality; children used words to cover up their true feelings; everyone avoided using words that spoke too bluntly about what was actually happening, so as to avoid triggering a violent or painful family episode.

Many of us may also have received early religious training that seemed to portray a reality that did not exist. On Sunday morning the adults intone, "I believe in one God, the Father Almighty, maker of heaven and earth."—What does this mean to a small boy whose father hits him? Where is this God they are all talking about? How does a child know that God is really there, that God is a person—a *he,* in fact—and that he made the earth (and heaven too—which may or may not really exist)? So again, we repeat what yet another group of people larger than ourselves has somehow decided is in our best interest.

Meanwhile, our own internal experience is raging. We

have feelings, experiences, fears, aches, yearnings—perhaps even prayers—that do not seem to correspond to any language that is being spoken in the world of grown-ups.

At our retreats, when I tell the stories of Jesus, or Moses, or the Desert Fathers and Mothers, or the Buddha, many people feel constriction or aversion. "I hate the Church for what it has done to me and so many women," said one woman. "When you quote the Hebrew Bible or the Christian New Testament, I think of all the passages in those scriptures that have been used as a weapon against me, against women, against gays, against children. When you quote those old stories, I just want to get up and run."

It is true that in my work I use many stories from the scriptures and sacred writings of Judaism, Christianity, Buddhism, Sufism, Native American traditions, and others. I use them to listen for the deeper experiences of being human. For thousands of years humankind has suffered famine, war, plague, hunger, and countless injustices; it has experienced numberless births and deaths. Each community of people has had to find some way to speak about those things that sustained them, that brought them grace—even in the midst of terrible sorrow. We all struggle to name what cannot be named: the universal force that makes the grass improbably push its way through concrete, the force that turns the earth, the energy that blesses all life, the essential presence in our deepest nature that can never be spoken of with perfect accuracy.

How can we begin to develop a spiritual language that feels accurate and precise in naming what we love? Perhaps it is only the essential qualities of the divine—wisdom, grace, fertility, compassion—that can even be approximated in words. When I was a student at Harvard Divinity School, Krister Stendahl was dean. He used to say that simple prayer, repeated over and over, may sound repetitious, uninspired, even boring. Yet if we were to listen to a couple making passionate love, we would likely hear a single name, word, or phrase repeated over and over and over. For this couple, Krister said with a slight twinkle in his eye, the repetition is not boring at all. In a way, he said, prayer is like making love with God. The important thing is not our flowery language, but rather that we are fully present and attentive to our companion. Often a single word or phrase is sufficient to focus our mind upon the object of our heart's desire.

A few lines of prayer, a devotional chant offered to the divine, a mantra repeated with mindfulness—these are enough. *Our father, who art in heaven. Hail Mary, full of grace. Om mane padme hum. Sri Ram Jai Ram. Jesus Christ, have mercy on me.* Calling out from our heart to the heart of God, we speak what cannot be spoken.

THE WORD *discipline* is related to the word *disciple,* one who follows what they love. Spiritual discipline, like spiritual language, is most authentic when it flows easily from the heart.

A regular practice of meditation, prayer, writing, giving, or simply reciting a mantra can allow our mind to rest in what we love. A good practice will naturally flow from what we love, so that it will not become a chore or guilty obligation, but rather an act of great joy and ease.

Shunryu Suzuki Roshi, a gentle pioneer of Zen in America, speaks of the essential character of spiritual practice:

> Our way is not to sit to acquire something; it is to express our true nature. That is our practice.
>
> If you want to express yourself, your true nature, there should be some natural and appropriate way of expression. Even swaying right and left as you sit down or get up from zazen is an expression of yourself. It is not preparation for practice, or relaxation after practice; it is part of the practice. So we should not do it as if we were preparing for something else.
>
> This should be true in your everyday life. To cook, or to fix some food, is not preparation . . . it is practice. To cook is not just to prepare food for someone or to cook for yourself; it is to express your sincerity. So when you cook you should ex-

press yourself in your activity in the kitchen. You should allow yourself plenty of time; you should work on it with nothing in your mind, and without expecting anything. You should just cook!

Eknath Easwaran, the beloved spiritual teacher, suggests that one simple practice readily available to those of us with busy lives is the recitation of a mantra. A mantra can be of great value in learning to keep the mind even and steady, for it gives the mind something to hold on to, something to steady itself by:

> In the Hindu tradition, we often compare the mind to the trunk of an elephant—restless, inquisitive, and always straying. If you watch an elephant sometime, you will see how apt the comparison is. In our towns and villages, elephants are often taken in religious processions through the streets to the temple. The streets are crooked and narrow, lined on either side with fruit stalls and vegetable stalls. Along comes the elephant with his restless trunk, and in one sinuous motion it grabs a whole bunch of bananas. You can almost see him asking, "What else do you expect me to do? Here is my trunk and there are the bananas." He just doesn't know what else to do with his trunk. He doesn't pause to peel the bananas, either, or to observe all the other niceties that Emily Post says should be observed in eating a banana. He takes the whole bunch, opens his cavernous mouth, and tosses the bananas in stalk and all. Then from the next stall he picks up a coconut and tosses it in after the bananas. There is a loud crack and the elephant moves on to the next stall. No threats or promises can make this restless trunk settle down.
>
> But the wise *mahout,* if he knows his elephant well, will just give that trunk a small bamboo stick to hold on to before the procession starts. Then the

elephant will walk along proudly with his head up high, holding the bamboo stick in front of him like a drum major with a baton. He is not interested in bananas or coconuts any more; his trunk has something to hold on to.

The mind is very much like this. Most of the time it has nothing to hold on to, but we can keep it from straying into all kinds of absurd situations if we just give it the mantra.

I HAVE ALREADY written about Easter morning at Santo Domingo, when Tim discovered the yellow sand. Now I would like to speak more about the dance itself, the green corn dance.

At Santo Domingo, the costumes for the dance are all made and worn with great care. Each piece of clothing—the colors, the designs, the feathers—and each headpiece is in its own way significant. Each carries a portion of the prayer of the people for a good harvest and prosperity for the pueblo.

In the summer, the plaza where they dance is hot and dusty. Some dancers pass out from the constant dancing and the prolonged exposure to the sun. In the winter, the plaza is cold and windy. Nonetheless, the dance calls for their bodies to be exposed to the elements, and so there are no coats, no jackets, no blankets to seal out the bitter cold. Only breechcloths and thin cotton dresses are worn, even in the snow. Regardless of weather, they dance.

Once a dear Indian friend explained that for the Pueblo people, dances are prayers to the Great Spirit, to Mother Earth, to Father Sky: "When we dance, we dance our love, our thanks for the many gifts from the spirit of the earth."

What if the weather is horrible? we asked.

"We will dance," she said, "whatever the weather. How can the rain stop our prayers? What would our prayers be worth if we only prayed when it was good weather? How can the snow or rain stop our love?"

The timing, the line, and the shape of the dance all

follow prescribed ritual. Men sing and drum and move with the dancers. The people of the pueblo gather to watch silently. They are in the dance, too. I recall watching as one old man, too old any longer to dance or sing, sat and looked on. He tapped the beat with his finger against his palm. He could not escape the dance, even in his weathered body.

This dance is not a performance. No admission is ever charged. It is not a show. It is a sacred prayer, born of the faith and devotion and love of the people.

WHEN I SERVED as a parish minister, every Easter season we would celebrate a Tenebrae service. Tenebrae is the ritual of extinguishing all the candles and sitting in silence in the ensuing darkness. This is to symbolize all that was lost with the death of Jesus. We sit together in quiet contemplation of the presence of loss and death, and we listen carefully for the teachings that arise only in our darkest hour.

The service was in the evening, and it was usually sparsely attended. But there was one woman in the parish, Ada, who came faithfully. She was one of our busiest volunteers, one of those people who gave tirelessly to the church community. Like many others, she asked for very little in return.

But every year, come Easter, she would make sure we were going to do a Tenebrae service. She had lost many people in her life, and it was a time of deep reflection for her. She would weep, and at the end she would quietly leave for home. This was the one day in the liturgical year that touched her more deeply than any other.

Some of us may ultimately discover that the only language capable of holding the enormity of our love is a language of no words at all, a language of quiet reflection, a language of silence. In silence, we hear the still, small voice of the divine.

In the early Christian monastic tradition of the Desert Mothers and Fathers, there is a story about the richness of silence:

One day, Theophilus of holy memory, the bishop of Alexandria, came to Scetis. And the brothers who gathered said to Abba Pambo: Say a word to the bishop so that his soul may be benefited here. The old man replied: If he is not inspired by my silence, he will not be inspired by my words either.

Of all that God has shown me
I can speak just the smallest word,
Not more than a honey bee
Takes on his foot
From an overspilling jar.

—MECHTILD OF MAGDEBURG

✦

Exercise: A Collage of What You Love

Gather up a pile of about a dozen old picture magazines. Take time to go through them, holding in your
mind this simple question: What do I love? With that
question in your mind, be aware of any image that,
when you see it, seems powerful or intriguing. You need
not understand why, nor do you need to censor your
choices. When you see any potent image, rip the page
out of the magazine and place it in a pile next to you.
When you feel you have all the images you need, cut out
the ones you want, and construct a collage on a large
piece of paper. Be playful. Move things around until
they feel right, accurate. Continue until all the images
have been integrated into the collage.

Take a break, then come back and look at what you
have done. What do you notice about what you have
chosen? How does it make you feel to look at it? Are you
pleased with what you love? Is there anything missing?
As you reflect on your life, does it include the things you
put in your collage?

At the end, pick the single image that seems most powerful to you in this moment. What does this image say to
you about your inner life? What does it reveal about
your love? Choose one image from your collage and resolve to try to include in your daily life more of what that
image holds. Each week you can pick a new image to
invite into your life.

✦

Love and Sadness

SOMETIMES WE LOVE things we have lost, things that are gone. Jessica was sad and angry when she came to see me. She had had a miscarriage. She had loved her unborn child very much, and it broke her heart to lose the baby. After a while her family insisted she get over it and get on with her life. Yet somehow she did not feel ready. I asked her to speak her feelings. "I am angry they won't let me grieve," she said. She spoke of how selfish and insensitive they were. She felt alone, abandoned.

And the child, I said. *What do you need to say to the child?* She was stunned. She had never spoken to her child; her attention was on her family, their reactions. She was quiet for a time, and tears filled her eyes. "I love you," she said quietly. "I miss you. I miss you." She wept, long and deep. She wept the truth of her love.

EILEEN MOELLER:

ten years ago

had you been born
I would have stayed a child
squinting through my mother's
steamy windows, barely visible
over the sill

instead I did what the rabbits do
in a drought
dissolved you with dread and fear
back into timelessness
your life no more than a startle

for both of us
a breeze rearranging everything
before it goes

little tadpole
gone back to the ghostworld
I went to the crossroads
could go no further
could go no further
left you as fine as a mustache hair
on your father's soft lipped mouth
saying no
ten years ago
I bled on a white padded table
and the crone sang her black song

and here I am now
still carrying you
a question mark curled asleep
in the keening dark of my mouth
a seed unspoken
you rise
pearl in the moon of my thumbnail
tiny mirror
I am still bleeding

When we love deeply, at times an inexplicable sadness arises within our love. It seems bittersweet. Why should we feel love and sadness at the same time?

We incorrectly believe that a life well lived will be always and continuously saturated with love. We think that the reward of all our spiritual practice—the correct alignment of our heart and spirit—will mean the elimination of all sadness, that because we are finally so clear and wise, we will now be spared the hurt and grief of a less spiritual life.

But often the opposite is true. As we open our hearts, as we attend to what is beautiful and necessary in our lives and the lives of those we love, we begin to feel more intimately the tender sorrows that fill any human life. We become less defended, more awake to the inevitable sorrows of being alive. We begin to feel how love and hurt often arise to-gether. People who love us are the same people who hurt us. When our heart opens in love, whatever is embedded in the heart will also spill out. The love that opens our heart will also open whatever sadness we have carried for a lifetime.

This can be confusing. If we touch love and find sad-ness, we reasonably conclude that this must not be love. But we are too quick to judge. Love is love, sadness is sadness, and both can be true at the same time. They do not cancel each other out. At retreats I sometimes have people in small groups introduce themselves with simple sentences begin-ning with "I am . . ." I ask them to speak for two minutes. People will say, "I am happy, I am sad, I am someone who loves music, I am strong, I am weak, I am courageous, I am frightened . . ." and so on. Many are surprised when they come up with things about themselves that seem so contra-dictory. I reassure them they are not necessarily suffering from multiple personality disorder. Rather, they are simply reporting a basic truth: We are a rich mixture of sensations, emotions, and experiences; we span a breathtaking range, from despair and hopelessness all the way to ecstasy and joy.

So it is with love and sadness, love and loss. They are simply fertile human feelings that sometimes arrive simulta-neously in the tender moments of our lives.

FRANK WAS A CHILD of a violent, alcoholic father. Frank spent a great deal of his early childhood with his mother, while his father was away at war. Frank remembers that when his father returned, in his sharp, clean uniform, Frank hid under the table. He was afraid of his father's explosive temper. Frank would often get hit and then go away somewhere to hide, to watch, to wait until it was safe. Often he had to wait a very long time.

Now, fully grown, Frank is a psychiatrist, thoughtful and gentle in his work with people. One day he told me about his daughter, Sarah, who was seven years old. He loved her very much. Frank explained that every weekend he would hike up Sun Mountain, just outside Santa Fe. It is a lovely mountain, with exquisite views of the city—a quiet, beautiful place. He said he was looking forward to the day when he could take his daughter to the top of Sun Mountain with him. As he spoke of his dream he began to weep, and there was a catch in his voice. His deep love for Sarah and his yearning to share the beauty of the earth with her combined to open a raw tenderness in his heart. His love and kindness came from the very same heart that had been hurt by his father. Love and sadness and hope and joy, all from the same spigot.

JACK'S WIFE, Elaine, had gone through a year of very difficult treatments for a brain tumor—radiation, chemotherapy, many alternative medications. Jack had passionately supported her throughout the course of her illness. They had worked together to find the right doctors, and Jack had fought on her behalf with the medical establishment to ensure that she received the best and most accurate treatments. They had laughed and cried and fought and surrendered their way through many battles together. And now, at the end of this exhausting, painful year, she lay dying.

One evening Elaine was upstairs; a nurse was with her. As often happens with protracted illness, it is not always clear when death will come. Often people linger for a long time, and the people who care for the dying must occasionally take space to breathe. This was one of those moments. Jack had gone downstairs to check on his daughter, Lucy, who was resting on the couch. Lucy was feeling scared and alone. She was three years old.

As his wife lay upstairs, Jack held his daughter. Lucy had known her mother only a short time, and much of that time Elaine had been very sick. As Jack held Lucy, his intuition—born of intimate communion with his wife—told him that the moment had come when Elaine would be leaving her body. He made a move to go upstairs to be with her, but Lucy insisted he stay downstairs and remain with her. She cried and screamed, "Don't leave me, Daddy, don't leave me." Jack didn't know what to do. He felt a powerful need to be with his wife as she died, and yet his daughter, his own responsibility now, wanted him to remain with her downstairs. Jack took a long breath. He settled into the pillow and held Lucy close to him. A few minutes later the nurse came down and told Jack that Elaine had died.

At times this is how it comes to us. Love and sadness are blended together in the waters of our life, and we must drink them together, just as they are. Neither cancels out the other. Love, added to the sadness, makes our grief bittersweet. Sadness, injected into our love, creates a love that burns the heart.

SOMETIMES OUR LOSSES open our eyes to what we truly cherish. Where before we may have felt confused or ambivalent, a moment of grief can galvanize our awareness of what is precious and valuable. Judy was pregnant by a man she had been going with for many years but who refused to marry her. She was confused about what to do. She was fearful of having the child alone, but after many long, tearful conversations with me and others who cared for her, Judy decided to carry the child to term. She felt that the life growing inside her was both a challenge and a gift. She would raise the child herself and give it all the love she had to give.

However, within a few weeks Judy began hemorrhaging, and the fetus was lost. Judy called me soon after the miscarriage. Her mood was quiet, reflective. There was a clarity and strength I had not heard before. "You know, Wayne, I feel strangely peaceful. I am so much clearer about my life, about who I am and what I want. I am grateful I decided not to abort, and at the same time I can accept what has happened. I just know now that my work in this life is to care for myself and for my body, and to forgive myself, to the best of my ability. I know now—more than ever before—that the central task of my life is to grow into the most wise, strong, and loving person I can be."

MANY YEARS AGO we all sat with Brian, who was dying. His mother and sister had flown to Santa Fe to be with him, to feel his presence, to remember him, to help him die. His friends all came in and out, several sitting for days, always a few remaining with Brian and his family. Some cooked, some cleaned, some nursed, fluffed pillows, cried, laughed, held Brian's hand, held one another.

Even as Brian became weaker, his breathing more difficult, his appetite gone, we all felt thoroughly and completely loved. Who was giving the love? And who was getting it? Clearly the question has no meaning. We were all in fear, in sadness, in grief—and we were all in love. Through the galvanizing enzyme of Brian's kindness and friendship, we were all reminded of how much love there was within us. Our love for Brian, for healing, for kindness, for family—indeed, our love for love itself—was born in the midst of our sorrow and our fear. This is how love is. It grows even in the soil of sadness.

You do not have to be good.
You do not have to walk on your knees
for a hundred miles through the desert, repenting.
You only have to let the soft animal of your body
   love what it loves. . . .

—MARY OLIVER

Love in Community
with Others

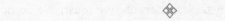

RED BARBER DIED TODAY. When I heard the news on the radio in my car, I started to cry.

I remember being in my grandfather's living room in the summer, watching baseball on WPIX, channel 11, sitting next to my grandfather in his big easy chair with the stand-up ashtray next to it. He always smoked, and he would die a few years later of emphysema on my thirteenth birthday.

We would watch the Yankees. Always the Yankees, never anyone else. The Yankees then were the best team in baseball, the best in the universe. Mickey Mantle, Roger Maris, Moose Skowron, Bobby Richardson, Yogi Berra, Whitey Ford—a whole generation of great baseball players. The game seemed mythic. The spectacle, the colors, the players were all majestic, somehow larger than the life I knew on Long Island.

Red Barber was the Yankee announcer, along with Mel Allen. They talked baseball—plays, players, strategies, rhythm, fly balls, grounders, shading fielders, relief pitchers, bunts, strikeouts, home runs. It was the dance, the music, the drama of life itself. I learned a great deal about the ebb and flow of human fortune in those afternoons by my grandfather's side, listening to Red Barber. But now he and my grandfather are both gone. Now, when I remember them both, I feel strangely alone.

MY FRIEND KENNETH died of AIDS this summer. A month later my friend Paul died of cancer. This has been a summer of death for our community.

I led the memorial services for both of these beautiful men. When people we love die, we gather in a circle. We

cannot bring them back; we cannot heal them of their passing. But we gather nonetheless, because we must. We do not
know what else to do. We need to hold something. We ache
to remember in our bodies and hearts those we loved. The
warmth of our bodies touching in this circle helps us to feel
safe when we are this close to the membrane between life
and death.

Being in community with others is an inescapable part
of a full and meaningful life. Gathering to observe ritual, cere-
mony, parade, pilgrimage, festival, these are the ways we
remember the rhythm of things, the triumph of the spirit,
the cycle of birth and death, the deepening of a life together.

Sometimes we gather to be in the presence of a particular person who holds something precious and valuable. This
spring I had the blessing to sit with Nyoshul Khenpo
Rinpoche. He is a great teacher, a revered master in the
Dzogchen lineage of Tibetan Buddhism. There were just a
few of us, in a garage temporarily redecorated in the fashion
of a meditation *gompa*. Each evening for three weeks Khenpo
would enter the garage at seven o'clock. We would all perform the requisite prostrations and then begin a period of
sitting and chanting that would last about an hour. Afterward
Khenpo would offer blessings to those in need.

Rarely would Khenpo actually discourse on the subject
of Dzogchen. Only twice in that period do I recall him teaching about the practice at all. More often we would simply sit
in his presence, gently quieting the mind, allowing our
awareness to rest in our original, perfect nature. Yet there
was something in this being—and something in each of us
that was awakened in the presence of this being—that defied
explanation. People felt touched in some intimate way; many
people reported they felt inexplicably changed in ways they
could not describe, though they knew something inside had
been irrefutably transformed. Khenpo's loving presence was
sufficient to awaken within us a lightness, an intrinsic spiritual wisdom. This, in the tradition of Eastern spiritual practice, is *darshan*—the transmission of grace through the loving
presence of an enlightened being. When these beings touch

us with their presence, we remember what is deepest and best in ourselves.

I saw Lyle Lovett at the Lone Star Café in New York City. People were lined up around the block for a lunchtime concert. Hundreds of hot, sweaty New Yorkers in August packed the Lone Star to see him, to be in his presence. We had all heard his music, we had his albums and tapes. So we were not there just to hear the songs—we wanted to hear *him* sing the songs, to see him do it. The transmissions I received from Khenpo and Lyle Lovett might have been different, but the act of gathering to share in the transmission was similar. This was *darshan*, too.

At the Lama Foundation, in northern New Mexico, where we often have summer retreats, about a hundred of us sit together in a large geodesic dome. We are not talking, not exchanging a word. Not comparing notes, not even sharing our feelings. But we have gathered to sit together, and that seems to matter.

We live in our body, and we live in the presence of the bodies of others. We cannot have a spiritual life that is completely separate from our corporeal selves. We need to see one another, to touch and be touched, to exchange some gift, some energy, some knowing that can be transmitted only in the physical body, from one to another. It is tangible, yet mystical; physical, yet immeasurable, invisible.

MANY WOMEN AND MEN who come to see me have been abused in some physical way. For them, the language of touch is at least confusing and is often frightening. They feel unsafe in their own bodies; their families were painful, they took suffering in through their body, and they are confused about the trustworthiness of the information they get from human touch. For them, the language of physical care was woven into a web of fear and pain that seems impossible to breach. The language of words comes more easily, or the language of quiet, of meditation. Only later, when there is someone unimaginably safe, can the language of the body become a language of love.

Susan Griffin:

To make love is to become like this infant again. We grope with our mouths toward the body of another being, whom we trust, who takes us in her arms. We rock together with this loved one. We move beyond speech. Our bodies move past all the controls we have learned. We cry out in ecstasy, in feeling. We are back in a natural world before culture tried to erase our experience of nature. In this world, to touch one another is to express love, there is no idea apart from feeling, and no feeling which does not ring through our bodies and our souls at once.

This is eros. Our own wholeness. Not the sensation of pleasure alone, nor the idea of love alone, but the whole experience of human love.

What do we get from one another? When we make love, what are we doing? Are we really "making" anything? Is it all physical sensation, pleasure, ecstasy? Or, in addition to that glorious sensory symphony, are we passing something from one to another, a deep remembrance of love, of care, of safety, of grace, of the divine? Through our intimate presence, we transfer a kind of knowing, a reminder of who we are at our deepest point. This does not always happen, of course. Sometimes it is just sex. (But sometimes prayer is just verbal daydreaming, too.)

In the imagery of St. John the Divine, spiritual practice can be like making love to the beloved. In the Song of Solomon, there are luscious images of bodies making love as devotion to God. The love of another's body can serve as a poignant doorway into a deep longing for God. Brother Lawrence, in *The Practice of the Presence of God,* uses the word *presence* to describe intimate communion with the divine. And so when we are afraid, when we meet death in our loved ones, when we ache for God, we sit in circles. We pass the kiss of peace. We hold one another's hands in prayer. We touch one another to remember. We remember our love in the company of the family of God.

MANY YEARS AGO, on a research grant from Harvard Divinity School, I visited the small pueblo of Yanque, in the mountains of south central Peru. I was visiting Sister Antonia—*Hermana* Antonia, as she was known in the village—a Maryknoll nun who had lived and worked with the people there for twenty years.

I had heard of *Hermana* Antonia and her work while I was serving as a volunteer editor at *LatinAmerica Press,* a small periodical that reported the struggles of the poor throughout the Americas. When I had a few weeks' hiatus from the paper, I flew from Lima to the interior city of Arequipa, and from there I arranged for a ride with Miguel, who was delivering supplies to remote villages. I rode in the back of his pickup truck, and it took about eight hours to reach the village from Arequipa. As we climbed along the edges of steep mountain passes, it alternately snowed and rained. We arrived well past dark in a town that had no electricity. I felt strange indeed, arriving in an isolated town, in the dark, in the rain, with only the name *Antonia* on a scrap of paper.

The first person we asked directed us to an old mission church, partially crumbling, where Antonia welcomed me as if I were an old friend. She was quite used to giving shelter to strangers, and in the light of a small candle Antonia described her life and her work with the people of Yanque.

Yanque was a small colonial town of fifteen hundred people. There were no lights, no running water, and only dirt streets. Antonia served as the village nurse, priest, doctor, therapist, and midwife. Without access to inexpensive vaccinations that we in the United States take for granted, people were susceptible to many infectious diseases. As it happened, I had arrived just at the end of a severe measles epidemic. Antonia said many, many children had died during this epidemic. She had been burying an average of three people a day for weeks.

The morning after I arrived, Antonia entrusted me with

several important tasks—cleaning the beans, turning the compost, and spreading the manure. She felt this would be a good complement to my Harvard Divinity School training.

When I had finished my work for the day, I went for an exploratory walk. I discovered the town was surrounded by terraces that climbed the sides of the mountain, terraces for growing corn and potatoes. They had been built by people who lived a thousand years ago. Twice a year all the able-bodied men of the village made their way high into the mountains to clear and repair the intricate Inca irrigation system, which was how the village got its water.

I was there in winter, and the men were gone for four days. They had to climb well above the snow line, working and sleeping in subzero conditions, with none of the benefit of technologically advanced clothing or equipment. They brought only shovels and blankets.

At the end of the four days, with the treacherous work accomplished, they began their descent. When the village was in sight, they blew a trumpet, which reverberated through the valley, announcing their return to the village later that evening. The people of Yanque excitedly prepared for a three-day fiesta.

On the day of their return, I was working in the fields behind the church. I was accompanied by ten-year-old Carlos, who was too young to go off with the men on their pilgrimage. That afternoon, when the sound of the trumpet spilled down the mountainside, we both stopped our work for a moment. Carlos looked longingly toward the mountain, to the place from which the sound had come. No doubt he was dreaming of the day when he too would be a part of the heroic company of *trabajadores.*

When nightfall came, the band began to play in the town square. The church bells were rung, and the workers arrived with a shout to parade around the square. The music played and the workers marched and marched, shovels proudly displayed like badges of honor across their shoulders. Since there was no electricity, all this happened in total darkness. Antonia and I, standing together in the square, could only feel, but not see, the entire procession. There was singing, eating, and drinking for three days, culminating in a grand *baile,* a dance for the whole village.

Water is sacred to the people of Yanque. Cleaning the irrigation system in a communal endeavor of great love (an endeavor I would later come to understand more deeply when I met Max Cordova and walked along the Truchas *acequia* in northern New Mexico). There is no confusion about the centrality of water in their lives. It is the fundamental center of gravity in their community. The mountains give them water, and water gives them life.

CONVENTIONAL POLITICAL WISDOM insists that the most potent way to unite a divided kingdom is to cultivate a common enemy. The fear and hatred of the evil outsider will galvanize the people into swift and unified action. It is a common ploy for leaders around the world to contrive an external war in order to forge a shaky domestic peace.

But what if the cultivation of a common love is ultimately both more efficacious and less costly? War inevitably produces casualties. Where are the casualties when we follow what we love? If we unite our families and communities through what we love, the results are so swift and sure that it can take your breath away.

When I first met Max Cordova, he wanted to start a weaving cooperative for the people of Truchas. Many families in these mountains had been weaving for seven generations or more. Sadly, they could sell their work only at a commercial tourist outlet near Santa Fe, which paid them about eighty cents an hour to weave rugs, blankets, and shawls. The store then sold the finished products to wealthy collectors at a tremendous profit.

Max and I went for a walk. "These families love to weave," he said. "Our ancestors have been raising sheep, dyeing wool, and building looms for hundreds of years. Now we work for almost nothing, so we have to give it up. We cannot afford to do what we love to do."

Max and I discussed the development of a weaving co-operative. We could build our own looms, get the wool cheaply in quantity, and let people sell what they made at the Truchas community center. The weavers would keep 75 percent of the selling price, and the store would retain 25 percent for operating costs. The weavers would make five times what they were making at that time, and the community would benefit greatly from the infusion of energy and creativity. Additionally, Max and his wife, Lillian, could teach young people how to weave, continuing a long tradition of passing wisdom to the next generation.

The only problem was cost. How much would it cost to set up an entire cooperative? Bread for the Journey concentrates on funding relatively small projects—and we were very small indeed when Max and I had this conversation. "Well," he began, "if we build the looms and use the community center for a workshop—and sell out of the community store—then all we will need is money for materials." I asked Max to calculate the proposed costs, and we would see if we could support it.

A few days later Max called me back. "I think we can do it for twenty-five hundred dollars." It was a ridiculously small sum. "I can get the lumber and the parts from a guy in Albuquerque. Lillian and I can work for free, and we can get the young people to volunteer in the store. If we can get that amount of money, we can start the cooperative."

Max loves the community; the weavers love to weave. Inspired by this love, the planning that would normally be a large bureaucratic nightmare became a simple act of faith. I had no doubt that, led by their deep love of the work, the people of Truchas would be able to make it happen.

We quickly raised the $2,500, and within a month the cooperative was up and on its way. Now, five years later, over eighty-five people belong to the group. The store has doubled in size, and the Truchas weavers have become well known for the quality of their work.

for colored girls who have considered suicide when the rainbow is enuf

i sat up one nite walkin a boardin house
screamin/ cryin/ the ghost of another woman
who waz missin what i waz missin
i wanted to jump outta my bones
& be done wit myself
leave me alone
& go on in the wind
it waz too much
i fell into a numbness
till the only tree i cd see
took me up in her branches
held me in the breeze
made me dawn dew
that chill at daybreak
the sun wrapped me up swingin rose light everywhere
the sky laid over me like a million men
i waz cold/ i waz burnin up/ a child
& endlessly weavin garments for the moon
wit my tears

i found god in myself
& i loved her/ i loved her fiercely

—NTOZAKE SHANGE

the
third
part

❖

How Shall
I Live,
Knowing
I Will Die?

❖

The Summer Day

Who made the world?
Who made the swan, and the black bear?
Who made the grasshopper?
This grasshopper, I mean—
the one who has flung herself out of the grass,
the one who is eating sugar out of my hand,
who is moving her jaws back and forth instead of up
    and down—
who is gazing around with her enormous and complicated eyes.
Now she lifts her pale forearms and thoroughly washes
    her face.
Now she snaps her wings open, and floats away.
I don't know exactly what a prayer is.
I do know how to pay attention, how to fall down
into the grass, how to kneel down in the grass,
how to be idle and blessed, how to stroll through the fields,
which is what I have been doing all day.
Tell me, what else should I have done?
Doesn't everything die at last, and too soon?
Tell me, what is it you plan to do
with your one wild and precious life?

—MARY OLIVER

The Clarity of a Life
Framed by Death

Here are a few journal entries from Forrest Hallmark, four years old. At the end of each day, his mother would ask Forrest if there was anything he wanted to remember, and she would write it down for him in his journal.

Thursday, 5 May 1994

I love dinosaurs. I love 'em love 'em love 'em. I love sharks. T Rex is the most fearess [fierce] hunter. It is Thursday today. My days are getting different now cause we're doing different stuff. Why do bunny rabbits hop? I just don't know how bunny rabbits hop.

Wednesday, 25 May 1994

I'm happy about my Stegosaurus. I don't know why my Pterodactyl's sick (only for 3 days). I love my dinosaurs.

Sunday, 12 June 1994

I'm happy today. I wish we goe'd on a hike and I wish there were butterflies in rain forests. Is there a rain forest in Micronesia?

I played on my tricycle. . . . I slipped and almost fell but I didn't. I ran over Sis's tail and hand. Sis growled. I said I'm sorry. I want to go to the rain forest sometime.

When we read this, we are undoubtedly struck by the natural curiosity and thoughtfulness of this four-year-old. Forrest's parents were considering moving the family to Micronesia to work for the government, and so he is wondering how it will be there. His name, Forrest, arose partly out of his father's deep love of nature. As it happens, Forrest has developed a fascination with rain forests.

If our time with Forrest and his journal ended here, it would be simply a sweet moment in the life of a bright and vital young boy. But two weeks after this final entry, Forrest was killed in an automobile accident. He died at the age of four—with his brother, Bryce, who was two years old, and his grandfather, who was seventy-five. Forrest's mother, who was driving the car, somehow survived. After the funeral, she and her husband gave me a copy of his journal.

Now, let us go back and read the entries, knowing that two weeks later this boy would meet his death:

> I'm happy today. I wish we goe'd on a hike and I wish there were butterflies in rain forests. Is there a rain forest in Micronesia?

> I played on my tricycle. . . . I slipped and almost fell but I didn't. I ran over Sis's tail and hand. Sis growled. I said I'm sorry. I want to go to the rain forest sometime.

What strikes us about the writing now? What emotions arise as the words touch our heart? What do we feel about the boy's life now that we know the circumstances of his death, which would soon follow? Does each word not become more poignant? Every event naturally carries more weight. Our attention is riveted on young Forrest, on these few moments from his brief life on earth.

Thus it is with a life framed by death. With death as its companion, each moment of life becomes instantly more compelling.

IN A PREVIOUS SECTION I spoke of Paul, who was dying of cancer. I described the afternoon when Paul realized his cancer was far advanced, when it became clear it was time for him to prepare for death.

Later, about a week before Paul died, I was visiting him one morning. I found him sitting up, propped against a mound of pillows. I sat on the edge of his bed. His bedroom had a beautiful porch with French doors that were always open to the summer sun and gentle breezes. Paul sat, silent, in the rays of morning light.

"I feel ready to go," he said finally. There was quiet in his face. "But sometimes," he reflected, "I just wish I had more time." Paul's voice carried so much sadness mingled with acceptance, melancholy softened with a gentle peace. In a moment like this, much is bittersweet. Some of our dreams have come true; some have not. There is a readiness to die, accompanied by an equally passionate wish to live. In the light of his few remaining mornings, Paul was reviewing the wishes of a lifetime. I was grateful to be near him.

"I've done so much work to prepare for this moment," he said. "I came to Santa Fe to deepen my life and to learn more about spiritual practice. I've learned yoga, practiced meditation with some wonderful teachers, and I have been loved by many beautiful people. I'm not unhappy with my life. I know I'm clear and whole inside, and when I feel that, I'm not afraid. I know it is time."

Again it was quiet. His words mingled with the morning light and the cool air. "But I also wish I could stay here," he added slowly. A tentative wish, offered against the growing impossibility of its coming true. "I wish I had ten more years, free of this illness. With those ten years, I could really live as I always wanted." We sat for some time in the wake of that wish. It vibrated in the air, this wish for life; it enveloped two men who would someday die. We each felt the truth of it from our particular vantage point that morning.

"What would you do if we could give you those ten years? What would your life look like?" I finally asked.

Paul spoke easily and certainly. "I would be kind."

"I would live my life with kindness," he said. "I would be kind to children. I would teach them to be kind, too. This

is all I ever really wanted to do, just to be kind, to be loving."
He was quiet for a moment. "A few months ago, when I was
still feeling strong, I thought I would treat myself, so I walked
into a bakery and ordered two of my favorite cookies. I told
the girl behind the counter they were my favorite, and she
said she loved them, too, but that they were very expensive.
When I left, I thought about it for a minute, went back and
bought another cookie, and gave it to her. 'This one is for
you,' I said. She was so surprised by my kindness. 'You are
such a kind man,' she said. I felt absolutely wonderful. Such a
small thing, such an easy thing to do. This is how I would
live my life, if only I had more time."

In the face of his death, Paul saw his life. His death
clarified his heart's desire: to be a kind person. Everything
else fell away, and he simply saw what was precious and
valuable. To be kind—this was the most sacred thing, the
most perfect and accurate offering he could make with this,
his single life.

The Buddha told this parable:

A man traveling across a field encountered a tiger.
He fled, the tiger after him. Coming to a precipice,
he caught hold of a root of a wild vine and swung
himself down over the edge. The tiger sniffed at
him from above. Trembling, the man looked down
to where, far below, another tiger was waiting to
eat him. Only the vine sustained him.

Two mice, one white and one black, little by little
started to gnaw away the vine. The man saw a luscious strawberry near him. Grasping the vine with
one hand, he plucked the strawberry with the
other. How sweet it tasted!

In Buddhism, the practice of *maranasati,* or "death
awareness," encourages us to use the fact of our death to
enrich and illuminate our life. Thus it is with many people I
visit who have HIV or cancer. When they receive a diagnosis

of terminal illness, they are suddenly shocked into mindful-ness. What have I done? What is my life about? What do I love? What do I place at the center of my life? Which people shall I invite as my companions, and which will I allow to fall away? Knowing the brief time I have left, what will I do with my days?

With so little time left, there is none to waste. Suddenly childhood trauma seems less compelling; money seems use-ful for daily needs, but greed seems silly—what can we really keep? Unproductive relationships are let go, and intricate ca-reer maneuverings seem wasteful, even comical. For those close to death, it becomes instantly clear that everything they do in their remaining days is precious. Every conversation, every action, every choice is pregnant with meaning and value. Only those relationships that are fruitful and loving are kept; the rest are allowed to fall away. Every act is a sacra-ment, every breath a gift. Nothing is taken for granted, noth-ing wasted.

What kind of life will we have? A human birth is a breathtaking gift. This singular life is a pearl of great price. How will we use this precious time? Sloppily careening from one day to the next, getting things done, checking off lists, buttressing our lives against trouble as best we can, until we die weary and wondering whether we were ever awake, ever truly alive at all? Or shall we live not by accident, but on purpose—naming clearly and courageously those things we cherish, creating a life of beauty and love?

Will we walk on the earth gently? Will we care for our children with understanding and wisdom? Will we seek out beauty and give thanks for it? Will we be generous with our talents for the good of all? Will we be patient and thoughtful with others? Will we be courageous in speaking what we know to be true? Will we be awake and alive? Will we leave a legacy of kindness?

Knowing we will die, how shall we live? The reality of our dying does not create these questions. Nor can our dying answer them. Rather, a clear perception of our death forces us to consider our life as something worth living; an active, creative, passionate event. "Life is impermanent," says Thich Nhat Hanh. "It is precisely because of its impermanence that we value life so dearly."

IN THE BHAGAVAD GITA, the question is asked: "Of all the world's wonders, what is the most wonderful?" The answer is simple and direct: "That no man, though he sees others dying all around him, believes that he himself will die." Death is something we expect to postpone until we have received our fair share of what life has to offer us. If we believe we will live as long as we wish, we can afford to waste time; we can spend precious days, months, even years engaged in mindless activity and fruitless relationships. We can wait until we arrange our career, our friends, and our possessions just the way we like. We can work for decades on our psychology, our spirituality, and our finances until we are perfectly content with our lives. Then—finally ready to begin our lives in earnest—we gather up the fruits of our labor and are rewarded with a happy and fulfilling life, free to enjoy for many years the harvest of all our good work.

If we buy this illusion that we will live forever, we can waste all the time in the world before we are ready to live. But this notion of "all the time in the world" is a seductive lie. Much of my time of late has been spent at the bedsides of women and men who embraced just this illusion; and now, long before retirement, before they have finalized all their plans—before they are ready—they discover they are dying of cancer, kidney failure, heart disease, or AIDS. They find they are dying before they have scheduled their time to live. Some feel cheated and are angry at God for not giving them their full measure, their slice of happiness and joy. They feel their mortality is coming too soon, before they really lived the way they wanted. It seems an untimely death, a tragedy, an injustice.

When Brian first got sick with AIDS, he was terribly frightened. He knew so many who had died, and now he was feeling his own life wrested from him. For many hours I would sit with Brian; he was dying, and we both knew it.

Still he would argue with death, yell at me that he wasn't ready to die. "I hate it all," he would scream. "I hate this stupid virus, the sickness, always feeling like I have no energy at all. I'm afraid all the time. I wake up sweating, terrified; I even hate that I'm afraid of dying!" This is not how Brian wanted his life to go, constantly wrestling with this fear and sadness. If he was going to die—and for Brian it remained, until the very end, a resounding *if*—then at least he wanted to feel at peace. He wanted to be healed.

Together we shared his anguish. We felt the fear as it gripped his body. Brian stayed with his fear, through the discomfort, through the unimaginable sadness. "I don't want to die, I don't want to be so afraid," he would weep. I held him, and we both felt the sadness, the powerlessness. Each time it came, he would first try to push it away; then, slowly, he would let himself feel it all, the grief, the confusion, the fear. After a million such surrenderings into the truth of his illness, there came into Brian a gentle courage, a courage born of knowing he had to do this now, for there was no other time. Slowly Brian made it through the worst of his fears, and emerged into a sense of calm and peace.

Now I was visiting Brian at home, as he was sick much more often. He was thin, his skin taut against his face. But there was light in his eyes, an unmistakable brilliance. He shone. "I still can't believe I'm dying," he confessed. "But I feel I can handle anything. It's funny—in a way, I wish I could have had this feeling, strong and brave, when I was younger and still healthy." Two weeks later, Brian died in his home, surrounded by friends who loved him. We were all quiet for a long time after he died, sitting together in a circle. It was a gray, peaceful winter afternoon.

Brian's courage was born in part from knowing he had little time. If he thought he could have postponed dealing with his fear and anger, he would have. We all do. But his impending death was the single enzyme that provided sufficient strength and determination to make it to the other side. While death can be frightening, it can also grant us great courage to face what must be faced this moment. For if not now, when?

In the doorway of many forest monasteries in Thailand, there is a sign with this admonition: "Don't waste your life." Pema Chodron, an insightful and articulate Buddhist nun, describes how the fact of impermanence can inspire us to be more fully alive:

> Life is very brief. Even if we live to be a hundred, it's very brief. Also, its length is unpredictable. Our lives are impermanent. I myself have, at the most, thirty more years to live, maybe thirty-five, but that would be tops. Maybe I have only twenty more years to live. Maybe I don't even have one more day to live. It's sobering to me to think that I don't have all that long left. It makes me feel that I want to use it well. If you realize that you don't have that many more years to live and if you live your life as if you actually only had a day left, then the sense of impermanence heightens that feeling of preciousness and gratitude.

FOUR YEARS AGO Kirsten received a completely unexpected diagnosis: During a routine mammogram, it was discovered she had a tumor in her breast. It proved to be malignant. Even worse, cancer cells had invaded her lymph system. The prognosis was not hopeful.

Kirsten instantly responded to this information in a variety of ways. She assembled a team of physicians and healers. She had the tumor removed and began a course of chemotherapy. She combined Western medicine with Chinese herbs, acupuncture, and other healing techniques. She addressed her illness with tremendous mindfulness and care.

But Kirsten then rearranged other things in her life. She cut back on her work. Since she was making less money, she simplified her days. She stayed home more, took walks, and worked in her beloved vegetable garden. She had tea with people she loved. She did yoga, she meditated, she lay in her hammock and listened to breezes. She started to paint. The reality of her cancer focused Kirsten's awareness on the fundamental quality of her life. She had always wanted to deepen her spiritual practice, she had always wanted to garden, she had always wanted to paint. If not now, when?

One day during Kirsten's lengthy illness, my friend Jai Lakshman and I were speaking together about how she was doing. We were both concerned for her survival, and we worried aloud how difficult it was to undergo chemotherapy. We admired her strength and courage. Then, after a period of quiet, we found ourselves confessing that we were both a little jealous of Kirsten. Because of her cancer, Kirsten was now doing exactly what she wanted with her life. When we reflected on all our meetings and phone calls and workshops and endless traveling, we both wondered if we were living the lives that would make us the happiest. We, without cancer, at times felt strangled by tasks and responsibilities we had no excuse to get out of. If we had cancer, we would have permission to live more gently and easily, not be so rushed. The diagnosis would somehow allow us to let go of many cumbersome responsibilities and begin to more thoroughly enjoy our lives.

Of course, we realized the absurdity of our predicament. We too would die. What more permission did we need to follow our own hearts? How many of us are secretly waiting for some magical permission—like a diagnosis of terminal illness—before we truly begin to listen to the quiet dreams, the desires of the heart?

Happily, Kirsten lived to heal from her cancer. Her life is again more busy, but the fundamental flavor of her enjoyment of life lingers. "I am so grateful for my life," she said to me the other day over lunch. "I don't take anything for granted. Every day is a miracle. Before, I would just make it through the day, as if it was all just work. Now I feel such joy to just be alive each day. I am much happier, life is lighter. I only give my care and attention to what is really important— being loving, being kind, creating beauty, being grateful '

❖

AS SUSAN ERTZ wryly observes, "Millions yearn for immortality who don't know what to do with themselves on a rainy Sunday afternoon." Sadly, those of us without the benefit of a diagnosis of terminal illness go about our lives as if we had all the time in the world to waste in unproductive work, joyless relationships, endless worries and plans for some distant future, obsessive goals and demands. Our presumed immortality permits us to be sloppy and imprecise in our actions and words; we can always clean up later. So we are not so careful with what we say and what we choose to do with our precious days on the earth. We give hardly any thought to what we hold sacred. We simply wait until the world turns our way before we take the tremendous risk of becoming fully awake and alive. But all this waiting and worrying and sloppiness is nothing more than a form of sleepwalking.

Some people, in their confusion, believe that their life is simply preparation for a sweeter, more pleasing afterlife. They treat this life like a waiting room, something to endure until we are liberated into the life hereafter. But this is nonsense. Any afterlife we encounter will undoubtedly present us with some refined manifestation of how we have lived in this one. The Buddha, in the opening verses of the Dhammapada, insists: "One who does good rejoices in this world and after death, joyful in both."

Thich Nhat Hanh admonishes those who wait for the salvation that comes after death:

> There are some people who believe that they will enter the Kingdom of God, or the Pure Land, after they die. I don't agree with them. I know that you don't have to die in order to get into the Kingdom of God. In fact, *you have to be alive to do so.*

Proximity to death wakes us up. Death dispels the most potent illusion about life—that it belongs to us, and that we have all the time we need to arrange it the way we want. But in many ways it is a gift that our life is limited, impermanent. We hold it more dear because this is so. When Shunryu

Suzuki Roshi was dying, he prepared his students in this way:

> If when I die, the moment I am dying, if I suffer that is all right, you know; that is suffering Buddha. No confusion in it. Maybe everyone will struggle because of the physical agony or spiritual agony, too. But that is all right, that is not a problem. We should be very grateful to have a limited body . . . like mine, or like yours. If you had a limitless life it would be a real problem for you.

Our liberation begins when we surrender to our own mortality. (Actually, no surrender is necessary; whether we surrender or not, we shall surely die.) More precisely, we must surrender our *illusion* that we will not die.

JUAN GARCIA, raised in a poor section of Santa Barbara, quickly deduced the unfavorable odds of living a long and healthy life as a young Hispanic male in a gang-infested neighborhood. On his own street, by the time he was thirteen, he had witnessed random violence, gang killings, knife fights, and drug-related deaths. Juan knew he could die at any time.

Every summer there is a fiesta in Santa Barbara, which is an occasion for parades, parties, and civic pride. However, in some neighborhoods, fiesta is also a time for enthusiastic and unbridled drinking, and a fertile occasion for roving groups of young men to vent their frustrations and hostilities upon one another. It is not unusual to see a pronounced increase in emergency-room admissions during fiesta.

One evening during his thirteenth summer, Juan found himself in the middle of two gangs trolling for action during fiesta. When he realized he had stumbled into dangerous territory, Juan tried his best to remain inconspicuous—no small feat in a situation where everyone is superalert, monitoring the position of each and every person, noting who is with whom, who is moving, and in what direction. Juan knew there was a fight in the making; he smelled the familiar odor of violence. But Juan also knew that whatever he did, he might not be able to get out of its way.

Suddenly it began to erupt—young men on both sides shouting and drawing weapons, everyone scrambling for position. Juan realized he had to somehow back out of the circle that was forming, and he turned to run behind the nearest house, hoping to avoid any stray bullets. It was then Juan noticed his little brother David standing on the sidewalk nearby, unaware of any imminent danger.

Juan turned quickly and raced back to where his brother was standing. As he ran, an armed member of one of the gangs took Juan to be an opponent in flight and shot in the direction of Juan and David. Juan jumped into the air in front of his little brother just in time to catch the bullet in his own body. Juan fell to the ground. The gang members scattered, leaving Juan bleeding. His brother was miraculously unhurt.

When I went to visit Juan later, he refused to be labeled a "hero." For Juan, dying was not a problem—life was the problem. Dying was part of the deal in his neighborhood. Doing the right thing—that was far more difficult to do. Being around death made Juan more determined to try to do the right thing.

"Dying's nothin', man," Juan told me as we sat in his kitchen. His wounded arm was healing, and despite himself, Juan seemed more than a little proud of his scar. "Everybody's dyin' around here all the time. You just gotta do what's right. I couldn't let my brother get hurt, man. There wasn't no choice about it."

CLAUDIA SLACK, a novelist and newspaper reporter in Santa Fe, wrote a piece in our local paper about her life with cancer:

> Like knowing you're to be hanged at dawn, cancer concentrates the mind wonderfully. . . . The world around me is suddenly delineated in sharper detail and more brilliant color. It has become more joyous, more poignant, more worthy of note and

admiration. Small things: a delicate lavender, wild penstemon, rare in my area, volunteered to grow beneath my front window—a precious gift to be cherished each day. An acquaintance's endearing puppy of my favorite breed is not just *this* puppy but an embodiment of *all* bull terrier puppies that have touched, amused and delighted me through my lifetime.

Big things: The loving care, help and support of family and friends, doubly appreciated because freely given, is a new-minted revelation of the goodness and kindness of most human beings I've always believed in but sometimes lost sight of in this cynical society. I can return little but love and thanks, and they say with mild surprise, "But that's what we're here for."

When she says that "cancer concentrates the mind wonderfully," the point, of course, is not the cancer; the point is the light the cancer sheds upon our life. If we follow what we love, if we live deeply and attentively in this moment, we will not feel bound by regret at the moment of our death. We will live with reverence for all things and a deep gratefulness for the gift of a single day upon the earth. Thus our death begs us to live well and with joy. As Jesus told his followers, the message of his life and death was simple: to remind them to be awake and alive. "I have come that you may have life," he told them, "and have it abundantly."

When I sit with people who are dying, I naturally become more aware of my own life—what I hold as sacred, what I name as important, how I use my time. I become aware that I have been seemingly given the inexplicable gift of more time on this earth. How am I using these remaining days, days that have been denied this being lying next to me? Why am I left behind—to do what, to be what? What gift or talent am I not using, what work needs to be done, what joy needs to be celebrated?

To embrace death is not morbid; to deny death is morbid. It is fearful and dishonest to pretend we will not face death. As a species, we have lived with death as long as there has been life. "Die while you are alive," writes Japanese Zen master Bunan, "and be absolutely dead. Then do whatever you want: it's all good."

If we know we will die, then we will know we are alive. From this mindful awareness can spring a variety of practices that deepen and enrich our time on the earth. In this section I would like to explore several facets of this daily awakening—practices that, held gently and easily in a succession of days, may contribute to a rich and potent spiritual life: acceptance, effortlessness, remembering, simplicity, and gratefulness.

When you consider something like death, after which
. . . we may well go out like a candle flame, then it
probably doesn't matter if we try too hard, are awkward sometimes, care for one another too deeply, are
excessively curious about nature, are too open to experience, enjoy a nonstop expense of the senses in an
effort to know life intimately and lovingly. It probably doesn't matter if . . . we sometimes look clumsy
or get dirty or ask stupid questions or reveal our ignorance or say the wrong thing or light up with wonder
like the children we all are. It probably doesn't matter
if a passerby sees us dipping a finger into the moist
pouches of a dozen lady's slippers to find out what
bugs tend to fall in them, and thinks us a bit eccen-
tric. Or a neighbor, fetching her mail, sees us standing
in the cold with our own letters in one hand and a
seismically red autumn leaf in the other, its color hitting our senses like a blow from a stun gun, as we
stand with a huge grin, too paralyzed by the intricately veined gaudiness of the leaf to move.

—DIANE ACKERMAN

PRACTICE: THE COMPANY OF THOSE WHO HAVE DIED

We begin to appreciate the value of our lives when we become more accepting of the inevitability of our death.

One gentle way to begin this process of acceptance is to gather up photographs of all the people you loved who have died—pictures of grandparents or other relatives, friends, people who touched you in some way who have passed away.

Arrange these pictures on a small altar. Perhaps you can add a candle or some incense. Sit down in front of this collection of beings.

Look into the face of each person who has died. Allow yourself to linger with whatever memories or reflections arise. If there is sadness, allow the sadness. If there are pleasant recollections that bring a smile, allow those to be fully present as well.

Take a moment to feel how all these beings have passed from this life. They have all died. Just as you will die. Be aware of the deep and abiding kinship of death. These beings are your family; they have merely gone before into a place you too will inevitably pass into. Be aware that you are on your way to meet them in your own time.

What feelings arise? Fear? Sadness? Freedom? Allow this altar to be a touchstone, a place of remembrance. Not only to remember those you loved, but to remember that they are not separate from you. Their death will be yours as well.

How does this affect the way you think about your life today?

Acceptance

35/10

Brushing out my daughter's dark
silken hair before the mirror
I see the grey gleaming on my head,
the silver-haired servant behind her. Why is it
just as we begin to go
they begin to arrive, the fold in my neck
clarifying as the fine bones of her
hips sharpen? As my skin shows
its dry pitting, she opens like a small
pale flower in the tip of a cactus;
as my last chances to bear a child
are falling through my body, the duds among them,
her purse full of eggs, round and
firm as hard-boiled yolks, is about
to snap its clasp. I brush her tangled
fragrant hair at bedtime. It's an old
story—the oldest we have on our planet—
the story of replacement.

—SHARON OLDS

IN THE EARLY YEARS of the AIDS epidemic, many young
men—terrified by the prospect of an impending death they
neither imagined nor understood—felt betrayed, angry, and
desperate. Few of the drugs now recommended to prolong
the lives of HIV-infected people were available. People were
dying rapidly from the opportunistic infections that ravaged

their bodies. At that time, death from HIV-related illness seemed swift and sure.

Anthony was in his late twenties when he was first diagnosed with Pneumocystis carinii pneumonia, a malady common to people with AIDS. When he was in the hospital, he felt resentful and afraid. His heart was hardened in anger against the possibility of his untimely death. He vowed to do anything he could to enjoy the rest of his life, however long that was going to be.

When he was well enough to leave the hospital, he began applying for—and receiving—dozens of credit cards through the mail. He would use the available credit to take trips to exotic places, buy a new stereo, get new furniture, and eat at only the best restaurants. He was going to die soon, he reasoned; no one would ever be able to collect from him. When he reached the credit limit on one card, he would simply get another. In those days, many in the AIDS community encouraged and supported this kind of behavior. What else was there to do in the face of such a tragedy? They felt that the prospect of dying young somehow bestowed the right to be less responsible to a larger spiritual ethic. It was time to milk from life whatever it had to give.

Still, even as Anthony jetted from place to place, there was an unquenchable sadness, an unmistakable desperation in his every move. There was little real joy in these remaining days. He responded to his illness with fear and despair. For him, there was only this hollow, desperate conclusion: Eat, drink, for tomorrow we die.

Of course, very soon Anthony did die. And after him Brian, and Tom, and Michael, and Tim, and Steve, and Diana, and Kenneth, and Jack, and Rick, and so many others in our community.

However, we eventually came to see that people with HIV could live more than a few months. In fact, many have now been living for more than a decade with HIV. We slowly began to realize that HIV did not mean instant death. Rather, it meant learning to *live* with death. While the presence of death remained unmistakably strong, there arose a corresponding realization that we needed to construct a vital, passionate life in the face of death. Death became a partner, a constant companion, a wake-up call. *Pay attention,* it whispered. *This is your life. How shall you live it?*

Soon after Anthony's death, we began conducting healing services for people with HIV and AIDS; support groups emerged from within the community, where HIV-infected men and women and their friends and lovers would gather to share their fear, their hope, their struggles with illness, life, and death.

Bread for the Journey helped people care for one another when they were sick, taking loved ones into their homes, sitting around the clock with those in need. We helped start assistance and meal programs for the homebound, provided access to alternative therapies, and provided residential care for those with no insurance or other support. Many in the community began to study meditation and develop spiritual practices that deepened their capacity to fully experience their sorrow and still feel a genuine sense of grace. We had more gatherings, times for prayer, chanting, and song.

In a few short years a more mindful, loving community gradually emerged from the ashes of the many we had lost. Quite a number of us, through a reluctant acceptance of our mortality, found ourselves drawn into a web of ethical action and response; we became more convinced we wished to use our remaining life to cultivate balance, kindness, and peace. Death—or, rather, an intimate engagement with the inevitability of death—was the awareness that catalyzed a community of fear and despair into a community of tremendous love and courage. If we are here for only a short time, what else have we to do but be loving and kind?

VICTOR FRANKL SPEAKS of the evolution of compassion that emerged within the Nazi death camps:

> We who lived in the concentration camps can remember those who walked through the huts comforting others, giving away their last piece of bread.

They may have been few in number, but they offer sufficient proof that everything can be taken from a person but one thing: the last of human freedoms—to choose one's attitude in any given set of circumstances—to choose one's own way.

Acceptance of death is acceptance of freedom—freedom to live each day with clarity and courage. Like those in the camps, we are awakened to the impermanence of our precious life, and in that impermanence we find the freedom to choose our own way. If we know we will die, all danger disappears. There is less fear about what can go wrong, because the worst that can possibly go wrong—our own death—is completely assured. All there is left to do is to live, and live well.

One day, as Achaan Chah—a Buddhist teacher from the forest monasteries of Thailand—was teaching, one of his students asked him, "How can you be happy in a world of such impermanence, where you cannot protect your loved ones from harm, illness, and death?" He held up a glass and said, "Someone gave me this glass. I really like this glass. It holds my water admirably and it glistens in the sunlight. I touch it and it rings! One day the wind may blow it off my shelf, or my elbow may knock it from the table. This glass is already broken. Even as I hold it in my hand I know it is already on the floor in pieces, so I enjoy it incredibly."

The glass is already broken. We are already dead, so certain is our physical demise. Seen through this lens, what is the hurry? What is the rush? Where is the fire? The fire has already come, and everything has already burned to the ground.

We are getting closer to death with every breath, and no strategy will exempt us from a sure and certain end to our life as we know it. Does this make us depressed? On the contrary, it can set us free—free from the illusion that one more phone call, one more meeting, another hundred dollars will buy us safety, happiness, immortality. It is all chasing after the wind. When we stop chasing the wind, we can begin to live in peace.

SHUNRYU SUZUKI ROSHI:

> *Life is like*
> *stepping onto a boat*
> *which is about to sail*
> *out to sea*
> *and sink.*

JAMES WAS DYING OF CANCER. There were times when he was at peace with this. Other times he felt lost and afraid, and he would come to see me. On this one particular day James was overcome with fear, and he could think of nothing else.

Tell me about the fear, I said to him. *What does it feel like?*

"I feel it most in my chest. It feels like pressure, and heat. There is burning near my heart. It aches."

If this burning could speak, what would it say?

"I'm afraid. I'm so afraid to die." He began to weep.

Let's try this, I suggested. *Instead of pushing away your death, let's try to welcome it. Allow it all the space it needs to live in your body. Try saying this to yourself: I could die today.*

"But I don't *want* to die today."

I understand, James. You know I do not wish you to die. But, like mine, your death will come when it comes. When you use all your strength to fight your death, you are losing all the energy you have left to live. Please, try this experiment. Repeat this to yourself: I could die today.

James was very skeptical. He was opposed to giving his death any power or acknowledgment at all. However, since he honored me greatly with his trust, he ventured this experiment. He said it softly, tentatively: "I could die today."

Good. Say it again a few times.

"I could die today. I could die today." James was quiet. Something seemed to be shifting.

One more time, James. Please.

James took a deep breath. "I could die today." Much to his surprise, he started laughing.

Tell me what happened.

"The fear goes away," he said. "My chest feels more

open and soft. It's true: I could die today. Or I might not. But it's totally out of my control, isn't it?" He smiled. He felt relieved of the burden of trying to control his own dying. Now, a great deal lighter, he could devote his energy to enjoying the time he had left.

James decided to use this as a mantra throughout his day. Whenever he woke up in the morning, he would say to himself, "I could die today." When he got into his car, when he sat down to eat, before he picked up the phone, he said the words—this phrase became a constant companion.

Later, when he came to see me again, he said the fear was almost completely gone. "Whenever I feel that fear arising in my chest, I just acknowledge it—'I could die today.' Somehow it sets me free. I feel more peaceful, not so sad about everything. I still don't want to die—but knowing that I could die makes living less of a battle against death. I just have this day, and so I do what I love with it. I visit friends, meditate, appreciate the mountains, call people who need my care. I'm not dying, I'm living."

WE MISTAKENLY believe that if we accept our death, we will begin to die. Curiously, the reverse is true: When we accept we are already dying, we are set free to live.

The preacher in Ecclesiastes speaks of the ever-circling rhythms of all things as they arise and fall away:

> *A generation goes, and a generation*
> *comes,*
> *but the earth remains forever.*
> *The sun rises and the sun goes down,*
> *and hastens to the place where it*
> *rises.*
> *The wind blows to the south,*
> *and goes round to the north;*
> *round and round goes the wind,*
> *and on its circuits the wind returns.*
> *All streams run to the sea,*
> *but the sea is not full;*

> *to the place where the streams flow,*
> *there they flow again.*
> *All things are full of weariness;*
> *a man cannot utter it;*
> *the eye is not satisfied with seeing,*
> *nor the ear filled with hearing.*
> *What has been is what will be,*
> *and what has been done is what*
> *will be done;*
> *and there is nothing new under the*
> *sun.*

Such is our life. What the Buddha names as our ten thousand joys and ten thousand sorrows, the preacher in Ecclesiastes names as vanities—those things that take form and flourish, only to die and be replaced by new forms, which will themselves fade in their own time.

Such is our life. Our dreams are born, and then they dissolve. Every edifice we build for posterity is eroded by time. Everything we try to remember is eventually forgotten. Each bulwark against illness and death is slowly corroded by the necessity of impermanence. Everything put together falls apart. And for everything that falls apart, something new and unexpected is born to take its place.

Sometimes in summer we go hiking in the national forest in the mountains behind Santa Fe. When I walk in these deep woods, I cannot help but feel engulfed in a thick orchestration of life and death. Fresh green things sprout beside the decay of fallen giants. The mulch of generations of leaves and branches fertilizes every manner of plant, fungus, tree, and flower. Life emerges from death, and death from life, at every turn in the trail. It feels as if the earth is absolutely incapable of not producing life at every opportunity. The constancy of it, the relentless expansion and contraction of life and death, is so insistently miraculous that I only become more and more quiet in the presence of this endless cycle.

Such is our life. Taken at face value, this perspective may seem to render our lives small and insignificant. In the midst of such impermanence, how can our meager, individual lives possibly achieve any real meaning? All beings live and die; billions of lives on the earth arise and pass away. Whole worlds are born and are then destroyed. Entire galaxies come into being and then dissolve. What possible value can a single, modest human life have in this breathtaking cacophony of life and death?

Indeed, the value of a single life shines brightly. A single rose, a single star, a single note of sweet music played at the right time—these are things of great beauty and wonder. All that we do becomes embedded in the whole; because of this, our every day—our every word, every act of kindness, love, or beauty—is an invaluable opportunity to contribute to the growth and beauty of all things. With our single life, we change the shape of the universe.

When we are aware that we too are part of this forest, part of this cycle of replacement, we feel at once the larger context to which we so thoroughly belong. We awaken to our portion in the larger impermanence of all things. The seasons of our life, like the seasons of the earth, are in constant motion. All is in flux. Fall becomes winter becomes spring becomes summer becomes fall. Leaves sprout, flowers bloom, trees grow, leaves fade and fall away, things go cold and dark, all is quiet and still.

DENISE TOOK CARE of her brother, Mark for many months before he died of AIDS. During that fertile and difficult period, Denise found that many of her habits and expectations had been challenged by Mark's presence in her home. First, Denise had been a very private person who lived alone, but Mark insisted that he wanted to live with Denise, and he demanded constant doses of care and attention. Mark had been a successful organizer and teacher, admired by many for his ability to create schools and learning environments for children. Because of his many talents, he was used to being in charge. Denise, however, was also used to taking charge of things—she was a supervisor at work, an organized woman who prided herself on her ability to make things come out the way they were designed—yet here was her brother, dying. In the realm of her brother's life and death, she clearly could not control much of anything. Mark, in his fear, became even more insistent upon retaining control of the details of his life, and so they fought passionately, and often, about who was calling the shots.

Finally Denise had to allow herself to see things just as they were: Mark was sick, he needed care, and she had to surrender. No amount of control or organization could alter the fact of his impending death. To surrender control meant finally admitting that her beloved brother was really going to die. The grief was almost unbearable. Denise wept in my office as she spoke of it. Mark and his illness could not be arranged or administered out of existence. The reality was larger than she could control, larger than she could imagine.

Denise would periodically stop by to report on her progress, and Mark's health. In fact, he seemed to be deteriorating very quickly. Denise had become more open to his needs, and she now felt that it was all right to simply sit with his pain, his fear, even his need for control. She told me a story from their childhood together. "I remember when I was five years old. I was standing in the living room, and for some reason it was dark. Mark, my newborn baby brother, was lying in a bassinet. I remember having an incredibly powerful feeling: I knew I would never be loved the way I wanted ever again. Now that this new child—Mark—was in our family, *he* was the baby, and he would get all the love I had now lost forever.

"But ever since Mark came back to be with me, in his life and now his death, he has given me all that love back. I feel such love now. It all came full circle, like some deep, healing destiny. I wish I could have known then all the love I know now."

Much later, after a long illness, Mark died. When Denise came again to see me, she was touched by a mixture of deep sadness and inexplicable joy. "His death was so beautiful. All his friends were there. My house was filled with people, and it felt so loving." She wept quietly at the memory. "He gave me so many gifts. Not just his love, but also in making me see how flexible I could be. Just having him in my home, our time together, our struggles, our talks late into the night—I have been stretched so much. I feel so much more soft and open, more flexible in the face of things I am given. My life feels less predictable. And even that doesn't sound so scary."

JOSEPH GOLDSTEIN, in his book *Insight Meditation,* proposes an extremely useful distinction between the practice of "letting it go" and "letting it be":

> Often in meditative language we speak of letting go of things: let go of thoughts, let go of emotions, let go of pain. Sometimes that is not exactly the right phrase, because letting go suggests that you need to do something. A better phrase to work with is "Let it be." Let it be. Everything comes and goes by itself. We do not have to do anything to make it come, or make it go, or to let it go. We just have to let it be.

So it is with life and death. When we die, we need not let go of anything. Death will come when it comes. We are simply letting it be. And it is the same with life. We need not let go of our illusions of immortality. They will go on their own soon enough. But if we can mindfully accept it all simply as it is—we live and then we die—then there is nothing to do at all, only to let it be. This acceptance brings tremendous freedom.

I WAS SPEAKING as the guest of a healing center. After the retreat was over, Nancy—the founder of the center—and I went out for dinner. She told me the story of how the center began.

Nancy had been a timid woman. She had always wanted to do good things for people, but she was often confused and unsure as to how to proceed with her life. She entered into a relationship with Mary, a woman she loved very much, and that seemed to bring her a great deal of security and peace. But Mary was soon diagnosed with cancer, and Nancy had to take care of her. Day after day, night after night, Nancy sat with Mary, coordinating her care, holding her, bathing her, feeding her. It was a deep and healing time for them both.

When Mary died, Nancy knew exactly what she had to do. She would start a healing center. There was no uncertainty now, no hesitation at all. "I was fearless," Nancy said. "I felt a clarity and determination I had never felt before. In the old days, I would get a good idea, then I would just get stuck. Now, in the face of Mary's death, I had no time to get stuck. Whenever I met an obstacle—and there were a bunch of them—I just kept on going. Instead of stopping, I would ask, 'How do we get past this? Let's try something else.' It was no more, 'Well, maybe we shouldn't be doing this, it's too hard.' Now it was, 'We're just going to do it. If we can't do it this way, we will do it that way.' Death helped me see more clearly what had to be done. After that, the rest was easy. All I had to do was just go ahead and do it."

JONE AND CULLEN are the parents of Forrest and Bryce, the young children killed in the automobile accident. After the tragic death of their children we worked together for many months, touching and gently healing the unspeakable grief of two parents who loved their children very much.

One day Jone came in and announced she was pregnant. She and Cullen spoke of how strange it felt to be inviting a child into a family where the child's older siblings had already died. "It will be hard in some ways. This child will be the youngest, and it will know it had older brothers. But it will also grow and, God willing, will grow to be the oldest in the family.

"But most important," Jone continued, "this child will grow up in a family that has known death. Because of that, we will always know this child is on loan, a precious thing and a gift. We may not change our parenting—we really had great times with Forrest and Bryce—but we will be even more aware how unbelievably lucky we are to have a child in our life each day."

ETTE HILLESUM, increasingly aware of her impending death at the hands of the Nazis in the death camps, wrote of the clarity, courage, and compassion that seemed to arise within her the closer she got to her destiny:

> Such words as "God" and "Death" and "Suffering" and "Eternity" are best forgotten. We have to become as simple and as wordless as the growing corn or the falling rain. We must just be.
>
> People sometimes say, "You must try to make the best of things." I find this a feeble thing to say. Everywhere things are both very good and very bad at the same time. The two are in balance, everywhere and always. I never have the feeling I have got to make the best of things, everything *is* fine just as it is. Every situation, however miserable, is complete in itself and contains the good as well as the bad. . . .
>
> Have I really made so much progress that I can say with complete honesty: I hope they will send me to a labour camp so I can do something for the 16-year-old girls who will also be going? And to reassure the distracted parents who are kept behind, saying, "Don't worry, I'll look after your children"?
>
> When I tell others: fleeing or hiding is pointless, there is no escape, so let's just do what we can for others, it sounds too much like defeatism, like something I don't mean at all. I cannot find the right words either for that radiant feeling inside me, which encompasses but is untouched by all the suffering and all the violence.

If I survive this life without dying, I'll be surprised.

—Mulla Nasrudin

Practice: I Could Die Today

Pick a simple daily activity, something you do every day, such as turning on the faucet, getting into your car, putting on your clothes, taking a drink of water.

Choose one of these activities. Then, for one week, whenever you perform one of these simple acts, say this to yourself: *I could die today.*

Stop for just a moment in the process of this action and reflect on the truth of this simple phrase: *I could die today.*

What if this was true? It is, you know. Any of us could die any day at all. What if you were to die today?

What feelings arise when you say this? Which people come to mind? What activities? What dreams? What responsibilities do you feel liberated from?

Pay attention to what arises when you say this to yourself each day: *I could die today.*

Next week pick another activity, then another. This is a good exercise to increase mindfulness throughout the day.

Effortlessness

JACK IS A PAINTER. When he came to me, he felt he was "going crazy." After decades of working hard as an artist and teacher, he found himself drinking alone at night and feeling suicidal. For years Jack had played the struggling artist in the scene of galleries, critics, and openings. After a great deal of intense effort, he felt the critics had never been fair to him, and from where he now stood, it looked as though he would never be the successful, famous painter he felt he should be. This crushing defeat was leaving him angry and desperate.

When Jack was small, he was beaten regularly and often by his angry father, with fists across the face, belts across the back. There was a sadness in his eyes that spoke of many nights of fear. There was a sorrow embedded in his spirit.

But Jack also grew up in a time when the artistic myth was strong: The struggling, hard-drinking artist, misunderstood by all, fights and claws his way through the jungle of the art world to redeem all the ills of a lost and evil world. Jack—driven to be good, to be worthy, to be recognized as a successful painter—pushed and pushed, drove himself beyond his capacities, worked until he was exhausted, and drank to soothe his disappointment and anger. In Jack the famous quote by Somerset Maugham came alive: "The artist produces for the liberation of his soul."

This was Jack the artist. But Jack the painter was much gentler. Painting was beautiful and easy. When Jack painted, he would quiet himself down and listen to how the color, the shape, the line spoke to him, following the brush as it sought out the spaces between things. He listened for the tiniest indication of what was necessary, what was required. Nothing more. Just as he was an excellent painter, he taught his students the same way. "Be easy," he would tell them. "Let the colors tell you where to go." He was sought out as a gifted master who helped students find the best in themselves.

Jack was torn between being a painter and teacher or being a "great artist." Painting and teaching, he was joyful and easy. But as soon as he tried to push and grind and force the world to recognize the great artist, he felt only misery.

The Buddha taught that one of the steps on the Eightfold Path is the practice of Right Action. First, Right Action is that act that is morally and ethically clear. We are admonished to abstain from destroying life, from stealing, from intoxication, from harming others, and from sexual misconduct. Above all, Right Action supports those activities that help others to be healed and to live a peaceful and honorable life.

In naming the benefits of Right Action, the Buddha does not list "Right Result." There is no such thing. We are in charge only of our actions, not the fruits of our actions. We can speak honestly and work diligently and still never be rewarded with worldly success. We can meditate daily and pray without ceasing and still be stricken with bodily illness. The fruits of the practice are not the results, only the practice itself. The benefit of Right Action is having performed right action. Nothing more, nothing less.

If we are patient and quiet, we can feel this. If we prepare a fine meal mindfully and with care, there is much joy to be derived from the preparation. If we take a walk, there is much reward in the walking, regardless of where we are headed. If we pray, the quietness that arises in prayer is reward enough, regardless of the "success" of what we have prayed for. Right Action is its own reward.

"What if," I asked Jack one day, "you allow yourself to live your life and your career in the same way that you paint? To push less, to allow what is necessary to emerge from the canvas of each day?" Jack looked skeptical. I continued, "Listen. If the Buddha was right, then you can only do what is right action, not right result. Action is painting; acclaim and recognition are results. You can't ever paint the result; you can only paint the canvas."

Jack seemed stunned by the suggestion. After a moment he said, "That's too easy. A great artist has to suffer." Then we both laughed. How insidiously this myth had penetrated his life. His painting—which he dearly loved—had somehow been kidnapped by this need to redeem his pain, his father's pain, the pain of the world—and to be universally acclaimed as an artistic savior in the bargain. It all seemed so unnecessary.

"Well, it is true that many people want me to teach," he admitted. "So if I just follow the rhythm of what is happening now, I should just teach and paint and see what happens." He laughed again. It seemed as if a great burden had been lifted from him.

When Jack returned the next week, he was so much lighter and happier. He held my hands in his and looked into my eyes. "I have never felt this good," he said. His eyes were misty. "For all these years I have lived with the burden of thinking I had to work against my grain and suffer to be successful. Now that I feel how easy it is if I just listen to myself and trust my own rhythm, I feel cheated out of the last twenty years." He paused, feeling again the pain of the struggle. "But now," he said, "I have the next twenty. And it feels great."

HOW SHALL WE LIVE, knowing we will die? Many of us simply do not know. Without the "aid" of a diagnosis of terminal illness, we may drift for years at a time, lost, frightened, and confused. So we seek to unravel our confusion—to amputate our inner "don't know"—by going to a host of workshops, seeking out a variety of therapists, reading piles of books, consulting with scores of teachers, friends, lovers, and acquaintances to fill in the blanks, to replace the gnawing emptiness of "don't know."

Many of us are exhausted by this desperate search for answers, as if our life is a big problem to be solved and we haven't yet found the trick to it, the perfect solution to the puzzle. After all our investigations, we have still not discovered the answer to our life. We figure we must not be working hard enough. So we push harder, hold on more tightly to the problem, hoping to eventually wring some wisdom from our struggle and set our life on the right course.

But what if "don't know" is not a signal to push and work and struggle, but rather an indication that it is time to be quiet, listen, and wait? What if the answers to our questions about life and path and practice are already speaking to us, and in our rush to find them elsewhere we miss the easy, gentle wisdom that would teach us all we need to know if we simply center ourselves and be still for just a moment?

Many of us naturally assume that a spiritual life is very hard work. This is not quite accurate. Rather, *trying* to have a spiritual life is very hard work indeed. *Trying* to pray, *trying* to meditate, *trying* to study scriptures, *trying* to get healed, *trying* to act spiritually at all times—this can make anyone exhausted and miserable.

We assume that the hardest, most difficult path will always be the most fruitful in the end and that the more we bring suffering on ourselves, the more generously we will be rewarded. But if we listen to the great saints and teachers of the world, we are struck by one common theme: They all speak of how gentle it can be. Jesus says, "Come to me, all you who are heavy laden, and I will give you rest. . . . My yoke is easy, and my burden is light." Thomas Merton says that in the moment we stop working for ourselves and begin working for the divine, we will be amazed how easily it all goes. Buddha begins the Dhammapada by observing that simple purity of thought will bring happiness that will follow us as reliably as our own shadow.

Here, Chuang Tzu tells a wonderful Taoist story that describes the benefits of not pushing, but rather following the openings that arise easily and gently along a spiritual path:

> Prince Wen Hui's cook
> Was cutting up an ox.
> Out went a hand,
> Down went a shoulder,
> He planted a foot,
> He pressed with a knee,

The ox fell apart
With a whisper,
The bright cleaver murmured
Like a gentle wind.
Rhythm! Timing!
Like a sacred dance,
Like "The Mulberry Grove,"
Like ancient harmonies!

"Good work!" the Prince exclaimed,
"Your method is faultless!"
"Method?" said the cook
Laying aside his cleaver,
"What I follow is Tao
Beyond all methods!

"When I first began
To cut up oxen
I would see before me
The whole ox
All in one mass.

"After three years
I no longer saw this mass.
I saw the distinctions.

"But now, I see nothing
With the eye. My whole being
Apprehends.
My senses are idle. The spirit
Free to work without plan
Follows its own instinct
Guided by natural line,
By the secret opening, the hidden space,
My cleaver finds its own way.
I cut through no joint, chop no bone.

"A good cook needs a new chopper
Once a year—he cuts.
A poor cook needs a new one
Every month—he hacks!

"I have used this same cleaver
Nineteen years.
It has cut up
A thousand oxen.
Its edge is as keen
As if newly sharpened.

"There are spaces in the joints;
The blade is thin and keen:
When this thinness
Finds that space
There is all the room you need!
It goes like a breeze!
Hence I have this cleaver nineteen years
As if newly sharpened!

"True, there are sometimes
Tough joints. I feel them coming,
I slow down, I watch closely,
Hold back, barely move the blade,
And whump! the part falls away
Landing like a clod of earth.

"Then I withdraw the blade,
I stand still
And let the joy of the work
Sink in.
I clean the blade
And put it away."

Prince Wen Hui said,
"This is it! My cook has shown me
How I ought to live
My own life!"

Effortlessness is the ability to slow down and listen for the spaces between the joints. Then—whump!—the blade passes through with no struggle at all. Deep within all things there is a natural rhythm, a music of opening and closing, expansion and contraction. Our heart, our lungs, the seasons, the oceans—all life expands and contracts, opens and closes, softens and hardens and then goes soft again. This potent opening and closing cannot be forced to happen, nor can it be stopped. It is simply the way of all things. It is happening inside you even now as you read this sentence.

The wisdom of this essential rhythm is called by many names: the Kingdom of God, our Buddha nature, the One, the Beloved, the still, small voice. This inexplicable movement permeates the life force that vibrates within all things; there is little we need do to make it happen. We need only remain clear and awake to listen for how things really are, to feel how the smallest changes of energy and attention move in us, in our relationships, in our work. Like the butcher, we can learn to follow the spaces between things. Not to fight and push and cajole, but rather simply to wait until the true way reveals itself easily and clearly in this moment.

Lao Tzu:

Whoever forces it spoils it. Whoever grasps it loses it.

IN OUR YARD in winter we sometimes get heavy mountain snows. During a storm snow accumulates on the branches of the junipers outside our window. The snow gently piles itself on each branch, flake upon flake, until the branch gets very heavy and seems to groan under the weight of the wet snow. The branch bends slowly, aching, almost to the ground. It seems it will break. Then a single snowflake, the one whose time has come, will add its infinitesimal weight to the already overwhelming bulk, and it will all reach critical mass. At that instant all the snow slips at once from the branch, a cloud of white. The branch springs upward, free of its burden.

In the fall, the golden locust turns bright yellow. The cool nights and failing light tell the leaves their work for the season is done. It is time for them to fall away. But of all the trees in the yard, those of the locust are the last to fall. The leaves of the aspen and cottonwood and plum and peach and crabapple all turn color and drop to the earth, but the leaves on the golden locust remain, tenacious, refusing to let go. Holding on for what? For the day that comes (and who can truly predict the day?) when suddenly they all fall at once, a bright, gleaming shower of time. Thousands of tiny golden leaves shimmering through the air, making their way home. It is as if they have all waited together until each was ready, and then, with some silent, invisible signal, the fullness of time is achieved, and they all fall free.

In the spring it is the same thing. From under the snow, as the soil begins to warm, first the crocuses, then the daffodils, then the irises, then the apple and plum and crabapple, then the lilacs, then the aspen, then the golden locust all return in their own time.

Who knows the timing of this readiness? If we are quiet and listen, if we are vigilant and watchful, we will feel our days are saturated with these moments of readiness: time to eat, time to rest, time to work, time to have company, time to be alone. All through the day there are these singular moments when it is time for change, time for something to be set free.

When is it time to let go of our parents? When is it time to be finished with therapy? When are we finished with our grief? When should we feel we are fully healed? These are not questions about pushing and working harder. These are questions about readiness. And for readiness, we must listen. If we plant corn in spring, our hungry demands for corn in June will be fruitless. The corn will come in August, or not at all. Regardless of how much we may desire it now, we cannot "decide" that it is time for corn. If you truly love corn, you will live with it for many seasons, watch for the sprouts on the stalk, await the appearance of tassels that drift in the wind, feel the ear in your hand as it fills out the husk. You will know when it is ready, for it will teach you, with unmistakable signs.

"Hasten slowly," said Milarepa, "and ye shall soon arrive." If we find we are struggling over and over with some aspect of our lives, perhaps we are working against the grain. Perhaps this is not what is called for, not what is necessary. If we are always tired, agitated, and discouraged, this is a good indication that we are doing too much. If we are doing all this work without success or satisfaction, most of us take this as an indication to work harder, faster, do more. But in reality, this is an unmistakable sign that it may be time to do less. "The trouble with the rat race," Lily Tomlin wryly observed, "is that even if you win, you're still a rat."

JACQUELINE CAME to one of our retreats. She had been hurt deeply as a child by her abusive parents. They had harmed her physically and emotionally. She felt she carried scars she could not even name, deep in her body and in her heart.

But Jacqueline had also done a great deal of work on herself. In therapy, with the support of others who had been harmed in similar ways, she had found within herself places of great strength and spiritual courage. She was ready to let go of her parents, she said; she had done forgiveness meditations, tried letting them go, tried saying good-bye to the past. Yet still, when she thought of them, she felt anger and hurt. She was frustrated and disappointed in herself. Why hadn't she been able to finally let them go?

I suggested she stop trying to let them go. She had done her part. She had explored the places where she had been harmed, and she had touched those places with kindness and healing. She had allowed herself to imagine that she could live her life without carrying around the story of how they hurt her. She was ready to let them go. I asked her if she could simply live with this readiness. "I get so impatient, I want this whole thing to be over," she replied. Her voice was tired, frustrated. "I just want to be finished with them."

"Perhaps it is merely this impatience that stops this process from moving forward," I suggested. "Maybe you could allow even this feeling of incompleteness to be enough for now. To simply rest in the readiness for it to happen, without pushing so hard all the time to make it happen."

Jacqueline seemed to relax. She smiled. "Actually," she admitted, "I wouldn't mind a little rest." Everyone laughed. They could all sympathize with how hard she was working. Everyone in the room had been working just as long and as hard. They all took delight in the concept that they could simply rest, even for just a little while.

Two weeks later, Jacqueline sent me a letter. "You'll never believe this—then again, you probably will—but I *did* stop pushing my parents to leave, and I just surrendered into waiting. And then, without me doing anything, one morning I woke up and I felt different. They were gone. My parents were completely gone. I hadn't killed them or forced them out; there was just a softness where there had been a hardness in my heart before. Now, when I think of them, I feel only sympathy for their pain. I don't necessarily want to be closer to them, but I don't need to push them away, either. They just fell away. It feels wonderful."

All Jacqueline needed was permission to stop pushing—to stop working so hard to make her healing happen the way she wanted it to happen, and to allow it to grow and unfold within her in its own time. Many times this is all we need—permission to stop pushing, to stop working so hard. There is wholeness here already. Let us wait for it to show itself.

We push because we believe pushing will make it happen. But would a woman in the sixth month of her pregnancy, weary of carrying this child and aching for relief, squat down and push, trying to force the baby out? This is absurd, for it is clearly not time, and this will only bring much suffering. The baby knows when it is time, and it will announce its readiness with signals few women have ever missed.

Can we attune ourselves to this unmistakable, gently insistent rhythm? Listening—listening to how things are, and how they move—is part of timing. If we listen closely enough to the subtle shifts in light and temperature, we can feel when it is time for the crocuses. We can taste when the lilacs are about to bloom. So, too, can we feel the seasons of our days, if we are sensitive to the movement of energy and awareness within our bodies and hearts.

THOSE WHO RECEIVE a diagnosis of terminal illness initially devote their every waking hour to uncovering any and all treatments, medications, or interventions that might prolong their life or heal them of disease. They mobilize every resource to seek healing. This is important and necessary work: finding the right doctor (or doctors); assembling a healing community; identifying precise and correct medicines and treatments; and cultivating a healthy, positive attitude. Many fortunate beings find their lives have been improved, even saved, by this good work.

But in some cases these efforts, while they bring some measure of emotional and spiritual healing, do not prove effective in eradicating the physical illness. We are now invited to surrender fully into the fact of our dying.

In this moment, all hurry ceases. All rushing evaporates. Where are we rushing to? We know how it ends. The only possible outcome is death. Why should we hurry to get there? When the future is taken away, fear and desperation naturally dissolve.

And so we slow down. There is no place to go but right here, no time left but right now. This does not mean that we become lazy or depressed, or that we no longer strive to accomplish anything useful or valuable. On the contrary, in our quiet we can see which actions are necessary and which are not. Effort is not wasted; it is simply applied only when it will prove most fruitful.

RYOKAN:

> *Too lazy to be ambitious,*
> *I let the world take care of itself.*
> *Ten days' worth of rice in my bag;*
> *a bundle of twigs by the fireplace.*
> *Why chatter about delusion and enlightenment?*
> *Listening to the night rain on my roof,*
> *I sit comfortably, with both legs stretched out.*

When we bring this consciousness into our daily life and use it to inform our living as well as our dying, we work more gently and effortlessly. Quietly attuned to the rhythm and the readiness of things, we become awake to what is useful and necessary. When we act in this way, the speed with which things happen can take our breath away.

LAST SUMMER Alvaro walked into our office at Bread for the Journey. He had heard that we helped people in northern New Mexico, and he wanted to know exactly what we did. Now, it is unusual for people to just walk into our office. It is small and inconspicuous, and most people contact us by phone or letter. Few people ever walk in unannounced. So it was a delightful break for us to sit with Alvaro that afternoon and explain who we were and what we were about.

When we had introduced ourselves and the work of Bread for the Journey, Alvaro spoke. "I have an idea," he began. "Maybe you could help us. My friend Orlando, he's a fly fisher, he told me about you. We have this group of fly fishers, we get together and fish, tie flies, collect equipment, things like that. Many times we bring our sons, and their friends come along. Some of them have had hard times, problems at home. Lately we started talking about how so many kids never get out to fish, never learn to be quiet and wait for things, never relate to someone older who wants to teach them. So we all decided we would try to find some kids that needed maybe a big brother or something, and take them out fly-fishing. Teach them to tie flies, to look for spots in the mountains to fish, to watch real good for where the fish are, and practice learning to catch them. Teach them patience, listening, respect, you know? What do you think?"

It is our belief that the right amount of support, given at the right time to the right people, can prove extraordinarily effective. Alvaro's idea was exactly the kind of project we wanted to support. As it turned out, Alvaro had about two dozen fishermen who were anxious to see the project work and would help in any way they could. We began by contacting the Big Brothers and Big Sisters program, which had many young people on the waiting list, more than would ever get to have a big brother or sister. So, with some financial and administrative support from Bread for the Journey,

Alvaro and his friends designed a two-month program and invited the boys and girls from the waiting list to join them for a summer of fly-fishing, tying flies, and the company of many good-hearted adults who would care for them and teach them things they could never learn anywhere else.

Two weeks after Alvaro walked into our office, over sixty young people were in the mountains learning to fish and to listen. They focused on developing a personal relationship to fishing. The adults taught the young people that it was not the amount or size of the fish that was important, but the connection to nature; they offered them a haven from the pressures of adolescence and taught them to connect honestly and deeply with themselves and others.

If Bread for the Journey had decided on our own to create a mentoring program for young people, it could have taken us a year to get all the pieces in place, with meetings, proposals, committees, and the like. We would have needed to constantly push our idea in order to make it happen. But now, simply by being prepared to listen to what was possible and seize whatever opportunity presented itself, in little more than two weeks we were able to be part of an exciting and spontaneous event that was thoroughly successful.

Readiness to move is the heart of this practice of effortlessness. If we strive to remain rested, awake, mindful, then we will see these spaces clearly when they emerge. We will recognize those moments when action will be most fruitful.

ANNIE DILLARD:

> The gaps are the thing. The gaps are the spirit's one home, the altitudes and latitudes so dazzlingly spare and clean that the spirit can discover itself like a once-blind man unbound. The gaps are the clefts in the rock where you cower to see the back parts of God; they are the fissures between mountains and cells the wind lances through, the icy nar-

rowing fjords splitting the cliffs of mystery. Go up into the gaps. If you can find them; they shift and vanish too. Stalk the gaps. Squeak into a gap in the soil, turn, and unlock—more than a maple—a universe.

Like the golden locust, like the branch ready to let go of the snow, if we are awake to this timing, then we will live in concert with those things that are ready, and the things we need will arise at once, with hardly any strain at all. A good golf swing, a good tennis stroke, a good swing of the ax to split the wood, a perfect word of kindness, a simple act of beauty—these will find the groove, the space, and hardly any effort will be required. We will not be exhausted, even after hours of this activity.

Not that spiritual life is not hard work. But this is not the pushing, driving, desperate kind of hard work, where we are out of breath, straining to get things done by artificial deadlines. When we are desperate to make something happen that is not ready, then inevitably we will feel weary, defeated, disappointed.

Effortlessness requires a good ear, listening quietly to the winds of change as they move through the people and events of our lives. The wind blows where it will, said Jesus, and we hear the sound of it. But we do not know whence it comes or whither it goes. Such is the way of the spirit.

There is a time to act and a time to remain still. There is a time to push and a time to wait. There is a time to engage and a time to retreat. If we can feel the truth of this fundamental law of expansion and contraction of all things, then we will be easy and at peace. And, much to our surprise and delight, we will see that much will be accomplished.

THERE ARE REGIONS of northern New Mexico where fruit trees blossom like the Garden of Eden—Velarde, Dixon, Embudo, places in the high desert mountains with names sweet as spring. Some years the fruit is beautiful and abundant. Other years, when the trees bloom too early or the frost comes late, the fruit is ruined, and there will be no harvest that fall. Levi Romero, a local poet, speaks with wisdom born of many years watching the fruit, how it is given, how it is taken away:

> **It is the 14th of May,**
> **already the days for planting**
> **are just about over**

> *winter has followed spring into this season*
> *with afternoon showers of rain, hail,*
> *and cold weather receding into promises*
> *of warm days that come for short spells*
> *and then disappear behind a cloak*
> *of dark clouds and damp weather*

> *the apricots bloomed early*
> *but March also fell prey to frost*
> *and so this year the tree in the backyard*
> *bears no fruit*

> *it is that way sometimes*
> *it is that way in what we have been told*

> > *"one year yes, one year no"*

> *it comes down to that*
> *a simple understanding of life's give and take*
> *and we in our lives move forward simply*
> *accepting and giving*
> *as the earth gives*
> *and rejecting and taking*
> *as the earth takes*
> *because we know nothing else*

> *there is nothing else to know*
> *it comes down to that*

> > *"un año si, un año no"*

and love too
comes in that similar way
and it remains
it remains in that way when it does
like that

so do not be fearful or impatient
learn how to sway
your life accordingly

you will understand what it means
the sound of a horse neighing
in the moonlight
when your season is come

love

you will know
you will know

Remembering

Mary called to tell me her father had died. He had suffered for many years with Alzheimer's, his memory had deteriorated terribly, and he had been in great pain. Mary felt grateful she had been able to hold his hand, to be with him when he died. As is the case with many deaths after a long illness, she felt a poignant combination of sadness and relief.

For years Mary had missed her father's presence, his ability to focus, to remember who she was. Many times recently when Mary would go to visit him, he would not even recognize her. It made her sad; still, she continued to travel to see him regularly. She was losing someone she deeply loved; he deteriorated before her eyes and heart. It was very painful.

Now, in honor of his death, Mary had decided to be very careful, conscious of what she did and how she moved through each day. She planned the memorial service, made arrangements for the cremation and the interment, and handled the myriad details that inevitably arise when someone dies. "I wanted to be fully awake, to be aware of how I acted, to watch and listen for what was simple and necessary."

At the time of her father's cremation, rather than delegate all the uncomfortable processes to the funeral parlor and insulate herself from the sloppiness of death, Mary insisted she be involved. On the morning of the cremation Mary arranged to be there when her father was placed in the cremation oven. She asked to speak with those who would be handling her father's body. "When you do this today," she said to them, "please remember that this was a man who was once full of life. He was my father. I would like to send him off with love. And I would like you all to help me. Perhaps we could together say a prayer, asking that his spirit go

gently and easily out of his body." The staff, unaccustomed
to this kind of attention to their work, were taken aback—
but they all agreed to honor Mary's request. For them, this
particular cremation became what we might hope every cremation could be—a powerfully sacred moment.

What had Mary done? She had taken an ordinary task—
one performed by millions of people all over the earth—and
infused it with attention and care. She had chosen to use a
commercial funeral parlor; no priests or shamans were present, and there was no incense, no liturgy. Still, an ordinary
moment had somehow been allowed to breathe, to become
rich and full.

Many of us incorrectly assume that a spiritual life begins when we change what we normally do in our daily life.
We feel we must change our job, our living situation, our
relationship, our address, our diet, or our clothes before we
can truly begin a spiritual practice. And yet it is not the act
but the awareness, the vitality, and the kindness we bring to
our work that allows it to become sacred.

The language of spirituality can seem other-worldly, inaccessible to those of us who must live ordinary lives. Words
and phrases such as *enlightenment, sin, redemption, karma, dam-
nation,* or *salvation* can feel either like an imposition or meaningless in the face of meetings, phone calls, piano lessons, car
pools, rent, errands, or problems in our primary relationship.
For others, the language of traditional religion can feel hurtful
or intrusive—or simply outdated and irrelevant. Conse-
quently, we come to feel that our lives, by their very "secular" nature, exclude us from the language and practice of
traditional spirituality.

Yet many of the saints and sages of the earth have ad-
vised that too much religion can impede true spirituality.
"Throw away sacredness and wisdom," counsels Lao Tzu,
"and people will be one hundred times happier." The heart
of a full, rich, spiritual life is driven less by what we do than
by how we do it. The implied tension between things that
are "religious" and those that are "secular" is often harmful
and inaccurate. Our actions at work, our decisions about our
children and our lovers, our choice of vocation, our use of

time, our ability to respond with wisdom and kindness—our every act is an integral part of our spiritual practice, our way of walking on the earth. "It is not the nature of the task," said Martin Buber, "but its consecration that is the vital thing."

Most spiritual traditions have developed a variety of practices to guide daily life. Buddhists prescribe the Eightfold Path; Jews the Ten Commandments; Christians the Sermon on the Mount; Hindus the Bhagavad Gita; Jains the Five Vows; Muslims the Five Pillars of Islam. In each case, the prescriptions are meant to provide a framework for each day, with ways to pay attention and to listen carefully as we try to do what is right and true.

The form and vocabulary of these prescriptions can make them feel stiff and inaccessible. The language of the Ten Commandments or the Eightfold Path can feel constricting, imposed from a distant, unforgiving past on our lives, which now seem more spacious and flexible. And yet these teachings can skillfully remind us that we must often make hard choices about our behavior and the way we live. Without these reminders, we can quickly lapse into laziness, fall asleep, and live sloppy lives that provide little benefit to ourselves or others.

Many of us, in seeking a spiritual life, feel compelled to adopt more formal practices—such as so many minutes or hours of prayer or meditation every day—which then make us feel guilty because we can't find the time to squeeze them into our schedule. The true measure of a daily practice is that the practice itself is joyful, loving, gentle. As St. Teresa said, "All the way to heaven is heaven." We need not be obsessed with whether or not we are doing the "right" spiritual thing, the thing that will "make us spiritual." We are already spiritual. Cooking can be spiritual; working can be spiritual; gardening, driving, answering the phone, making love, cleaning out the refrigerator can all be spiritual activities. It is our belief they are not that brings us a sense of separateness from our selves.

Many Native American languages have no word for *religion* at all. For them, the path of being alive is so inextricably infused with spirit that to imagine anything that was *not* reli-

gion would be folly. Our words, thoughts, and actions are
our prayers. Our moments in the company of others are our
church. Our time alone is our meditation. We are at this very
moment engaged in the most exquisite of spiritual practices—the art of being fully, passionately alive.

BARBARA GATES is a seasoned meditation practitioner and
teacher. A few years ago, she discovered she had breast cancer.

> I was ashamed to notice on several occasions how I
> looked forward to telling people that I had cancer,
> as if that would trick out of them their hidden love
> for me, their feelings of guilt for having ignored or
> jilted me. At times, the prospect of becoming seri-
> ously ill, or even possibly of dying—just to get a
> break from my own constriction—felt exhilarating.
> There had been an excitement about all the atten-
> tion and expressions of love I was getting from
> friends and relatives at the time of the surgery. I
> would catch myself imagining my memorial ser-
> vice, people meditating, reading aloud from my
> journals. And seeing this, I was scared. If I failed to
> embrace life now, would I prevent myself from
> healing?

And so Barbara resolved to remember, to use her days
more mindfully, to watch more carefully. This careful watching became her practice. When the time came to have surgery, she resolved to pay attention to each detail, touching
her breast with kindness and sweet recollection:

> Instead of simply telling the surgeons to cut the
> breast out of my awareness, I wanted to be present
> with what I might lose. And so I remembered. I
> conjured up the delicate nipples of adolescence like
> tender pink stars, the new breasts, velvet to the
> touch under my nightie, the erotic breasts caressed

by my husband Patrick and past lovers over these many years, the milk-filled mother's breasts which suckled my daughter Caitlin. Cautiously, I wanted to experience the history of this embodiment, at the same time seeing the impermanence. . . . Could I learn to honor the body without insisting that it stay young or healthy or never die?

As it happened, the news from surgery was hopeful, and she was able to keep her breast. Barbara's daily practice, which now includes napping in the grass beneath her daughter's climbing tree in the backyard, is clearer than ever. She strives to remember fully the unfolding gifts of the day.

Today I want to notice everything, the Mexican primroses with their soft pink faces and yellow tongues, the dead rat shriveled by the tomato patch. Again and again, I am confirmed that mindfulness—bringing my awareness to whatever is there—is the most healing practice for me.

The heart of most spiritual practice is simply this: Remember. Remember who you are. Remember what you love. Remember what is sacred. Remember what is true. Remember that you will die, and that this day is a gift. Remember how you wish to live.

WHEN JESUS was sitting with his disciples at the Last Supper, he instituted the sacrament of communion by proclaiming, "With this sip of wine and this piece of bread, I want you to do this: Remember me. When you do this, remember that I make my home in you, as you make your home in me."

In a similar way, before he died, Neem Karoli Baba, the playful and wise Indian guru, told his followers to maintain their spiritual practice by doing just three things: "Love, serve, and remember."

Which practices help us remember who we are and what we know? Which act, when we perform it—meditation, prayer, song, writing, walking, cleaning, making tea, gardening, caring for children, making love, helping others—helps us recall our spiritual intention and centers us on our path?

Gary Snyder describes how following even a single breath can refresh and renew our sense of clarity and purpose:

> In this world of onrushing events the act of meditation—even just a "one-breath" meditation—straightening the back, clearing the mind for a moment—is a refreshing island in the stream. Although the term *meditation* has mystical and religious connotations for many people, it is a simple and plain activity. Attention: deliberate stillness and silence. As anyone who has practiced sitting knows, the quieted mind has many paths, most of them tedious and ordinary. Then, right in the midst of meditation, totally unexpected images or feelings may sometimes erupt, and there is a way into a vivid transparency. But whatever comes up, sitting is always instructive. There is ample testimony that a practice of meditation pursued over months and years brings some degree of self-understanding, serenity, focus, and self-confidence to the person who stays with it. There is also a deep gratitude that one comes to feel for this world of beings, teachers, and teachings.

We all need some touchstone, some simple act that helps center us into a remembrance of what is already whole and beautiful. This morning I picked some daffodils, early gifts of the spring, growing in the warmest places along the south face of the house. I cut a few and put some on Christine's desk, some on mine. The stems are supple and green, fresh from the warm soil of early spring. The cups are the most brilliant yellow, loud, exuberant, unselfconsciously yellow. Beautiful things such as daffodils catch our attention; they fill our eyes and our noses and surprise the body with a delightful, unreasonable glee. When we allow ourselves to slow down and be touched by this singular springtime moment, we glimpse a different perspective on our true nature. For an instant, without even meaning to, we realize that this is prayer.

Thich Nhat Hanh playfully notes that even doing the dishes can become a meditation practice:

> To my mind, the idea that doing dishes is unpleasant can occur only when you aren't doing them. Once you are standing in front of the sink with your sleeves rolled up and your hands in the warm water, it really is quite pleasant. I enjoy taking my time with each dish, being fully aware of the dish, the water, and each movement of my hands. I know that if I hurry in order to eat dessert sooner, the time of washing dishes will be unpleasant and not worth living. That would be a pity, for each minute, each second of life is a miracle. The dishes themselves and the fact that I am here washing them are miracles!

To live a day, to care for a single day, is to shape a life. Each day is an opportunity to choose where to place our care. What shall we do today? What simple acts of remembrance will we use to punctuate our time and enrich our walk upon the earth this single day?

JASON IS INFECTED with the HIV virus. Since his diagnosis, he has made it a practice every night to lie in bed before he goes to sleep and review the events of the day. He makes a point to give thanks for any gifts or blessings he received and to be grateful for the people who brought them. He also listens for any unfinished business—any conversation or interaction that felt in some way unpleasant or incomplete. Then when he awakens the next morning, he sets himself to resolving whatever is in need of his attention. "I don't know how long I'm going to live," Jason told me. "Hopefully it will be for a very long time. But because I do not know, I feel I have to stay clear in my life, with other people and with myself. This is one simple way to do that." For Jason, this is a useful meditation.

BROTHER LAWRENCE:

> It is not necessary to have great things to do. I turn
> my little omelet in the pan for the love of God.

Many years ago I was privileged to meet Archbishop Desmond Tutu. It was at the height of the anti-apartheid movement in South Africa. He spoke to a group of us at Harvard Divinity School about the spiritual practice of seeking peace and justice. One of my friends asked, "You seemingly work so tirelessly on behalf of your people, and there is constant pressure being a spiritual leader and a spokesperson for peace around the world. What sustains you? What keeps you going?"

Archbishop Tutu smiled quietly. "Two things sustain me," he said. "First, I begin each day with a period of meditation, prayer, and reflection. I cannot imagine starting a day without this time of quiet contemplation. And second," he added, "I am sustained by knowing that I am doing what is right."

BOB, A PEDIATRIC NURSE, works with terminally ill children in the hospital. He told me about one little girl with cancer. Her name was Emily. Emily loved playing with Bob. She felt safe with him, and they soon became fast friends. Once in a while Emily would speak of the time when Chucky Lee was going to come. Bob didn't know Chucky Lee, but he assumed he was a friend or member of her family. One day, after she had repeatedly mentioned Chucky Lee, Bob asked her to tell him about Chucky Lee. "Chucky Lee comes to see me sometimes," said Emily. She was quiet for a moment. "Chucky Lee," she finally continued, "is death. Someday Chucky Lee will come and take me away."

Emily had personified death into a character she could understand. "Are you frightened of Chucky Lee?" Bob asked her. "Yes, very much," Emily replied. "But he mostly comes at night. That's when I see him." Bob was moved by her clarity and innocence. He wanted to protect her, to shield her from such sorrow. "At night, when you feel Chucky Lee coming, is there anything you can do to feel better?" Bob asked. "Oh, yes," Emily replied brightly. "You have to sing 'Jingle Bells' and other love songs."

After that, whenever Bob saw Emily, he would ask her about the night before. How was she doing? "Well," Emily would reply with a conspiratorial whisper, "I had to sing 'Jingle Bells' three times last night—very loud."

Sometimes we must water the garden. Sometimes we must prepare a meal. Sometimes we must speak with those we love. Sometimes we must make tea. Sometimes we must be very quiet and pray our most secret prayer. Other times we need to sing "Jingle Bells" and other love songs very loud. Each time we do this, it can be an opportunity to remember what we love and to give thanks for the miraculous gift of an ordinary life.

MY FRIEND MICHAEL told me that as an activist in the civil rights movement, he and his friends were regularly arrested and put in prison. Many were imprisoned illegally, simply as intimidation for their beliefs about justice and equality.

Whenever they were in prison, they would sing. The guards would come in and yell at them and sometimes even beat them, demanding that they stop. They felt the prisoners' songs were dangerous. And in a way they were right: These courageous beings were singing of joy in the midst of sorrow, freedom in the midst of imprisonment, life in the midst of death. The singing insisted there was a more potent truth than jail or oppression.

And so they would sing. Their singing upset and disturbed the jailers, for when Michael and his friends sang, even as they were being beaten, it meant they had not been broken. They had not been defeated. In the larger game of power, the jailers had lost to the relentless hopefulness of song. The prisoners would keep on singing, because their song was their spirit. And their spirit would not die.

This is how we live, knowing we will die. We are in prison, bound by the bars of our mortality. And still we sing. Singing helps us remember who we are—children of spirit, people of God, here for a short time, and then gone. What else can we do but sing?

I went to the woods because I wished to live deliber-
ately, to front only the essential facts of life, and see
if I could not learn what it had to teach, and not,
when I came to die, discover that I had not lived. I
did not wish to live what was not life, living is so
dear; nor did I wish to practice resignation, unless it
was quite necessary. I wanted to live deep and suck
out all the marrow of life. . . .

—THOREAU

EXERCISE: PLANNING YOUR MEMORIAL SERVICE

Because I am ordained, many people request that I preside at their memorial services. When we gather to remember a human life, we invariably recall the kindness, playfulness, endearing quirks of personality, shared conversations, passionate conflicts, moments of tenderness and love. What people recall are ordinary moments, particular configurations of vitality and grace that arose in the life of this person.

Your memorial will reflect your life, and a life is made of days. Each day is like a droplet of water filling the chalice of our legacy. How do we live, knowing we will be remembered for how we have lived each day?

Take an hour or so to plan your own memorial service. As you think about the structure and content of the service that will honor your life, reflect on the following questions: Do you want to be mourned or celebrated? Do you want music or tears? Do you want people to miss you or to be grateful for your company? Who would you especially like to be there? What would you like them to say? About which accomplishments would you be most proud? What would you like to be most remembered for? If you leave anything—money, property—to whom will you leave it, and how do you want it used? What is the primary legacy of your life? What footprint would you like to leave in the community of beings who would gather to remember you? Finally, what would you like your epitaph to say?

Your "memorial service" may give you some surprisingly clear ideas about the kind of life you wish to have lived. What single thing could you do to begin this life today?

Simplicity

God is not found in the soul by adding anything but
by a process of subtraction.

—Meister Eckhart

Every year, in early spring, our friend Molly comes out to the
house for dinner. It is the time of year to prune our fruit trees,
and Molly is the only one who can do it. She has a particular
wisdom, an uncanny ability to see the tree that will grow out
of the tree that now is. When she sees this, she is able without hesitation to cut from the tree what simply must go, and
allow to remain what must remain.

Every year, as I cook dinner on the grill in the backyard,
I argue with Molly as she moves from tree to tree. "You're
cutting too much!" I always protest. I am afraid she will take
more than the tree can do without, and it will not grow. She,
of course, understands that things often grow taller and
stronger with less, not more. This is something I still have
trouble accepting completely, although I understand it con-
ceptually. But Molly knows this for a fact. And so she cuts
and cuts, leaving a trim, firm shape behind. Sometimes she
leaves a little extra, just for me. The tree doesn't need it, she
insists; it is just so I won't get so upset.

Much of spiritual practice is just this: cutting away what
must be cut, and letting remain what must remain. Knowing
what to cut—this is wisdom. Being clear and strong enough
to make the cut when it is time for things to go—this is
courage. Together, the practices of wisdom and courage en-

able us, day by day and task by task, to gradually simplify our life.

Carl Jung:

> I have done without electricity and tend the fireplace and stove myself. Evenings, I light the old lamps. There is no running water, and I pump the water from the well. I chop the wood and cook the food. These simple acts make man simple; and how difficult it is to be simple.

One winter morning I was standing in line at a local coffee shop. I was hungry, it was late, I was in a bit of a hurry. Santa Fe is a small town, so whenever you go out you are almost certain to run into a friend or someone you know. That morning I was a little grumpy, so I was hoping to get in and out of the shop without meeting anyone. I hunkered down in my coat, trying to be invisible. Just as I was about to order, I saw someone get in line behind me. It was Diana, a friend with AIDS. I have spoken about her in earlier chapters. She was a courageous and impassioned fighter who held on for many years before she died.

I turned around and asked how she was. She said she was sad, sick, and very tired. In that moment she reached for me. I held her, she held me, we stood there in the coffee shop with our arms around each other. She melted into me, allowed herself to feel my company in her life. She was quiet. Neither of us said anything. Then, after a few moments, she whispered in my ear, "Thank you."

What had happened? I was immediately reminded that this was a precious moment. This simple encounter with Diana completely transformed my mood, my perception, my entire day. In the beginning, I had simply offered a moment of my attention out of habit, perhaps even out of obligation. But Diana experienced the deeper truth of the offer; living close to death, she opened and enriched a very simple gesture of care. The gesture was simple—a moment, an arm, a kind word—but the texture was deepened. This was true love.

She woke me up to the preciousness of the moment. I too felt held by the astonishing simplicity of this shared kindness.

A LIFE IS MADE OF DAYS. Each day is an opportunity to say something honestly, to make something more beautiful, to create something precious, to give a gift only we can provide for the family of the earth. To dedicate a single act to the healing of others is a day well lived.

People who know they will die live very carefully. Not careful as in fearful; careful as in full of care. Every word, every act, every relationship holds the possibility of giving birth to something filled with great care. And that thing need not be showy or dramatic, for the most potent spiritual acts are often acts of breathtaking simplicity: a simple prayer, a sip of wine and a piece of bread, a single breath in meditation, a sprinkling of water on the forehead, an exchange of rings, a kind word, a hand on the cheek, a blessing.

We often mistakenly steer our spiritual ambitions toward some great exhibition of spiritual power or skill, some great feat or accomplishment—meditating for hours without a break, fasting for weeks, remaining strictly celibate or vegetarian, wearing robes or performing elaborate rituals and ceremonies. At times these practices may help some of us remember who we are and what we are doing. They may center us more deeply into a life of the spirit.

But just as often the most spiritual thing we can do is offer a bowl of soup to someone who is hungry or a kind word to someone who is frightened. Or say a prayer when we are in need. Touch the earth. Prune a tree. Sing a lovely song. Hold the hand of a small child.

These may seem like small and ordinary things with little spiritual import. But any of these, done with mindfulness and care, may open the doors of our spiritual perception and experience wider than a thousand ceremonies could do. One Zen master summarized the simplicity of the spiritual life in this remarkable way: "When I am hungry, I eat. When I am tired, I sleep. That is all."

GARY AND HELEN were very much in love. They had endured all of the usual hardships in the course of their ten-year marriage and were just now beginning to feel they were headed for smooth sailing. They felt close, and they knew it was time to finally start a family. They had Jennifer, a beautiful baby girl. They were very happy. Later that same year, they discovered Helen had an inoperable brain tumor.

It was determined that Helen should undergo a variety of treatments, including radiation and chemotherapy. Gary and Helen were worried about the cancer, and they were also concerned about the effects of the treatments. As often happens during chemotherapy, Helen's hair started to fall out. She grieved the loss of her thick black hair. Gary and Helen were the kind of people who naturally attended to each other's comfort. When he saw her sadness, Gary sought for ways he could ease her sorrow.

Then Gary decided he would shave his own head so that they would go bald together. He would support her loss by taking on the same loss himself. They shaved their heads together, in a ritual of mutual support. Years after Helen died, Gary still has the box that holds the hair they shaved that day.

Our lives are made of these moments. Simple words and actions, taken together, weave a single day, and our days become our life. Every gesture is a seed, and the seed determines the harvest. As Rumi reminds us, "Let the beauty we love be what we do."

NANCY WILLARD:

How to Stuff a Pepper

Now, said the cook, I will teach you
how to stuff a pepper with rice.

Take your pepper green, and gently,
for peppers are shy. No matter which side

you approach, it's always the backside.
Perched on green buttocks, the pepper sleeps.
In its silk tights, it dreams
of somersaults and parsley,
of the days when the sexes were one.

Slash open the sleeve
as if you were cutting a paper lantern,
and enter a moon, spilled like a melon,
a fever of pearls,
a conversation of glaciers.
It is a temple built to the worship
of morning light.

I have sat under the great globe
of seeds on the roof of that chamber,
too dazzled to gather the taste I came for.
I have taken the pepper in hand,
smooth and blind, a runt in the rich
evolution of roses and ferns.
You say I have not yet taught you

to stuff a pepper?
Cooking takes time.

Next time we'll consider the rice.

Often we are overwhelmed by the complexity and speed of our lives. When we become aware of this complexity, we often respond by working harder, moving faster, adding new things that we hope will help us cope with the old things. In our frantic search for peace, we always seem to do more; rarely do we ever do less. And yet the Tao Te Ching proposes we make do with fewer, simpler things:

> *To attain knowledge,*
>   *add things every day.*
> *To attain wisdom,*
>   *remove things every day.*

Someone once asked Jesus about the true meaning of the Ten Commandments. If one was unable to follow them all, which single commandment was really the most important one to follow? What should they do? Jesus answered, "Simply this: Love God, and love your neighbor as you love yourself." This, he said, is all that is required.

JACK KORNFIELD, my friend and a respected teacher of Buddhism, took a sabbatical in Thailand with his family. They stayed for six months, visiting some of the forest monasteries where Jack had studied. They also toured many beautiful villages and took some much-deserved time to rest together as a family.

When Jack returned, we had a conversation about his transition from Thailand to America. "It was very disturbing at first," he told me. "I found I was always losing things—my car keys, my appointment book, locking myself out of the house because I had forgotten my keys. This was unlike me, and I was getting a little worried about it.

"Then I realized," he said, "that in Thailand, we got used to doing one thing at a time. Each day was easy and natural. We had enough time and attention to give each thing as it arose whatever care it needed. So we simply did only one thing at a time, and when that was done, we went on to the next.

"But in America we do many things at once. We drive and listen to the radio, we eat and read, we talk and plan and run errands all at once. I wasn't used to doing more than one thing at a time, so everything was getting lost."

OUR FRIEND Debbie was spending the night. She had to get up the next morning to teach a class at the college. In the morning we were all rushing around to get out of the house, as is all too often our normal procedure. Our four-year-old son, Max, who had participated in many of these morning dashes, was now watching Debbie. He said to her, "If you go too fast, things get lost." Debbie laughed. Everyone hurried into their respective cars and was about to drive away. Then Debbie got out, knocked on our car window, and said, "Could you please open up the house again? I left my appointment book in there." Max looked out at Debbie from his car seat in the back. "See?" he said.

When our days are complicated and fast, things get lost. All too often it can be precious things that get lost—a sunset, a walk, a gentle word, an opportunity to be kind, the touch of grass on bare feet, the smell of lilac, a cup of tea by the fire, an embrace.

When we are busy with our important work, who has time for such things? And yet if we do not have time for such things, what can be the value of our work at all? As the preacher reminds us in Ecclesiastes, "Better is one hand full of quiet than two hands full of striving after wind."

THE DALAI LAMA:

> Just as Buddha showed an example of contentment, tolerance, and serving others without selfish motivation, so did Jesus Christ. Almost all of the great teachers lived a saintly life—not luxuriously like kings or emperors but as simple human beings. Their inner strength was tremendous, limitless, but the external appearance was of contentment with a simple way of life.

RECENTLY I HAD an opportunity to visit Frank Waters at his home in Taos. I have always loved his writing—*The Book of the Hopi* and *The Man Who Killed the Deer* are classic examples of spare, simple prose that is at once powerful and revealing. On a crisp fall day in the shadow of Taos Mountain, I was invited into his house. He was ninety-two years old.

I am drawn to his desk. We sit among his papers and pencils; an old Olivetti portable is the only significant mechanical device adorning this old rectangular pine table. No drawers, no compartments—just a single wooden surface.

The light from the window falls gently on a few letters

and an apple from the tree, stem and leaves still attached. His library is filled with books on Mayans, Anasazi, Hopi, peyote, mystics, altered states of consciousness, Vivekenanda, Carlos Castenada, the Bhagavad Gita, Ramana Maharshi, the Tibetan Book of the Dead. I am struck by the wide swath of Eastern scriptures in the library of a man known for his astute observations about Indians. Clearly he feels a deep connection to the mystical traditions of many cultures.

For a moment I wonder if I too will end my life as a writer, with shelves of books, a table strewn with letters. When I was seventeen, an English major at the University of Rochester, this is the life I used to dream about. A typewriter, a window—an English major's vision of heaven.

And it is so quiet. I am struck by how quiet it feels at this desk, in this room full of books and windows. How could anyone ever truly write without such quiet?

I ask him, how do you begin? He speaks slowly, no rush. "First thing, I sharpen my pencils. I take out my pocketknife, and I sharpen my pencils. I take my time. I look out the window, I think about nothing in particular. No need to be in a hurry," he said with a twinkle, "the muse will be waiting. First the pencils need to be sharp. Then we can start to write."

A simple act. A pocketknife, a pencil, a glance out the window. "Stay close to the elements of your craft," he reminds me.

What are the elements of our craft? What few simple tools are necessary to live a full and happy life? Which few things, if we choose them, would be able to sustain our creativity, enthusiasm, and passion? Why not begin to simplify our life so that we can hold these few precious things more surely in our hands?

PHILIP WAS sixteen years old when his parents requested he come talk with me. Lately he had been sporadically flying into uncontrolled rages, tearing up furniture and breaking windows in the house. He seemed an angry young man, confused and frustrated by some inner demons that were tugging at his spirit. He was at a loss to explain to his parents what was happening, nor could he seem to stop the violent outbursts. He and his parents decided that coming to see me might at least give them some useful information.

Philip's mother was an alcoholic who had recently stopped drinking. She herself had been abused as a child by her father. So in Philip I could witness at least three generations of sorrow and hurt coming to fruition in his young soul. After a session or two it seemed as if Philip needed to breathe, to leave the family constellation and be out on his own. He was intelligent, creative, and resourceful. His anger seemed to be his only way of naming the need he felt to leave. To say it out loud would have been too hard, so his unconscious rage spoke for him.

His parents, marshaling no small amount of faith, arranged for Philip to go away to school for a year, to be away from his familiar surroundings, to uncover those parts of himself that were waiting to be born. It was perhaps the most important year of Philip's life; in new surroundings, unencumbered by his family's history or his family's expectations, Philip blossomed. He became strong, clear, and much more at peace. For a year he was able to follow his own yearnings and intuition. He learned a great deal about who he was, and when he returned he was, in many ways, wise beyond his years. He had merely needed to extricate himself long enough to discover his particular identity. Then he could safely and productively return home.

Speaking about his trip afterward, Philip and I discussed his relationship with his family, how important they were to him. "I feel so connected to my whole family. I know where my ancestors came from, I know what they did, what kind of people they were. I even visited some of the places they lived. I feel them like they are part of my body. I just had to detach from them all so I could find my own self. Then I could reconnect. We all get along much better now."

I bring up this story of Philip partly to illustrate how sometimes one simple act, correctly timed, can do a great deal of healing. But I also include this story because of something else Philip said to me—something that helped me understand a particular aspect of spiritual practice.

As we were ending our conversation, Philip mentioned he had heard from his mother that I was writing a new book. He asked what it was about, and I told him I was writing about the spiritual practices we encounter in our ordinary lives. I told him I felt many of us desired to live with more spiritual awareness.

"Oh, that's easy," Philip said. "You just need to know how things work and where they come from," he added. I asked him to explain. "Well, for example, if you turn on the tap, and you really know where the water comes from, how it gets there, who brings it, where it goes after it leaves your house—you eventually feel connected to everything. If you just know how things work, then you can have a spiritual life."

I was struck by the simplicity and power of what he said. Philip's experience, so clearly named, was to feel the natural interconnectedness of all things: his family, the earth, his ancestors. If we know how things are connected, we will feel a part of all things. How many spiritual teachers had struggled for years to speak the truth of this, and with less precision? I felt I had received a blessing from this young man.

The more we know about how things work, the more carefully we will walk on the earth. When we see how our words affect our friends and family, we will be careful with our language; when we see how our actions ripple out into our work and our community, we will be more mindful of what we choose to do and not to do; when we see how our thoughts create the inner atmosphere in which we move each day, we will be more aware of which thoughts we give our energy to and which thoughts we simply allow to fall away as uninteresting and not useful.

When we feel where our precious water comes from, we will use it with gratefulness and care. The simple act of turning on the tap becomes a practice of remembrance—remembering the gift of water, the people who dug the well, the rain that fed the groundwater, the clouds, the sun, the earth. A single act can unite us with the universe.

THE BUDDHA:

> In the discipline of living alone, it is the silence of solitude that is wisdom. When the solitude becomes a source of delight then it shines in all the ten directions. Listen to the sound of water. Listen to the water running through chasms and rocks. It is the minor streams that make a great noise. The great waters flow silently. This is the sound of wisdom.

FOR THE PAST few years Bread for the Journey has had an arrangement with St. Elizabeth's, our local shelter for the homeless. Many homeless individuals and families are in fact working but cannot put together enough money all at once to pay the first and last months' rent and security deposits for the gas and electricity in a new apartment. And so they languish in the shelter, unable to start a new life.

We started a program with St. Elizabeth's that works like this: Whenever the directors of the shelter become aware of anyone who is working and saving to move into an apartment or trailer but cannot meet these initial payments, Bread for the Journey will donate the difference. This enables the working poor to find permanent housing. In the past three years, we have helped many people who would otherwise be homeless to secure a place to stay. Since they are working, they are able to keep up the rent payments once they are in an apartment. Most of those we have helped have never returned to the streets.

On the face of it, the program seems too simple. We always assume that the problems of homelessness are too complex for any real benefit to arise from our good intentions. But here it is, years later, and the program still works.

ANNE MORROW LINDBERGH, in her classic *Gift From the Sea,* found that the greatest blessing she received from her time of reflection by the shore was the serenity and nourishment provided by the simplicity of her life there:

> One cannot collect all the beautiful shells on the beach. One can collect only a few, and they are more beautiful if they are few. One moon shell is more impressive than three. . . . Gradually one discards and keeps just the perfect specimen; not necessarily a rare shell, but a perfect one of its kind. One sets it apart by itself, ringed around by space— like the island.
>
> For it is only framed in space that beauty blooms. Only in space are events and objects and people unique and significant—and therefore beautiful. A tree has significance if one sees it against the empty face of sky. A note in music gains significance from the silences on either side. A candle flowers in the space of night. . . .
>
> My life in Connecticut, I begin to realize, lacks this quality of significance and therefore of beauty, because there is so little empty space. The space is scribbled on; the time has been filled. There are so few empty pages in my engagement pad, or empty hours in the day, or empty rooms in my life in which to stand alone and find myself. Too many activities, and people, and things. Too many worthy activities, valuable things, and interesting people. For it is not merely the trivial which clutters our lives but the important as well. We can have a surfeit of treasures—an excess of shells, where one or two would be significant.

A Little Stone in the Middle
of the Road, in Florida

My son as a child saying
God
is anything, even a little stone in the middle of the road,
  in Florida.
Yesterday
Nancy, my friend, after a long illness:
You know what can lift me up, take me right out of despair?
No, what?
Anything.

—MURIEL RUKEYSER

❖

PRACTICE: EXPLORING A LIFE OF SIMPLICITY

Arrange for some time to sit quietly in a place of refuge. Allow yourself to become calm and attentive, using the breath to settle yourself into your body and heart.

Then, in a gentle way, review your current life. Bring to mind each of several areas, including your work, your relationships or family life, your finances, your leisure activities, your possessions, your goals, and your spiritual life. One by one, as each area comes to mind, ask yourself the following questions: What would it be like to simplify this part of my life? What could I let go easily? What could I do to make this part of my life more quiet and simple?

Reflect on the choices that arise within you. Notice which feel immediately comfortable and which feel difficult or frightening. The object is not necessarily to change anything immediately. In this moment you are simply noting where you desire more simplicity in your life and where this is possible. How can you make room for this simplicity? Take as much time as you need with each area of your life, becoming aware of what steps you might take. Then make a resolution to make changes in each area.

❖

Gratefulness

The clouds above us join and separate,
The breeze in the courtyard leaves and returns.
Life is like that, so why not relax?
Who can stop us from celebrating?

—Lu Yu

WHEN KENNETH FIRST MOVED to Santa Fe from New York six years ago, he involved himself in the community with playfulness and enthusiasm. Kenneth had been a model, a designer, and an artist, and was enthusiastically committed to serving people with AIDS. He helped many of our AIDS organizations get off the ground. His energy was contagious; even the state legislature was not immune to his charm. He was one of the first AIDS lobbyists we ever had. The first year he stormed the legislature for more AIDS funding, they more than doubled their allocations.

This year Kenneth himself began to get very sick. He had been deteriorating slowly, and by this point he had lost much of the use of his legs. He could hardly walk. He had to have nursing care in his home around the clock.

One afternoon he told Betsy, the nurse who was staying with him, that he was going out for a walk. Betsy knew perfectly well Kenneth could not go out alone, if at all, and she insisted he needed to stay in bed. But Kenneth's stubbornness was legendary. It was a warm spring day, and Kenneth knew what he wanted; he rarely let anything so insignificant as minor paralysis ruin his plans. Before Betsy knew it, Kenneth was out the screen door and hobbling toward the street.

After only a few steps, Kenneth collapsed in a heap, like a pile of old clothes. Betsy ran out the door. "Kenneth, are you all right?" she screamed. She was sure he must have done terrible damage to himself.

Kenneth did not immediately respond. He lay still and quiet on the grass. Then slowly he turned his head and looked calmly up at Betsy. He smiled. "The sun feels so good on my face," he said.

This is an enlightened moment. Close to death, his body failing, Kenneth is so present and awake that he is simply grateful for the warm sun on his cheek. This moment he is alive. In less than a week he will die. But in this instant, as the sun touches his cheek, he is thankful.

DRIVING DOWN Old Las Vegas Highway in the early evening, headed home from work, I am occasionally met by the appearance of a full moon, bright orange, rising up from behind the Sangre de Cristo Mountains. I am always surprised. Even though I understand the cycles of the earth, sun, and moon, even though I have traveled this road for many years, when I first see the moon at its fullest I am inevitably astonished at its appearance. It seems unusually big, unexpectedly delightful. Without thinking, I exclaim aloud—to whom?—how magnificent it is.

Later in the evening, when I see the same moon, it seems somehow smaller, not quite so spectacular. I enjoy the sight of it, but I have lost the earlier sense of awe and delight. I now expect the moon to be there. I have already seen it, I know it rests in the sky. There is no surprise. With expectation, our delight in seeing the very same moon is somehow diminished.

We can so quickly lose our capacity for surprise and delight. Beautiful things become commonplace, and we cease to be amazed at the color of the sky, the smell of the earth after a rain, the gift of a fine meal, the touch of a friend. We assume that because we have been given these gifts before, we will be given them again. We feel these gifts now belong to us; everything we have is safely catalogued in our personal inventory. And so we feel no wonder, we do not fall to our knees in gratitude.

Instead we focus on what we do not yet have, what we have not yet been given. Why don't we have more money? Why can't we get more respect? Why have we not achieved the success we deserve? Why wasn't our childhood the way we wanted? Why can't our family love us better?

Some people have had so much sorrow in their lives that they feel they have nothing to be grateful for. They feel angry and bitter because they were given suffering they did not want. So they close down in resentment, becoming tight and brittle. *Wait until I am fully healed and finally get what I want,* they say. *Then I will be grateful.*

But acknowledging our sorrow need not diminish our gratefulness. Look at Kenneth lying on the grass, fallen in a heap, his legs paralyzed, his body racked with infection. *The sun feels so good on my face,* he said. He did not insist he be cured of AIDS before he gave thanks for the warmth of the sun. In that moment he was spacious enough to hold both things that were true: He was dying, and he was grateful. The gratefulness did not eliminate his sorrow, nor did his suffering prevent him from giving thanks.

Gratefulness arises naturally from this fertile balance of honoring both our sorrow and our joy. We name our sorrows so that we can bring care and attention to our wounds, so that we may heal. And at the same time we give thanks for the innumerable gifts and blessings bestowed upon us daily, lest we forget how rich we are.

Pema Chodron, a thoughtful and articulate Buddhist nun, speaks of waking up, being fully present and alive in this way. Here she describes a traditional Buddhist teaching regarding the effects of impermanence, one of which is to heighten our sense of gratefulness:

> Joy has to do with seeing how big, how completely unobstructed, and how precious things are. Resenting what happens to you and complaining

about your life are like refusing to smell the wild roses when you go for a morning walk, or like being so blind that you don't see a huge black raven when it lands in the tree that you're sitting under. We can get so caught up in our own personal pain or worries that we don't notice that the wind has come up or that somebody has put flowers on the dining room table or when we walked out in the morning the flags weren't up, and when we came back, they were flying. Resentment, bitterness, and holding a grudge prevent us from seeing and hearing and tasting and delighting.

I VISITED PAUL often in the last few weeks of his life. His tumors were growing. There was a great deal of swelling and pressure, and gradually his pain became terrible. We used breathing meditations to help him soften the area around the pain, but still, it was unpleasant at best.

Occasionally the pain would abate for a short time. "I feel so grateful for a single pain-free moment," he would tell me. "Sitting here in my chair by the window, feeling the sunlight, I am so very grateful for a single breath that is not filled with pain."

This exquisite attention to the quality of each breath was paid for with great sorrow. But the corresponding joy and thankfulness he experienced within a single moment was humbling. How often had I felt such gratitude for my own breath, I, who was sitting next to him, cancer-free? His gratitude, like the gratitude of so many others who have known their own mortality, wakes me up.

GRATEFULNESS SLOWS TIME. For those close to death, there is little time to waste. When we give thanks for each moment, when we say a silent "thank you" for every meal, every touch, every morning, then we truly feel the richness and breadth of our lives, and things do not go by quite so fast.

Last summer I was teaching at the Omega Institute. After a long morning session on Saturday, I was hungry and anxious for lunch. I walked the path from the cabin to the cafeteria with food on my mind. I passed by a lush variety of flowers, trees, and bushes along the path, but I did not really see them. I was thinking only of what I was wanting—lunch—and not at all about what was in front of me.

After lunch, properly fed, I walked the same path back to the cabin. I saw the reds and purples and greens, touched the flowers, smelled the August humidity in the air, watched the clouds change shape in the summer sky. I felt tremendous gratitude for such beauty. When I got back to the cabin I realized the walk back had taken no more time than the walk to eat. The walk to eat had felt rushed and stilted; the walk back had felt spacious, restful, and easy. The only thing that had changed was my appreciation and gratefulness for what was around me. Gratefulness slows time.

E.E. CUMMINGS:

> i thank You God for most this amazing
> day:for the leaping greenly spirits of trees
> and a blue true dream of sky;and for everything
> which is natural which is infinite which is yes
>
> (i who have died am alive again today,
> and this is the sun's birthday;this is the birth
> day of life and of love and wings:and of the gay
> great happening illimitably earth)
>
> how should tasting touching hearing seeing
> breathing any—lifted from the no
> of all nothing—human merely being
> doubt unimaginable You?
>
> (now the ears of my ears are awake and
> now the eyes of my eyes are opened)

WE WERE INVITED to dinner at Shona's house. The roof of their home in the pueblo had been leaking badly. All six of their family had slept crowded into one room, because the summer rains would drench the rest of the house. When a friend told us about this, we had helped Shona and her family get a new roof. That night they were making us dinner as a gift in return.

As we sat in the living room, Shona's daughter came out of the kitchen and quietly offered cornmeal to the corners of the house. Nothing was said. But in that house, regardless of the poverty, the Native American way was always to honor the relationship between the gift and the receiver. The cornmeal was a prayer of thanksgiving, an act of gratitude. The cornmeal affirmed that the food we ate was not a right, not a boring repetition of some chore, but an honor, a gift of food and life. The offering of cornmeal was part of that gift. When we ate in that way, it took no more time, but the food tasted sweeter, and the nourishment was multiplied a hundredfold.

Lao Tzu:

> Be content with what you have;
> rejoice in the way things are.
> When you realize there is nothing lacking,
> the whole world belongs to you.

My first job as a therapist was working at a street clinic in Rochester, New York. It was a drop-in center for runaways and teenage drug users. Sometimes, after taking in a stray teenager, we would have no place at the center to put them. As often as not I would end up taking them home with me. At the time I lived on a small commune, located in a farmhouse outside the city.

People questioned the wisdom of my bringing these teenagers into our home. The young people could certainly be irresponsible, and it was true that sometimes they stole from us. But more often they seemed so desperate to belong somewhere, anywhere. We would give them chores on the farm, and they would end up being part of the family.

Dolores was severely epileptic. Her mother was very poor, not well educated, and unable to care for her daughter properly, so Dolores ended up on the street at the age of fourteen. She was heavily medicated, and she would often focus her rebellion by refusing to fill her prescriptions. When she came to the farm we worked closely with her doctors, trying to recalibrate her medications. Whenever Dolores went into a seizure, we would sit with her, hold her head, and keep her from swallowing her tongue. For those minutes she was shaking, we would sit with her and keep her safe. Dolores quickly became a member of our family.

Maria was abused by her father. She was hurt so badly, she ran away at thirteen. She was a very angry young woman, and it was somewhat of a risk to bring her out to the farmhouse. At first she refused to help with any chores. Whenever I went to work in the barn, I asked her to come along. She would follow me, but she would never help. She just watched me, her eyes darting from side to side like a frightened bird's. Maria rarely spoke, but she watched everything.

Then one day, when Maria and I were walking toward the barn, we saw that one of the chickens, smaller than the rest, was getting pecked by the others. This hen was at the bottom of the pecking order, and the other chickens were merciless. The small one would come away from these sessions bleeding from the top of her head. Maria was clearly moved by this. She asked questions about it, about why the others harmed it and how it protected itself. After that, she went out every morning to check on the chickens. She would try to protect the young one, and they seemed to develop a bond. She would bring in eggs for breakfast for us. Through her own hurt, she began to discover a sense of compassion for others.

At the farm we had an enormous table in the kitchen that seated about fifteen people. Most nights, between those of us who lived there and the various runaways we had staying with us, the table was full. Before we ate, we would all gather around the table and say grace. Everyone would name something for which they were grateful; with so many people, it would take a long time to go around the circle. People such as Dolores and Maria were not used to giving thanks. They were uncomfortable at first, even angry. But after a while they would gradually chime in. Dolores would give thanks for having one less seizure that day than the day before, and everyone would cheer. Maria would say she was glad to be in a place where no one hit her. We added our silent assent. By the time we were all done, the food was always cold.

Sono:

> Every morning and every evening, and whenever anything happens to you, keep on saying, "Thanks for everything. I have no complaint whatsoever."

A traditional prayer before meals in Buddhist monasteries begins with this phrase: *First, seventy-two labors brought us this food; we should know how it comes to us.* We are thoroughly dependent upon the gifts and labors of others, even for our most basic necessities. Our meals come from the farmers, the gardeners, the plumbers who brought water, the people who pulled the weeds and turned the compost, those who harvested, migrant workers, poor children, those who made the boxes to carry the vegetables, those who made the cars that transported the food, the truckers and their families, the grocers, the cooks, the servers—innumerable labors indeed. So many stand silently with us at every meal, and we are indebted to each and every one as we partake of the gift of nourishment. To feel their presence and be thankful for their many gifts to us is to be more accurately aware of our place in this large and generous community of beings.

Can we feel this connection? People who are dying often describe a deep thankfulness for the many who care for them, seen and unseen. We constantly rely on others for our well-being. Farmers rise at dawn to grow our food, poor immigrant women work in sweatshops to sew our clothing, truckers leave home for days to bring us whatever we need, men and women work in sun and rain and cold to build our homes—these people are offering their labors to us every day, people we never know but who give us their gifts that we may simply live.

People who are dying simply see more clearly what has always been true: *We are in the perpetual care of others.* They are grateful for any and all kindnesses, and they do not take the generosity of others for granted. They feel the care of those who cook for them, bathe them, clean their linens, nurse them, hold them. In all ways and in everything we are immeasurably interdependent; to give thanks for those who serve us is not mere sentimentality—our offering a word of grace is both spiritually accurate and necessary.

RUMI:

> *Your lamp was lit from another lamp.*
> *All God wants is your gratitude for that.*

Our life is not a problem to be solved, it is a gift to be opened. The color of the sky, the song of a bird, a word of kindness, a strain of music, the sun on our face, the companionship of friends, the taste of sea air, the shape of clouds in summer, the reds of maples in fall—there are so many gifts in a single life. If we are preoccupied with what is missing and what is broken and wrong, we lose the miraculous harvest of all these tiny gifts, piled one upon the other, that accumulate without our acknowledging them. If we listen more carefully for the infinite blessings of a single day, this will not discount or obliterate our sorrows. But it will help us remember how strong and rich we can be, even in the midst of suffering. A single word of gratefulness can transform a moment of sorrow into a moment of peace. Try this; you will see it is true.

THICH NHAT HANH:

> We often ask, "What's wrong?" Doing so, we in-
> vite painful seeds of sorrow to come up and mani-
> fest. We feel suffering, anguish and depression, and
> produce much more seeds. We would be much

happier if we tried to stay in touch with the healthy, joyful seeds inside of us and around us. We should learn to ask, "What's not wrong?" and be in touch with that. There are so many elements in the world and within our bodies, feelings, perceptions, and consciousness that are wholesome, refreshing and healing. If we block ourselves, if we stay in the prison of our sorrow, we will not be in touch with these healing elements.

Life is filled with many wonders, like the blue sky, the sunshine, the eyes of a baby. Our breathing, for example, can be very enjoyable. I enjoy breathing every day. But many people appreciate the joy of breathing only when they have asthma or a stuffed-up nose. We don't need to wait until we have asthma to enjoy our breathing. Awareness of the precious elements of happiness is itself the practice of right mindfulness. Elements like these are within us and all around us. In each second of our lives we can enjoy them. If we do so, the seeds of peace, joy and happiness will be planted in us, and they will become strong. The secret to happiness is happiness itself. Wherever we are, any time, we have the capacity to enjoy the sunshine, the presence of each other, the wonder of our breathing. We don't have to travel anywhere else to do so. We can be in touch with these things right now.

MY FRIEND KATHRYN introduced me to the writer Reynolds Price when he was visiting her at her home last Christmas. He was confined to a wheelchair, and he seemed a strong and cheerful man. I knew nothing about his life, however, until Kathryn gave me his latest book—*A Whole New Life*—in which he recounts his pilgrimage through a battle with unspeakable physical pain and an insidious cancer.

In 1984 they discovered a tumor wrapped around his spinal cord. After several difficult operations, radiation, and various drug therapies, he gradually and completely lost any use of his lower body. He lived with relentless, excruciating pain for years. Yet the weight of hopelessness and despair— so heavy at times that he wished to die—never quenched his spirit. He continued to struggle to regain some measure of health, and eventually, through biofeedback, hypnosis, and sheer strength of will and spirit, he managed to slowly get the pain under control to the point where he could abandon the massive doses of pain medication he had relied upon. Now he could once again write and get up in the morning thankful to be alive. This is how Reynolds Price concludes his story, in the final paragraph of *A Whole New Life:*

> I've long since weaned myself from all drugs but a small dose of antidepressant, an aspirin to thin my blood, an occasional scotch or a good red wine and a simple acid to brace my bladder against infection. I write six days a week, long days that often run till bedtime; and the books are different from what came before in more ways than age. I sleep long nights with few hard dreams, and now I've out-lived both my parents. Even my handwriting looks very little like the script of the man I was in June of '84. Cranky as it is, it's taller, more legible, with more air and stride. It comes down the arm of a grateful man.

Welcome Morning

There is joy
in all:
in the hair I brush each morning,
in the Cannon towel, newly washed,
that I rub my body with each morning,
in the chapel of eggs I cook
each morning,
in the outcry from the kettle
that heats my coffee
each morning,
in the spoon and the chair
that cry "hello there, Anne"
each morning,
in the godhead of the table
that I set my silver, plate, cup upon
each morning.

All this is God,
right here is my pea-green house
each morning,
and I mean,
though I often forget,
to give thanks,
to faint down by the kitchen table
in a prayer of rejoicing
as the holy birds at the kitchen window
peck into their marriage of seeds.

So while I think of it,
let me paint a thank-you on my palm
for this God, this laughter of the morning,
lest it go unspoken.

The Joy that isn't shared, I've heard,
dies young.

*—*ANNE SEXTON

PRACTICE: A GRATEFULNESS MEDITATION

At the end of the day, sit in a place of quiet. Take a few moments to review the day. Recall all the pleasant people and events, noting also those that were difficult or unpleasant.

Close your eyes and allow the significant people or events to arise one by one. Viewing the pleasant experiences one at a time, let yourself give thanks for whichever gifts may have touched your life today. Silently name any gratefulness you may feel for each person or event, taking the time to let your heart open and receive the richness and nourishment of that experience. Let yourself appreciate and give thanks for each gift, allowing each image to arise and fade away until you feel complete.

Next, begin to recall any unpleasant experiences from the day. Focus your attention on one particularly painful encounter or event. Now, try to touch that memory with gratefulness. What do you notice as you practice giving thanks for something painful? What emotions arise? Does it make you peaceful or angry? Does it feel easy or hard? Stay with one image, repeatedly giving thanks for the fact that this person or event was a part of your day. Be thankful for whatever teaching they brought, whatever they helped you notice about yourself. One by one, touch each memory with some gratefulness.

Finally, give thanks for your life. Take a moment to explicitly name all the qualities of your life for which you are grateful. Practice being thankful for your breath, your body, the people who care for you, your spouse, lover, children, friends, for the colors of the day, for your home, for your food. Reviewing as many gifts as come to mind, speak a word of silent thanksgiving for everything you have and for all that you have become.

Notice what happens in your body as you practice giving thanks. What emotions arise? You may practice this meditation every day. At the end of a week, what do you notice? Using the practice of gratefulness, we plant the seeds of abundance in the soil of our daily lives.

the
fourth
part

What Is My Gift to the Family of the Earth?

Naming Our Gift

> There is a light in this world, a healing spirit more powerful than any darkness we may encounter. We sometimes lose sight of this force when there is suffering, too much pain. Then suddenly, the spirit will emerge through the lives of ordinary people who hear a call and answer in extraordinary ways.
>
> —MOTHER TERESA

THIS WINTER Dottie Montoya called me to ask if I would come and meet with the newly formed HIV task force for Española, in northern New Mexico. When, last summer, her son Roger had openly declared he was HIV-positive, a group of people responded by organizing a task force to stem the growing threat of HIV, particularly among young people.

The Española Valley is a relatively small community. Nevertheless, Dottie began by reporting that in the two weeks prior to our meeting, four people in the valley had died of AIDS. For such a sparsely populated region, this is of epidemic proportions.

After the meeting, Dottie's husband, Jose, said he wanted to talk to me. I naturally assumed he wanted to talk about Roger. Initially Jose had felt frightened and confused by his son's infection. But I knew that since then Jose had deeply examined his feelings and was now a passionate supporter of both Roger and the task force. Jose and I quietly moved away from the group so he could share his thoughts with me in private.

"I want to talk to you about apples," he said. Now it was my turn to be surprised. What did apples have to do with Roger's illness? "A few of us up here have been seeing the pictures on the news, all those poor children in Rwanda," Jose began. "I know a lot of apple growers around here, and we thought we could send some of our apples to them. We organized some elementary-school students to help us peel and dry the apples so we could send them to the children in Africa. But we cannot figure out how to get them to where they need to go. Do you think Bread for the Journey could help us?"

At first I could not respond, I was so touched by his generosity. This was a man whose son was infected with HIV, someone who had every reason to feel angry and bitter. Yet this seemingly unquenchable impulse to be generous flourished even in the midst of his sorrow. Even more, I knew that Jose would never have named this as generosity at all, but rather as a simple and necessary response to the suffering of children. He saw a need and knew he had something that could help fill that need. He did not think twice about offering his gift of apples—even though I knew that the apple growers had had a bad season, with heavy losses from the early frost. From what they had, they wanted to give.

THROUGHOUT MY WORK with people who have been hurt, the most painful thing I witness is their deep conviction that, because of their hurt, they have no real gift, nothing of value to offer the family of the earth. This festering reluctance to comprehend the true value of their gifts is, I would argue, more costly than the original abuse, the neglect, the incest, the alcoholism. Their sorrows, while poignant and real, are not unbearable. With faith and kindness, patience and wisdom, aided by the miraculous resilience of spirit, these wounds can heal. The greater tragedy is that each person, in their own way, believes they have been broken by their suffering. As a result, they are convinced they have nothing useful to bring to the world in which they live, and they feel isolated and useless.

When we feel hurt or afraid, we are reluctant to come

to the table, ashamed our gift is insufficient. We feel empty and scarce, needing to hoard every scrap to feed ourselves, convinced we have barely enough resources to survive. We are certain that we must first be repaired, detoxified, perfected; we wait and wait, until we are finally filled, finally acceptable, before we feel worthy to offer our gift to others.

Melissa is a talented musician and writer, with a delightful sense of humor and a laserlike wit. Melissa was also sexually abused by her stepfather when she was a young girl. As a result, she feels frightened, unsure of her many abilities and talents. Hiding behind a lingering conviction that she is deeply damaged, Melissa rarely allows herself to shine. She finds jobs that do not use her skills, work that will not challenge her. She is afraid she will not have what it takes; she fears that when the moment of truth arrives, she will have nothing valuable to offer.

Sara is a passionate artist. She uses art media in new and challenging ways. However, growing up with a raging and violent alcoholic father, Sara also learned to get small, to make herself invisible. She feels timid and unsure of herself, which then stops her from imagining that her work—striking and original as it is—could possibly be of any real interest. As a result, Sara rarely shows her work to anyone.

James is remarkably kind. He always remembers people's birthdays and is sure to send a card, even if he hardly knows them. He is the first to volunteer to help whenever anyone is putting together a benefit or a fund-raiser for some worthy cause. But James also struggles with habitual unemployment. Raised in an abusive household, he learned to feel he was essentially worthless. Thus, even in the face of many job offers from people who know his strength and kindness, he always finds some excuse not to get hired. He is afraid he is really not smart enough, not good enough to be worthy of a real job.

I have listened to countless such stories. When we feel broken, we feel useless, and so we undervalue our gifts. Many of us believe there is no gift, no light at all inside us.

JESUS WAS FIRM in this declaration: We are the light of the world. We must let our light shine, he insisted, and not hide it under a bushel. Our sorrow does not contaminate our gift. In fact, in my experience the opposite is often true: Our sorrow can break us open, illuminating our gift. From deep within our suffering and loss, we can become more aware, more sensitive, more attentive and kind. From within our hurt we learn to listen more carefully for what is needed; we become exceptionally mindful of the right word, the most precise gesture of compassionate action.

Alberto is a recovering alcoholic. He drank for fifteen years, destroying two marriages and severely damaging his relationship with his two children. Now sober, he helps other alcoholics find their path to healing. And, having mended his relationships with his children, he is now helping his son start a new business.

Brenda is an elementary-school teacher. Her parents were abusive and unkind. Through counseling, travel, and meditation, she found a place in herself that was not broken by her childhood, a place she knew was strong and whole. She joined the Peace Corps and served children in Ethiopia for two years. Now back in the United States, Brenda brings a special awareness to her students. She believes children should be aware that they can be part of building a better world, and so she teaches them about how communities work, and she shows them how to solve the problems that arise when people try to live together in peace.

To protect himself from his family when he was young, Jeff learned to disappear inside his head, to retreat into his own thoughts. He learned to weave stories that would keep him company in the privacy of his own world, where he felt safe. Now grown, Jeff goes to schools and camps and communities and tells stories—stories about Native Americans, about the Southwest, about Coyote. He collects old Spanish, Anglo, and Native American stories and shares them with children and adults alike. He freely offers these playful, wise stories—stories of triumph over treachery, just like the stories he used to comfort himself with as a small and frightened child.

Thus our sorrow becomes our gift. From within our tender hurt there can spring kindness, generosity, and love for others. In our grief and confusion, we may mistakenly believe we have no offering to bring to the family of the earth. But mere suffering cannot extinguish the priceless gift of our true nature. As soon as we begin to heal—the instant we experience some degree of inner clarity or spaciousness—in the very next breath, generosity naturally arises. As we feel the measure of our own strength, we simultaneously experience a natural impulse to share it. This is not faith, this is simple spiritual physics: As we are fed, so do we wish to feed others.

"LOVE," WROTE JEAN VANIER, "doesn't mean doing extraordinary or heroic things. It means knowing how to do ordinary things with tenderness." Many of the gifts we offer to others are small, ordinary things: a kind word, a simple meal, a comforting visit, a gentle touch. We give from what we have. If we have apples, then apples are our gift. If we have good humor, then laughter is our gift. If we can cook, then food is our gift. If we can make music or hold a hand or listen or build or love well, these are our gifts. The currency of our kindness flows from what we are, what we love.

Some of us stop our natural impulse to be generous because we are afraid our offering will not be large enough, not impressive enough. But the most beautiful gifts are the small, lovely things. Juanita cooks for the dancers and the guests at Santo Domingo. Molly prunes my fruit trees. Cora, our neighbor, invites our son, Max, to come over and play. Anne, when she is making dinner, turns around when her children ask for her attention. Jim, when he has a fight with his wife, apologizes if he has hurt her. Jeff tells stories to children. Kathy makes sure to visit her friends when they are sick. Small gifts; yet how could we live together on the earth without these simple offerings?

ALICE WALKER:

> Grandma sleeps with
> my sick grand-
> pa so she
> can get him
> during the night
> medicine
> to stop
> the pain
>
> In
> the morning
> clumsily
> I
> wake
> them
>
> Her eyes
> look at me
> from under-
> neath
> his withered
> arm
>
> The
> medicine
> is all
> in
> her long
> un-
> braided
> hair.

MY FRIEND KATE is a community organizer in the poorer sections of Boston. She lives in a small home in Dorchester. A few years ago, I called her around the time when the riots were exploding in Los Angeles after the Rodney King verdict. She told me there had just been a murder in her neighborhood the night before. What could we ever do, we wondered aloud, that would be significant and healing in the face of such suffering and violence? Kate responded, "I am going to plant a garden in my yard. I don't know how it will help, but I feel like I just have to plant something and help it grow." Her garden is now a simple gift to the neighborhood, a quiet statement of color, fragrance, and love in the midst of poverty and hardship.

Every single day forty thousand children die of hunger and hunger-related illnesses on the earth. Every two seconds the light in a child's eyes goes out, often in the helpless arms of a starving mother, for lack of food or inexpensive vaccines. Even in the United States one child in five lives in poverty. People are dying of cancer and AIDS. Children need tutors. Shelters need people to cook for and house the homeless.

In New York City there is a graveyard where they bury the poor, the indigent, those without family or identification. In this graveyard there are buried over eight hundred thousand people who died alone and unloved in the city of New York. We need people to sit with those who are dying. We need people to plant a garden, to cook a meal and share it, to hold a hand and create a moment of sanctuary, to sing a song, to speak a single word of kindness into a moment of fear or sadness, to perform a single act of courage, to hum a tune, to dance, so we can remember how light and loving and alive we can be together on the earth.

Some of us wish to wait until our gift is potent and comprehensive enough to solve all the world's problems. Seeing that our gift does not stop all the suffering, we decide it is inadequate. But every gift is a drop of water on a stone; every kindness, every flash of color or melody helps us remain hopeful and in balance. Each of us knows some part of the secret, and each of us holds our small portion of the light. We can thrive on the earth only if we each bring what we have and offer it at the family table.

It is impossible that you have no gift. Perhaps you are unsure of your gift, or you are afraid to share it, afraid it will be refused, afraid it will not be good enough. Perhaps you are simply waiting for the perfect opportunity. What are you waiting for? It is alive inside you at this very moment.

SEVEN YEARS AGO I started Bread for the Journey. I was in private practice as a psychotherapist and decided to dedicate a portion of my fee to local charities. This way I would be reminding myself and my clients that we were all, even in the private seclusion of our individual healing, connected to the sorrows of others in the community. It bestowed a different kind of integrity on our counseling relationship, honoring our kinship with all who were in need of healing.

This was a small step, nothing dramatic. I believe the first year I raised $200. I was very proud when I sent off two checks at the end of the year, one to the local food bank, one to the soup kitchen. Soon others in the community, hearing of my little plan, offered to give me money to give away, trusting that I would find those people who needed it most. Gradually, without any publicity or fund-raising, Bread for the Journey began to grow. Now, years later, we help dozens of communities in need.

The plan was small and simple, nothing much at all. But if our gift has a life, it will grow; regardless of the size or scope of our offering, it must first be offered before it can take root and flower.

A gift is like a seed; it is not an impressive thing. It is what can grow from the seed that is impressive. If we wait until our seed becomes a tree before we offer it, we will wait and wait, and the seed will die from lack of planting in the warm, moist earth. The miracle is not just the gift; the miracle is in the offering, for if we do not offer, who will?

ALBERT CAMUS:

> Perhaps we cannot prevent this world from being a place where children are tortured. But we can reduce the number of tortured children. And if you don't help us, who else in the world will help us do this?

We begin by choosing to honor our gift. We each have something to offer. If we compare our gift with those who served in the concentration camps or those working with lepers, our gift may seem quite small and insignificant. But however large or small, dramatic or simple, if we ignore or suppress our offering, something deep and vital within us will wither and die.

EVERY DAY we are given countless opportunities to offer our gifts to those at work, in our families, our relationships. Miguel and I were stacking wood for the winter. Miguel brings the pine, cedar, and piñon for the wood stove every fall, as the air turns crisp and the nights get colder. Santa Fe is situated in the Sangre de Cristo Mountains at seven thousand feet. Preparing for winter is a ritual everyone shares. We talk about how much wood to bring in this year, and we all speculate when it will start to snow.

Miguel told me about his daughter, how smart she is. Last year, in first grade, she got all A's on her report card. This year, in second grade, she got many A+'s. His eyes moistened when he told me this. He is so proud of her.

Being a parent is one of Miguel's gifts. While he works extremely hard helping many of us get ready for winter by cutting wood all year, the thing that most surely warms his own heart is to see his children do well. He is from Mexico, and he has lived here twelve years. He still speaks English with a thick Spanish accent and is more comfortable with Spanish than with English. "But my daughter," he says proudly, "on her report card it says she reads and writes and speaks perfect Spanish and perfect English." This is his legacy. His children will do well.

This is the gift of many parents, quietly building and preparing so their children will do well. So many gifts unnoticed, decisions made and offered without the children even knowing what was given, or that there was anything given at all. Still, the gift remains, embedded in the lives of countless children who were sent forth with the love of caring parents.

These people I have spoken about are not saints—not in

the traditional sense that they are somehow better or more holy than we. Rather, they are ordinary people following the natural impulse of kindness that rises within them. Each of us has a gift to offer to the family of the earth. For some of us, that gift appears in a clear, dramatic way; for others, we may stumble from place to place in search of our strength, our talent, our offering. Still, while the size, shape, flavor, and texture of the gift undoubtedly changes from person to person, the certainty of that gift is, in my experience, undeniable.

Eknath Easwaran:

> The other day our children were telling me about the importance of trees. If they were not always releasing oxygen, they explained, life on earth would perish. A person whose mind is free from negative thinking spreads life-giving oxygen in the same way. On a smoggy day in California, the trees along the freeway look gray and drab in the haze; they do not seem to add anything valuable to the landscape. Yet if they were gone, our big cities would suffocate from their own activity. In the same way, although a selfless man or woman may seem to go through the day doing nothing extraordinary, such people are life-giving. Without them, nothing would revitalize the atmosphere in which we think. By being very vigilant, trying never to support or encourage negative thoughts, all of us can play a part in this vital service, which benefits everybody around us.

WHO ARE YOU? What do you love? How do you live, knowing you will die? Your gift will necessarily emerge from your response to these questions. This is your life, and so this is what you have to offer. You cannot offer other than what you are. If you try to pretend to be more than what you are or give more than you have, then you will be lying, and this will also make you feel very tired. On the other hand, if you give less than what you are, you dishonor the gift of your own precious life, and you will end your life in regret.

One way to name our gift is to pay close attention to what we love. Annie Dillard, a lover of language, tells the following story:

> A well-known writer got collared by a university student who asked, "Do you think I could be a writer?"
>
> "Well," the writer said, "I don't know. . . . Do you like sentences?"
>
> The writer could see the student's amazement. Do I like sentences? I am twenty years old and do I like sentences? If he had liked sentences, of course, he could begin, like a joyful painter I knew. I asked him how he came to be a painter. He said, "I liked the smell of paint."

YESTERDAY I WENT to visit Simon, who is dying. He is frightened. He regrets dying alone, with no partner to hold him when he awakens in the night, afraid.

As I sat with him, he wept. He is angry and sad about so many things that he cannot seem to feel the blessings. He is used to controlling the things in his life, and now there are things that cannot be controlled. He is losing energy, losing weight, and he cannot make this stop. I spent much of our time speaking with him about how we can feel the rhythm between sadness and joy, to not get caught in the reasons why. Toward the end of the morning, I felt that some healing had happened; he felt lighter. I believed my words had brought him some comfort.

Then, just before I left, he said, "You know, Wayne, I really don't understand most of what you say." He paused. "But I like your company and the sound of your voice." All the time I thought I was being wise and inspirational, it turned out Simon was soothed by my voice and my companionship. For my part, I rarely believe my companionship is enough, so I feel compelled to say clever and meaningful things. He wasn't interested. My company and my presence were enough.

Clearly we do not always know our real gift. I assumed my hard-won theological and spiritual wisdom would be the balm that would bring Simon comfort. As it happened, he felt cared for not because of my words but rather in spite of them. As often happens, I went away with a potent lesson, another reminder that I need not work so hard to sound so wise, because that may not be what really heals, not what others need at all.

SOMETIMES ONE OF our gifts is obvious, while another, deeper gift lies hidden behind it. Susan Jeffers, a dear friend, writes books about overcoming fear. Many people write to her and tell her that she saved their lives with her message of courage and hope.

But few know that Susan is also a cancer survivor. She had a mastectomy. She rarely speaks of it—not because she is ashamed, but because she does not take her identity from being a cancer victim. She quietly works with those who have cancer, often playfully. "I never saw losing my breast as a big problem," she told a gathering of women recently. "After all, I get half price on mammograms." In this way, too, she gives people courage, in a less visible but equally powerful way.

Jean Vanier founded L'Arche, a network of communities for developmentally disabled adults. He has seen countless people join these intentional communities, offering their skills and talents to those in need. Usually they bring those gifts for which they are known, talents that have long been recognized. According to Vanier, these obvious talents may only serve to mask what he calls our "deeper gifts":

Some people have outstanding talents. They are writers, artists, competent administrators. These talents can become gifts. But sometimes the individuals' personalities are so tied up in the activity that they exercise their talent chiefly for their own glory, or to prove themselves or to dominate. It is better then that these people do not exercise their talents in community, because they would find it too hard to use them for the good of others.

What they have to discover is their deeper gift . . . is not necessarily linked to a function. There are people who have the gift of being able to sense immediately, and even to live, the sufferings of others—that is the gift of compassion. There are others who know when something is going wrong and can pinpoint the cause—that is the gift of discernment. There are others who have the gift of light— they see clearly what is of fundamental concern to the community. Others have the gift of creating an atmosphere which brings joy, relaxation and individual growth. Others again have the gift of discerning what people need and supporting them. Others have the gift of welcome. Each person has a gift to use for the good and growth of all.

SOMETIMES OUR GIFT is pulled from within us by circumstance—often in ways we would never have imagined.

In 1989 Al Wooten Jr., a thirty-five-year-old security guard trainee, was killed in a drive-by shooting in Los Angeles. His mother, Faye, in the face of such random, senseless violence, vowed that her son would not die in vain. She sold her two-bedroom home in south central Los Angeles to raise money to open an after-school learning refuge for children ages seven to eighteen. She gathered a corps of mostly black college students and professionals to donate their time teaching courses in spelling, math, entrepreneurship, black history, and community and family responsibility.

Faye had always wanted to be a teacher, but as the eighth of nine children born to a minister father and a homemaker mother in Chisolm, Texas, she had to drop out of school in the ninth grade when she could not afford the bus fare to get to the segregated black high school. Instead, she washed glasses in a restaurant. Now, years later, with the tragic death of her son, came the moment for Faye to offer her luminous gift of teaching to a community torn by violence, poverty, and despair.

Helen is a nurse in the emergency room at a local hospital. She told me that whenever there was a "code" in the ER—when a patient needed emergency treatment to be resuscitated, to save their life—the doctors and emergency medical technicians (EMTs) would often make jokes or exchange nervous wisecracks to ease the tension. At that moment, everyone involved was frightened. A human being could die if things were not done perfectly. The cynical joking would mask the pain and the anxiety.

And yet Helen knew many of these doctors to be fundamentally caring, committed healers. They would not intentionally be hurtful or unkind. So Helen suggested a new practice: Whenever there was a code in the ER, she would invite the family members of the patient to gather around as the patient was being resuscitated. Working in the presence of the family members, the doctors and EMTs were suddenly softer, more concerned, more present. They were more aware of the personhood of the patient and the impact this particular human being had on the immediate lives of others. With this simple shift in procedure the atmosphere was dramatically enriched; what had been a time of discomfort and joking now became a moment of mindful, careful attention to the body, heart, and spirit of the patient and loved ones. The very difficulty of the situation actually gave birth to Helen's gift.

I FIRST MET Stewart Guernsey at Harvard Divinity School. He and I were both first-year seminarians after having had previous careers, I as a psychotherapist, he as a civil rights lawyer in Mississippi. We were there to explore the spiritual and ethical dimensions of our work, using the seminary as a place of reflection and contemplation.

Stewart had an incisive legal mind that was coupled with a keen moral sense. In 1982, the year we began our studies, Stewart happened upon the disturbing fact that there were no shelters for the homeless in Harvard Square. Winters in Cambridge can be bitter, and the lack of shelter for those in need—in the midst of such academic wealth and supposed moral authority—struck Stewart as fundamentally intolerable. And so Stewart set to work (all but ignoring his studies), single-handedly arranging for a Lutheran church in the Square to donate space, organizing several dozen volunteers from the seminary and the surrounding community, and talking local markets and restaurants into donating the necessary food.

As one of Stewart's volunteers, I was in charge of Sunday nights, helping prepare the food, getting the beds ready, fitting the residents with donated clothing. Since the shelter was in the basement of a church, we had no shower facilities. One night a man came in with lice and sores all over his body. I remember having to wash him, holding him up in a bathroom stall while I used a hose attached to the sink to bathe him. Such an intimate act, to bathe a stranger. I only now realize what trust he must have had in me, someone he never met, to allow me to wash him in this way. I also realize that none of this—the feeding, the clothing, the bathing, the shelter for over twenty-five homeless women and men— would ever have happened without the curious and unpredictable marriage of this desperate need with Stewart's moral courage.

Clearly this was something Stewart had never intended—in fact, did not necessarily want—yet the circumstances drew him there, and there we all were. During the next ten years, Stewart would begin many such shelters and become an articulate national spokesperson for the growing needs of the homeless.

❖

SOMETIMES OUR GIFT is pulled from us by more intimate needs. Here Jack Gilbert writes about caring for his beloved wife, Michiko, who is dying:

Finding Something

I say moon is horses in the tempered dark,
because horse is the closest I can get to it.
I sit on the terrace of this worn villa the king's
telegrapher built on the mountain that looks down
on a blue sea and the small white ferry
that crosses slowly to the next island each noon.
Michiko is dying in the house behind me,
the long windows open so I can hear
the faint sound she will make when she wants
watermelon to suck or so I can take her
to a bucket in the corner of a high-ceilinged room
which is the best we can do for a chamber pot.
She will lean against my leg as she sits
so as not to fall over in her weakness.
How strange and fine to get so near to it.
The arches of her feet are like voices
of children calling in the grove of lemon trees,
where my heart is as helpless as crushed birds.

Loving kindness, sympathetic joy, compassion, mercy: These are the unmistakable footprints of our spiritual life. We now regularly see churches and Zen centers turn themselves into homeless shelters and hospices, naming care for the dying and service to those in need as natural extensions of zazen practice and Christian prayer. People such as Stewart, who live and work with the poor, hungry, and homeless, now meditate and fast in community with others even as they strive to impact key legislation. Many people are becoming aware that the clarity and courage born of their own healing can also be made available for the healing of those in need.

A few years ago Sidney Poitier was given the Lifetime Achievement Award by the American Film Institute. Afterward he was asked what advice he would give to young black filmmakers just beginning their careers. Poitier—well aware of both the opportunities and responsibilities that confronted his audience and his profession—said simply, "Be true to yourselves." And then he added, "And be useful to the journey."

To the Spider in the Crevice/
Behind the Toilet Door

i have left you four flies
three are in the freezer next to the joint of beef
the other is wrapped in christmas paper
tied with a pink ribbon
beside the ironing table in the hall
should you need to contact me
in an emergency
the number's in the book
by the telephone.

p.s. i love you

—JANET SUTHERLAND

Practice: How We Give

Dedicate one single day to the exploration of the way you feel about giving. Be aware how your relationship to giving changes as you move through different situations, through varying aspects of your life.

From the moment you awake, use this day to examine how you give. Notice when the impulse to give first arises. Does it feel as if it emerges naturally from within or if it feels like an obligation imposed from without. Be aware of the situations in which it seems most easy to give, in which it feels more troublesome or complicated. Which gifts are given most freely? Which carry reluctance or resentment?

How often is there an impulse to give? Which impulses do you acknowledge? Which do you refuse to acknowledge? Why?

Notice especially the feelings before, during, and after each exchange. Does the offering of a gift produce happiness or well-being? Does it result in weariness or anger? Try to explore what seems to produce these different results.

Giving and
Receiving

The fragrance always remains in the
hand that gives the rose.

—GANDHI

REUBEN WAS BORN to a family of ten children. As one of the
oldest, he was often the mediator between his mother and
his violent, alcoholic father. He learned to look after his siblings, most of whom were younger and did not understand
what was going on. He felt tremendous responsibility to ensure that they were safe, and he spent much of his time
caring for their needs.

Today, grown and married with children of his own,
Reuben still watches for what is needed. He takes care of
many people in his village—he works with young people, he
brings food for the elderly. Last week he called me about a
fourth grader who was going to drop out of school. "Fourth
grade, Wayne! Can you imagine? But we got him involved in
our little after-school basketball program, and he loved it, he
started coming every day. I told him he had to stay in school
if he wanted to keep coming. So today he is still in school!"
Such a small thing, a priceless thing.

But Reuben has also had heart problems. He is always
pushing himself very hard, and he does not feel permission to
stop or take it easy. Always striving to make everything right,
he feels it would be unkind, even irresponsible to rest, to take
time to heal his own body. His deep compassion for others
does not always so readily flow toward himself.

I have met so many like Reuben, people who are noble

in heart and generous in spirit but who have difficulty allowing the love they bring to the world to touch themselves
as well. They push so hard for the healing of others, with
little regard for themselves. Then, continually giving without
any thought of receiving, they become exhausted, they burn
out, they fall apart.

When Jane was young, her mother was constantly and
seriously ill. Because her mother was unable to provide a
mother's care, Jane grew up very fast, in part to take care of
her mother, and in part to amputate any of the tender needs
of childhood that would never now be filled. Jane became the
mother in the family, taking care of the relentless needs imposed by the chronic illness of a family member.

Not surprisingly, Jane grew up to be a nurse. After a
lifetime of service, she has learned to subordinate her own
needs and desires in order to better care for others. Jane has
an authentic, compassionate gift. But now, middle-aged, she
is also beginning to feel trapped by her gift. Compelled to
give without receiving, Jane feels deeply out of balance.

Many of us believe that giving somehow means we
must stop receiving. "Giving" people never ask for anything
in return, according to the popular image of the kind and
saintly giver. We imagine giving as a purely altruistic, self-
sacrificing gesture that precludes any nourishment, playfulness, or personal benefit. Charity seems to want a tinge of
martyrdom attached to it: Give till it hurts. This is both dangerous and impossible—dangerous because it invites us to try
to live without receiving care and nourishment, which is insidiously suicidal, and impossible because all life is intimately
connected in a web of giving and taking, and as long as we
are alive we are an integral part of that web. We cannot live
on the earth and not give; we cannot live and not receive.

David Steindl-Rast speaks of the intricate and necessary
balance between giving and receiving:

> Life is give-and-take, not give or take. Spasmodic
> gasping is one thing, healthy breathing another.
> When we take a hearty breath, we give ourselves to
> the air we inhale; and when we give it out again,

we take a quick break from breathing. This balance of giving and taking is a key to healthy living on every level of life. In fact, balance is too mechanical a word to apply to the intimate intricacy of this give-and-take. We are talking about a giving within taking and a taking within giving. Once this is spelled out, it is hardly necessary to stress the fact that we are not playing off giving against taking. By no means. We are playing off a life-giving give-and-take against a mere taking that is as deadly as a mere giving. It matters little whether you merely take a breath and stop, or give a breath and stop there. In either case, you're dead.

When we give without taking, it invariably leads to re-sentment, anger, and frustration. There is no joy in it. Gener-osity becomes synonymous with sacrifice. It is instructive to recall that Jesus counseled against this kind of spiritual repa-ration. In fact, as the priestly elders of the temple were de-manding ever more costly sacrifices from the people as part of their religious obligations, Jesus—recognizing the deep suffering created by these requirements—rebuked them, say-ing, "Go, and learn the meaning of this: I desire mercy, not sacrifice."

THE FUNDAMENTAL LAWS of kindness are merciful; they insist that the most beautiful and life-giving acts are those that bring rich and fruitful blessings to both giver and receiver. Sharon Salzberg, a devoted teacher of Buddhism in the West, echoes David Steindl-Rast as she clarifies the central Buddhist concept of *metta,* or loving-kindness:

> *Metta* does not mean that we denigrate ourselves in *any* situation in order to uphold other people's hap-piness. Authentic intimacy is not brought about by denying our own desire to be happy in unhappy deference to others, nor by denying others in nar-cissistic deference to ourselves. Metta means equal-

ity, oneness, wholeness. To truly walk the Middle Way of the Buddha, to avoid the extremes of addiction and self-hatred, we must walk in friendship with ourselves as well as with all beings.

We can use this wise counsel to examine how we ourselves approach an act of kindness. How do we give? In the following passage, Robert Coles, a psychiatrist and social theologian, describes a critical moment in his training where he began to clearly recognize the essential need for an honest and proper balance between giving and receiving:

> When I was an undergraduate, I tutored some children in English and math. Billy, one of the youngsters with whom I worked, was eleven years old, I remember, and in the sixth grade. His parents had been born in Boston's North End neighborhood, though all four of their parents had come to the United States from Italy. They were hard-working people, and they were ambitious for the children and grandchildren, I began to realize, in more than a social or economic or educational way. They wanted Billy to be a decent, honorable, conscientious person.
>
> As for the future, if he were to become the tradesman his father had become, that would be wonderful—so the boy himself told me one day as we chatted. Indeed, several times he reminded me that schooling was not all that essential to his plans and that soon enough, in his teens, he'd be contemplating which of the trades he'd pursue. At the time, I recall, he had in mind becoming an electrician.
>
> Again and again, as I realized how very intelligent Billy was, I tried to persuade him to look carefully at his life, develop some second thoughts about what he might do with it. I talked to him about going to college and even about attending a high school that would give him a good chance of being

accepted at college. I talked with him about the opportunities particular professions offered. And I kept reminding him how bright I felt he was; his poor schoolwork was a result, I'd figured out, of general lack of interest.

He listened politely but said little, and he constantly tried to change the subject. . . . One afternoon, after we'd finished our arithmetic lesson and I'd made yet another effort at persuasion, I found myself decidedly on the defensive. Billy said not a word in reply to my comments until I was through, and then he put this question to me, one I still remember after all these years and I have thought about rather intently and with some perplexity. "I was wondering something," he began—and then he paused politely for me to give him the nod that meant yes, I'd love to hear more. With that signal, he asked, "Why do you come here?"

Though I was usually able to talk with some fluency, I was suddenly utterly quiet. I looked across the table at a wall . . . and then toward the window. . . . I avoided the boy's eyes and was unable to reply for so long that we both became embarrassed. . . . I was still quite unable to muster a sound, let alone a coherent reply. Finally, ever tactful and considerate (more so than I had been, with my constant stabs at self-important, self-serving propaganda on behalf of college attendance), he said, "Well, I guess I shouldn't ask."

By then I was ready to insist on Billy's right to be as inquisitive as he wanted to be. (Hadn't I been telling him so all along!) I spent much time assuring him along those lines, but all the while I was trying, in vain, to think of an answer to his question. He never pressed the matter further—and a loud bell, telling us that everyone in that after-school program ought to be leaving, saved my neck for that day.

The young Robert Coles returned to Harvard to see his college adviser, Dr. Perry Miller, a professor of American literature. Robert shared the boy's question and confessed his inability to answer. When asked how he would now reply if given a second chance, Robert replied, "I don't know."

After that confession, Robert and his tutor had a long talk. As Robert described his confusion, Professor Miller nodded his head several times and said, "Yes, yes, I understand," and then spoke about the need to honestly acknowledge the real human needs of all parties in any kind of teaching situation.

> He wanted me to consider this—and I have certainly kept in mind the gist of his reasoning; what we do on behalf of others may be a big puzzle to them, perhaps because we patronize them, condescend to them, convey to them our sense of lofty *noblesse oblige,* even hector them with it, while refusing to acknowledge (to ourselves, perhaps also to them) our own purposes and reasons and, very important, our own needs. He concluded with these words, an odd and compelling mix, I thought then and still do, of relatively fancy talk and quite earthy talk: "There's a moral asymmetry that takes hold of us teachers rather too commonly—we think of ourselves as offering service to others, giving them our best, and forget what's in it for ourselves, the service that we're receiving from our students."

The next time I saw Billy I used my own words to echo my professor's. I said I liked coming to that school, liked leaving the place where I lived (a college dormitory filled with talkative, aspiring, and not always humble young men), and I liked especially, stopping on my way back to that world for some strong coffee and some Italian pastry at a nearby eating place. Billy liked that last bit of information, liked my thoroughly indirect suggestion of the nurturance I was getting—or so I interpreted by his big smile much later in my life. He was telling me indirectly that he hadn't wanted some long-winded, introspective *apologia* from me, or some big-deal analysis and explanation. He wanted only a sign that I was a human being, flawed and even voiceless, like others, like him, and capable of plenty of confusion, as he knew he was, and, yes, as hungry in my own way as he was.

WHEN I FIRST MOVED to Santa Fe I served as the director of a family therapy program for juvenile delinquents. One of my first clients was Carlos, a fourteen-year-old who was habitually truant, getting into fights and stealing. He would cut school, jump on the four-wheel motorcycle his grandfather bought him, and be gone until evening. Carlos was not a mean young man; he was simply fascinated by doing things he was not supposed to. He didn't even seem to care if he got caught; his real enjoyment came from breaking the rules. I called his family, his grandfather, his siblings, and we all worked together on trying to help Carlos become a more responsible member of the family and the community. Slowly—reluctantly—Carlos began to turn around. I never really thought he was a hardened criminal. He and his family simply needed a few guidelines. Years later I saw that Carlos had settled down and had two children of his own.

Last year a new bakery and coffee shop opened near my office. The first time I went in, there was Carlos, working as the cook. Now, whenever I am in a hurry and need a sandwich or a cup of coffee, Carlos makes sure to take care of me. Sometimes, if he is near the register, he does not even charge me. "It's on the house, man," he tells me. "You did so much for me, I want to do something for you." He always thanks me for what I did. I feel embarrassed. I feel I did not do anything much at all, certainly nothing to deserve this kingly treatment. I am clearly gratified he is doing well, but I am afraid Carlos gives me too much credit. As always, I am confused about how much kindness I can accept without feeling as though I am getting more from Carlos than I ever gave to him. And I also know this is an old problem of mine—learning to receive from others the natural kindness that arises in response to whatever I have given them.

I am uncomfortable because I feel I am getting back from what I gave. Like Coles, I must constantly confront my misguided sense that giving is always better than receiving, more noble somehow. When I am always trying to protect my position as "giver," this marginalizes Carlos, keeping him imprisoned as a teenage delinquent client rather than a human being whom I spent time with, who now wants to give back to me. I am forced to enter into the stream of giving and receiving. My reluctance to fully participate in the exchange enables me to remain separate and different—I am a giver. But when I also become a receiver—when I take from Carlos in return for the gift—the walls between us soften, the boundaries disappear, and I am simply one of the family.

There is a rich web of giving and receiving, a deep ecology of give-and-take that permeates all life. On biological, social, political, and spiritual levels, we are always part of something that gives and receives oxygen, food, clothing, shelter, goods, services, prayers, morning light, dew on the grass, touch, color, moisture, music, love—the exchange goes on and on. It is impossible that we do not participate. So the question "What is my gift?" is not about coercing us into giving more and more, but rather about becoming more mindful of how we are already intimately connected with everything and everyone. In this marketplace of care and kindness, what are we already bringing to the family of the earth?

True kindness is rooted in a deep sense of abundance, out of which flows a sense that even as I give, it is being given back to me. We are always giving, we are always receiving. When I am spacious and easy with my offering, I am assuming that it will always return to me in some form. It is a statement of my deep faith and belief—nay, experience—

that this is the truth of how things are, an abiding sense that all is provided.

After the death of the Buddha, his followers instituted a practice that continues to this day: Monks must beg each day for their food. They go from house to house with their begging bowl, accepting whatever they are given as their daily bread. Most important, monks are not allowed to keep food overnight. Each day they must trust again in the delicate rhythm of giving and receiving. Within this balance, just as the monks send out their prayers for the healing of all beings, so will food come to them for their nourishment. If they remain empty, like the bowl, ungrasping, then the river of giving and receiving will flow through them.

Similarly, in the Hebrew story, the Israelites were fed in the desert with manna from heaven. The Israelites had to rely on God to keep and nourish them. There was only one rule about manna—it could not be kept overnight. If they hoarded the gift out of fear that there would be no more, the manna would spoil by morning. Thus receiving is grounded in faith; faith that there is enough, faith that we can be generous in our offerings and there will still and always be enough left for us.

The Buddha explains that within giving, there is always receiving:

> Hard it is to understand: By giving away food, we get more strength; by bestowing clothing on others, we gain more beauty; by donating abodes of purity and truth, we acquire great treasures.

> The charitable man has found the path of salvation. He is like the man who plants a sapling, securing thereby the shade, the flowers, and the fruit in future years.

JUST AS OUR GIVING naturally invokes receiving, so can an authentic act of receiving give birth to a rich and generous gift.

I was leading a retreat with a small group of men and

women, people who had been hurt as children, now grown, who were seeking healing and peace. Michael, who had been quiet for much of the weekend, finally spoke up on Sunday morning. He described the particular terrors of his childhood, wounds still reluctant to heal. Then, after a poignant silence, he added: "I have AIDS." He told us he had been very sick the past winter. He felt alone and frightened. But Michael had been raised never to ask for help, only to be strong and bear up under whatever he was given. So while he was in tremendous need of love and care, he could not ask for it.

I invited Michael to go around the circle, to say to each and every person there, "I need your care." It was very hard for him; at first he refused to do it, because it was terrifying to admit to such a weakness. If he were truly strong, he felt, he would need no such thing. To say to anyone "I need your care" felt so selfish, so prohibited, so impossible.

It was a powerful moment for Michael. Overcoming this ancient prohibition, this refusal to be in need of care, took enormous courage. Slowly, one by one, he spoke to each person in the circle. "I need your care," he said. Looking into his eyes, we could see he was tender and frightened, and we could sense Michael's genuine need for love, kindness, and attention. A rich and potent generosity began to emerge from within the circle. Some moved to hold him, cry with him, speak softly to him. For much of that Sunday morning we cared for Michael. As he softened, he gradually allowed himself to receive from the abundance that was being offered him.

But while Michael was drinking from this fountain of care, something else just as important was happening in that room. As people opened their hearts to Michael, everyone else began to feel cared for; they each received care as they gave it. The room filled to overflowing with compassion, saturating all of us. Michael's asking for care freed a river of loving-kindness within us all. His receiving allowed the care in all of us to come forth. His needing care gave birth to a roomful of love.

In this way, we can see that to refuse care when it is offered can be an act of selfishness. Michael, sick with AIDS, was trying to be independent, to do it all himself. We all had to convince him it was acceptable for him to receive our care. When he finally did, his acceptance of that care actually gave birth to a reservoir of healing for everyone.

SHARON SALZBERG:

> Generosity's aim is twofold: we give freely to others, and we give freely to ourselves. Without both aspects, the experience is incomplete. If we give a gift freely, without attachment to a certain result or expectation of what will come back to us, that exchange celebrates freedom both within ourselves as the giver and in the receiver. . . . In a moment of pure giving, we really become one.

When we are resting easily in the rhythm of giving and receiving, it becomes difficult to tell who is the giver and who the receiver. Visiting Santo Domingo pueblo for a green corn dance, it is clear the dancers dance because the people need food, the earth needs rain. The dancers dance for the people and for the earth. The men gather and sing for the dancers, they sing and drum, their gift to those who dance. The women and children and those too old to dance gather and witness the dance, not as spectators but in a communal prayer of support. This is their gift to those who dance. The elders descend into the kiva, drumming and singing deep in the heart of the earth. Others stay home and cook so that everyone may eat. A single home may feed a hundred dancers and visitors in a single day. Those who stay home and do not dance offer their jewelry for the dancers to wear so that they may all be beautiful. Then, as the jewelry worn by the dancers is blessed by the dance, the giver receives it in return with a blessing from the dance, from the prayer of the people, from the earth. Where is the giver, the gift, the receiver? It all flows.

Each moment we live, we are entwined in a rich and intricate web of giving and receiving. Early Christians recognized this when they articulated the fundamental economy of spiritual community: "From each according to their ability, to each according to their need." We give from what we have, we take from what we need. This sounds so simple; but we can easily learn to block our natural generosity, just as we learn to block our receiving what we need. Either way, it does not flow.

If we take all the time, this is selfish and will bring suffering. If we give all the time, this will lead to resentment and exhaustion and will bring suffering as well. Real joy is to be found in the balance between giving and taking. Like breathing, we must both inhale and exhale. Inhaling is not superior to exhaling; one is no more noble or good than the other. They are both necessary. To name our gift is to also name our need.

I am the one whose praise
echoes on high.

I adorn all the earth.

I am the breeze
that nurtures all things
green.
I encourage blossoms to flourish with
ripening fruits.

I am led by the spirit to feed
the purest streams.

I am the rain
coming from the dew
that causes the grasses to laugh
with the joy of life.

I call forth tears,
the aroma of holy work.

I am the yearning for good.

—HILDEGARD OF BINGEN

❖

Dedicate this day to watching the balance between giving and receiving.

As in the previous exercise, watch how you give, to whom, and the circumstances in which it feels as if you give most easily and freely. But now try also to become aware of what you seek to receive in return. As you follow the impulse to give, notice also what the heart desires to take in.

Does the giving and receiving feel out of balance? If you feel you have given too much, pay attention to that moment—what is your response to the imbalance? Do you get tired? Resentful? Hurt? What would you need to be given in return? What gift would allow you to feel cared for in this moment? How can you ask for this?

If you feel you are receiving more than you give, what stops you from offering your gift? What are you waiting for? The right moment? An invitation? Some assurance that it will be appreciated? When will you feel ready?

❖

Offering Our Gift

> The founding of temples is meritorious, meditations
> and religious exercises pacify the heart, comprehen-
> sion of the truth leads to Nirvana—but greater than
> all is loving-kindness. As the light of the moon is
> sixteen times greater than the light of all the stars,
> so is loving-kindness sixteen times more efficacious
> in liberating the heart than all other religious accom-
> plishments taken together. This state of the heart is
> the best in the world.
>
> —The Buddha

The Buddha said that if we truly understood the power of
giving, we would never let a single meal pass without sharing
it. The power of giving is not measured by the size or expense of the gift, but rather in the beautiful freedom that
takes birth in a moment of genuine kindness. In a freely offered gift there is nonattachment, love, surrender, a sincere
wish for the well-being of another, sympathetic joy, selfless-
ness, effortlessness—a virtual catalogue of the spiritual vir-
tues.

From wherever we stand, if we perceive something necessary, and if we have it, then we can offer it. Giving need be
no more complex or difficult than this. We cannot save everyone; we cannot do it all. Often one small gift is all that is
required to sow a garden of well-being.

Ben Whitehill is a doctor, his wife, Carolyn, a social
worker. They have spent the better part of their lives as
Christian missionaries traveling around the world bringing
medical care and compassionate advocacy to many in need.

Their children, raised in the company of the sick and hungry, have grown up to become teachers and healers as well.

Thirty years ago, working as a doctor in Hong Kong, Ben was driving along a rural road on the way home from the clinic. Along the way he happened to see a pig farmer walking along the side of the road. As he slowed down to offer the man a ride, Ben could see he was a leper. Ben asked him to get in. The man hesitated and then slowly got into the car.

Thirty years later, Ben and Carolyn—after many years in Santa Fe, he as medical director for the Indian Health Service, she as director of a program for developmentally disabled adults—retired, and as part of their retirement returned to Hong Kong to volunteer their skills. Even after thirty years, many people recognized Ben and Carolyn and came to them and thanked them profusely for their innumerable kindnesses, one man proudly recounting how Ben had repaired his severed hand, one woman weeping as she recalled the flowers Carolyn had given her in a time of terrible pain.

One day a man came up to Ben. "I remember you gave me a ride. I had leprosy, and you let me get into your car. I was tired, and you stopped and helped me get home. No one had ever let me in their car before, no one ever gave me a ride. You were the only one. I have always remembered you." Ben told me this story with characteristic humility, focusing not on his generosity but rather on the grace he felt in the presence of this man's deep, loving remembrance. Clearly the simplest gesture—a ride, a flower, a word of comfort—can be a miraculous gift.

A gift is not a contract. A contract is a negotiated, reciprocal exchange: If I give you this, you will give me that. While contracts are useful in developing working relationships with our coworkers, friends, and family, a contract creates an obligation. A gift, by definition, is given freely and without condition. The gift of life, the gift of love, the gift of the earth—these can never be earned. They are given freely.

In Buddhism, it is said there are three kinds of giving. Here Joseph Goldstein briefly describes the qualities of each:

The first are beggarly givers. They give only after much hesitation, and then just the leftovers, the worst of what they have. They think, "Should I give or shouldn't I? Maybe it's too much?" And finally perhaps part with something they don't really want.

Friendly givers are people who give what they themselves would use. They share what they have and with less deliberation, with more open-handedness.

The highest kind of givers are kingly givers who offer the very best of what they have. They share spontaneously and in the moment without needing to deliberate. Giving has become natural to their conduct. Non-greed is so strong in their minds that at every opportunity they share what is treasured most in an easy and loving way.

St. Paul reminds us that we are at our best when we feel the unspeakable freedom embedded in giving, offering whatever we have from a deep sense of abundance, acutely aware that there is enough for everyone and that whatever we give will be returned to us a thousandfold:

The point is this: he who sows sparingly will reap sparingly, and he who sows bountifully will reap bountifully. Each one must do as he has made up his mind, not reluctantly or under compulsion, for God loves a cheerful giver. And God is able to provide you with every blessing in abundance, so that you may always have enough of everything and may provide in abundance for every good work.

A kingly giver, a cheerful giver, is one who feels the truth of abundance. As we give, so do we receive. We will always be given enough, and we will always have enough to give.

As we explore the nature of our gift, our goal is to move toward this kind of giving: cheerful giving that flows gently and easily, kingly giving that flows surely from who we are. As we answer the questions—Who are we? What do we love?—the gift we bring will be easy, because our gift naturally emerges from who we are. The offering we bring is ourselves, just as we are. Our gift is our true nature. There can be no other gift than this.

LESLIE WAS A NURSE AND MIDWIFE. She worked with a strong, gentle wisdom that women came to love and to trust. Leslie seemed to be on call at all times for whoever needed her. She especially loved the poor, making extra room for those single, underprivileged women who could never pay her any money. When Leslie was a young girl in New York City, she would buy balloons and hand them out to strangers on the street. Whenever she was given anything, she felt a natural impulse to give it away.

When Leslie was pregnant with her second child, she discovered early in the pregnancy that the fetus had Down syndrome. Part of her did not want to believe it; the other part knew it was true. She wrestled with herself deep in her heart, agonizing over what she would do. Should she abort? This was certainly an option—arguably kind to the child, clearly easier for her. Could she keep the baby? With so many responsibilities, where could she find the energy, time, and patience to raise a Down syndrome child?

Leslie prayed. She spent countless hours in quiet meditation. She knew that she would need to be absolutely precise in her action. Whatever she chose, it had to be from her deepest heart—it had to be right, it had to be true. In the end, after many weeks of some of the most mindful inner conversation she would ever have, she made her decision. As one who had helped so many women through the excruciating pain of bringing life into the world, she was not someone who could stand in the way of yet another life aching to be born. She would carry the child, give it life. Raising the child would be her practice.

Fred was a carpenter. A few years ago he was working on a house here in Santa Fe, framing the roof, when he lost his balance and fell. He hit the ground with a great deal of force and was knocked unconscious. His co-workers on the job rushed him to the hospital.

As it turned out, his injuries were massive, and Fred died on the operating table. Like many who have had this experience, Fred continued to be aware of his surroundings, even after his clinical death. He felt his spirit rise, and he was able to watch the emergency room staff pronounce him dead. He then began to feel a pull toward a great light and was washed in an indescribable feeling of peace and well-being. Just as he was about to enter this warm, gentle light, a thought entered his mind: *I have a wife and two children who need me.* "As soon as I heard that thought in my mind," Fred said, "I felt myself instantly transported back into my body. It was so fast—the connection between my need to care for my family and my being pulled back into my body. It was like my self as father, as husband, brought me back to life here on earth."

Like Leslie, like Fred, we each in our own way do what we can. Whatever gift we bring necessarily arises from who we are. These four meditations—who we are, what we love, how we live, naming our gift—all flow into one another. What we love teaches us how to live. What we give helps us learn about who we are. In this way, perhaps we may learn to drink from the immeasurable grace of a single human life.

THE BUDDHA:

> As the bee takes the essence of the flower and flies without destroying its beauty and perfume, so wander in this life.

THERE ARE TIMES when our offering is not necessarily some tangible gift or helpful act, but rather simply a peaceful manner. If we are clear and present, if we are quiet and centered, then others may be nourished simply by our lack of agitation.

The world is so agitated that to be in the presence of a single person who is at peace can feel remarkably healing, a great blessing. If we are still, others will come when they need to remember who they are.

William Butler Yeats:

> We can make our minds so like still water that be-
> ings gather about us, that they may see their own
> images, and so live for a moment with a clearer,
> perhaps even with a fiercer, life because of our
> quiet.

Our work on ourselves can be an invaluable gift to those who are in need of strong and faithful company. When I sit with the dying, I do not really do anything at all. I sit without expectation. I listen, I hold their hand, I let them cry. I really cannot do anything "significant." I cannot cure their disease. I cannot save their life. I cannot take away their pain. I cannot make them not be alone at night. I cannot do anything.

So why do they ask for me? I believe it is because for a few moments, in the quiet of our shared company, they can finally hear themselves. Beneath the noisy distractions of their own habitual fears and worries, they can listen more clearly to what is true. They speak to me of what they love, and they remember what is important. This moment it is not about medicines and treatments and diagnoses and prognoses. It is about how it feels to be alive, and only yet for this short time. And I, one who will also die, sit and wait with them. We wait together.

Another quiet gift we bring is the gift of simply doing no harm: to refrain from judging ourselves and others, not to use sarcasm or anger to advance our cause, not to be hurtful in our speech or our actions. If we simply refrain from causing suffering, then the limitless potential for natural healing can quietly arise unimpeded.

My friends Stephen and Ondrea Levine have given much of their lives in service of those healing from loss and grief. In *Embracing the Beloved,* their exquisite book on relationship as a path of awakening, they speak of monogamy as an absolute necessity for clarity and healing in the relationship. As dedicated practitioners of monogamy in their own lives, Stephen and Ondrea have "gone for broke," to quote Stephen, to allow for the kind of ecstasy born of trust and commitment.

Here Stephen describes a moment in their work together when, simply as a result of their personal commitment to do no sexual harm, others who have been reluctant to trust seem to find healing:

> When you no longer see others as sexual objects, there is a level at which you can be trusted by those who have, through sexual cruelty, learned to distrust. Perhaps that's why so many sexually abused men and women have offered Ondrea and me such a profound degree of confidence, and allowed us so deeply into their healing. Perhaps that's why, as the room emptied after a very intense grief workshop, a woman who had been severely abused approached me and asked if we could speak. She said she had not allowed a man to touch her, to literally *touch* her in any way, in more than seventeen years. "It's just too terrifying." She asked if I would just touch her hand. And then if I would hold it. And after a few minutes of quiet, she leaned into my arms and we rocked back and forth crying together for the pain we could hardly contain in the mind and only had room for in our hearts. "You're the first man I've let hold me since I've been an adult, since I left home!" Crying together with this woman, I looked toward Ondrea, a dozen feet away cradling in her arms a gay man who sobbed that his lover and more than fifty friends had died of AIDS, that his world was collapsing. He said he couldn't stand to take another breath, breathing softly into Ondrea's tear-soaked hair. The lack of any sexual intention emanating from us allowed a

trust into which many released their fear and long-
held grief. It was another example of how the work
on ourselves is for the benefit of all sentient beings.

THE OPPORTUNE MOMENT for kindness and generosity seems to
present itself clearly, if only we are able to hear and are prepared to respond. Maria Mathis, an elementary-school
teacher in Pecos, New Mexico, read about a young girl in
Chicago who had AIDS. She told her class about this girl
named Whitney, who was sick with the life-threatening virus. They all decided to invite her to come to New Mexico.
So they raised money from students, their parents, and other
community members and brought Whitney for a visit to
meet the children in the class. For several days they listened
to Whitney tell her story about how it felt to have AIDS,
what it was, and what it meant to her. All the children had
questions, and they made a deep and lasting friendship with
Whitney. When Whitney returned to Chicago, they all continued to write to her, and she wrote back. The correspon-
dence continues today, enriching the lives of all the children
involved.

Marcy Grace—a close friend and longtime associate of
Bread for the Journey—heard about this event and was able
to meet with Maria and her students when Whitney was
visiting. She was deeply moved by the exchange; while so
many adults Marcy knew had died or were dying from this
terrible illness, here were eager young children speaking honestly and lovingly about life and death, sickness and health. It
seemed so full of hope and promise. Marcy immediately decided to start a project—her fifth in as many years dedicated
to serving those with AIDS—and came straight to Bread for
the Journey. Would we be willing to support, with financial
and legal assistance, the Whitney Project?

Marcy and several other dedicated volunteers began arranging for children with HIV to visit and correspond with
children in classrooms across New Mexico and throughout
the country. Children learn about AIDS through the lives of
other children just like them, children who are bravely facing

illness, hospitals, drugs, doctors, life, and death. Clearly all the children feel touched by the healing that comes from this intimate, loving contact. Now in its second year, the Whitney Project has paired thirty HIV-impacted children across the country with six hundred students in classrooms in New Mexico alone.

LIKE MARCY, Priscilla Logan loves children. She is a creative elementary-school teacher who came to Bread for the Journey last year and explained that she and her class wanted to build a wetlands on the grounds of their school. They wanted to see how active, natural wetlands could serve as real alternatives to chemical sewage disposal plants.

As soon as we agreed to support the project, an enthusiastic group of students, parents, teachers, and community members worked together for many days, digging, trenching, hauling dirt, and planting. Soon the wetlands was well established and became a functioning "outdoor classroom" for the entire school. Children in the lower grades learn spelling and vocabulary through pond observations they describe in their journals. The older children study biology and continue to explore the viability of using constructed wetlands in community water treatment systems. They are also using the wetlands to investigate a curious lack of aquatic life in a particular stretch of the Santa Fe River.

The wetlands became an integral and beloved part of school life. Many children had never been so involved in making things grow. Each day they would go out and talk to the plants. Things grew that were not supposed to. Corn that was planted the year before came back.

All this started with a single idea, then a conversation, then an enthusiastic collaboration, and finally a new world was created for the school community. Priscilla, the students who planted, the parents who hauled dirt and volunteered time, the teachers who coordinated lessons and projects— each brought their singular gift. These are not the kinds of dramatic projects that make the evening news. It did not require an enormous financial grant or an army of expert consultants. Rather, through the simple hope to build something useful and beautiful, people who live together, young and old, brought their particular gifts to the table.

Again, these are ordinary people, Maria and Marcy and Whitney and Priscilla, following what they have been given. All the resources are there; all that is required is to realize this is a moment in which a gift may be offered, and to offer it. This is not a moment to collapse in fear that we have no gift, or that it will be inadequate, or that we need to be more special or dramatic or extraordinary. Many of our projects were started by ordinary people who simply saw a need and felt they had something to offer. There are no guarantees they will work. Some work, some fail. But the success or failure of any single project is far less important than the offering of the gift. The project can always be altered, re-vamped, resurrected. But a gift not offered dies in the heart.

This may not be the message we received in our child-hood. Perhaps there were members of your family or other people in your life who said, "We do not need you. You are not important." Even worse, perhaps they said, "We do not want you. You are the cause of our problems. You bring us only suffering."

This was never true. It is not true now. The family of the earth aches for your gifts. We all need what you have. We cannot survive unless you join our circle and bring who you are to our gathering. Do not be afraid. This is the phrase used more often than any other in the Bible: Be not afraid. A kind life, a life of spirit, is fundamentally a life of courage—the courage simply to bring what you have, to bring who you are.

David Williams:

Privacy

So what if I outsmarted a fish
I found beautiful and didn't need to eat?
The pickerel's mouth was around the hook—
another instant he'd bite and be torn.

I jiggled a warning down the line,
and he backed off quick and smooth.

Across the pond a woman came down,
waded in so far and stopped,
but kept throwing out a stick
for her dog to return
while light off the water
dappled her thighs.

She thought she was alone
so I turned away.

I remember how my father always entered the water
shyly, carefully wetting his skin
like a shepherd smearing an orphaned lamb
with another ewe's blood so she'd claim it.
Once he swam out so far alone, he didn't
know the way back when dark surprised him.
Then someone on shore he'd never met,
thinking of something else,
flicked on a light and he didn't drown.

IN MY OWN LIFE I have been blessed with friends who have offered me so much. I am touched—amazed, even—by what I have been given when I was most in need of it. A flood of moments fills my mind as I write this. I remember when Richy held me as I wept long and hard after my divorce. I remember Peter Falco, Peter Guardino, Michael Napolillo, and many others who, when I was younger, taught me to sing and play guitar. I remember several others who put me up in their homes as I wandered around the country pursuing who knows how many dreams and projects. Countless others have helped me raise money for people in need. I recall wonderful teachers who taught me music, meditation, love of language, prayer, kindness, new ways to think about myself and the world. Still others hired me to join them in their work, helping me to learn and grow, because they saw something in me and believed in me, even when I did not always know what they saw. My wife, Christine, is eternally patient with my many comings and goings, my chasing after the wind, my periodic unconsciousness. Still, she stays close and loves me. Sherah, my daughter, whose devotion to me is one of the greatest gifts of my life, always has a twinkle in her eye as she teases me—and reassures me—about all my worries. Max hugs me and says, "I love you, Papa." I have been given a wealth of gifts for any lifetime.

Our greatest gift is to allow ourselves to feel alive in this sea, moving with the tides of loving kindness as they move into us, through us, out of us into others, only to return again and again. The kindnesses of others fertilize our soul—they become a part of who we are, and we carry them and their love. We feel this when people die, how their gifts remain alive in us. I feel the blessing of Peter, who sang with me and loved me. I miss terribly my friend Eddie, who played hard and with passion and who taught me to challenge the edges of life. In my heart I feel Paul, who laughed and smiled, and in his smile you always felt everything was all right. I still miss my grandfather, who taught me to love photography and gave me my first camera. All these and so many more have left their gifts in my body. I feel a tender sadness as I write this; I miss them, and yet their gifts remain.

My friend Peter Falco died when we were both twenty-nine years old. Our mutual friend Peter Guardino found this poem, which we read at Peter's memorial service:

MERRITT MALLOY:

Epitaph

> When I die,
> give what's left of me to children
> and old men that wait to die.
> And if you need to cry,
> cry for your brother walking the street
> beside you.
> When you need me,

put your arms around anyone
and give them what you need to give to me.

I want to leave you something,
something better than words or sounds:
look for me in the people I've known
or loved.
And if you cannot give me away,
at least let me live in your eyes
and not on your mind.
You can love me most
by letting hands touch hands,
by letting bodies touch bodies,
and by letting go of children
that need to be free.

Love doesn't die; people do.
So that when all that's left of me is love,
give me away.
I'll see you at home in the earth.

To offer our gift is to affirm that, yes, we are a part of all this. Here, alive on the earth, we receive and we give. We receive the care of so many, and we too—in our life and in our death—open our hand so that our gifts may fertilize joy, kindness, and healing for ourselves, and for all our family on the earth.

We are visitors on this planet. We are here for ninety, a hundred years at the very most. During that period we must try to do something good, something useful with our lives. Try to be at peace with yourself and help others share that peace. If you contribute to other people's happiness, you will find the true goal, the meaning of life.

—The Dalai Lama

Praying the Sunset Prayer

I'll let you in on a secret
about how one should pray the sunset prayer.
It's a juicy bit of praying,
like strolling on grass,
nobody's chasing you, nobody hurries you.
You walk toward your Creator
with gifts in pure, empty hands.
The words are golden
their meaning is transparent,
it's as though you're saying them
for the first time.

If you don't catch on
that you should feel a little elevated,
you're not saying the sunset prayer.
The tune is sheer simplicity,
you're just lending a helping hand
to the sinking day.
It's a heavy responsibility.
You take a created day
and you slip it
into the archive of life,
where all our lived-out days are lying together.

The day is departing with a quiet kiss.
It lies open at your feet
while you stand saying the blessings.
You can't create anything yourself, but you
can lead the day to its end and see
clearly the smile of its going down.

See how whole it all is,
not diminished for a second,
how you age with the days
that keep dawning,
how you bring your lived-out day
as a gift to eternity.

—JACOB GLATSTEIN
Translated from the Yiddish by Ruth Whitman

Sources and Permissions

Every effort has been made to trace copyright holders of material in this book. The author apologizes if any work has been used without permission and would be glad to be told of anyone who has not been consulted.

Page xii: Rilke, Ranier Maria. *Letters to a Young Poet*. New York: W.W. Norton & Co., 1954.

Page 6: Kornfield, Jack. *The Eightfold Path for Householders*. Dharma Seed Tape Library. Used by permission of the author.

Page 15: Feldman, Christina and Jack Kornfield, eds. *Stories of the Spirit, Stories of the Heart*. New York: HarperCollins Publishers, 1991.

Page 18: Casals, Pablo and Albert E. Kahn. *Joys and Sorrows*. New York: Simon & Schuster, 1970.

Page 20: Moyer, Linda Lancione. "Listen" from *Christianity and Crisis*, March 3, 1986.

Page 21: Brown, Joseph Epes. *The Spiritual Legacy of the American Indian*. New York: Crossroad, 1982.

Page 23: Bly, Robert. *The Kabir Book*. Boston: Beacon Press, 1977. Copyright © 1971, 1977 by Robert Bly. Reprinted by permission of Beacon Press.

Page 34: Emanuel, Lynn. "Silence. She Is Six Years Old" from *The Dig*. Urbana-Champaign, Ill.: The University of Illinois Press, 1992. Copyright © 1992 by Lynn Emanuel. Used with the permission of the author and the University of Illinois Press.

Page 38: Oliver, Mary. "Poem" from *Dream Work*. New York: Atlantic Monthly Press, 1986. Copyright © 1986 by Mary Oliver. Reprinted by permission of Grove/Atlantic, Inc.

Page 43: Hanh, Thich Nhat. *Peace Is Every Step*. New York: Bantam Books, 1991. Copyright © 1991 by Thich Nhat Hanh. Used by permission of Bantam Books, a division of Bantam Doubleday Dell Publishing Group, Inc.

Page 44: Vanier, Jean. *Community and Growth*. New York: Paulist Press, 1979.

Page 50: Walker, Alice. "For Two Who Slipped Away Almost Entirely" from *Horses Make a Landscape Look More Beautiful*. Orlando, Fla.: Harcourt Brace Jovanovich, 1984. Copyright © 1984 by Alice Walker. Reprinted by permission of Harcourt Brace & Company.

Page 53: Brown, Joseph Epes. "Becoming Part of It" from *I Become Part of It*, D. M. Dooling and Paul Jordan-Smith, eds. New York: PARABOLA Books, 1989. Copyright © The Society for the Study of Myth and Tradition, Inc. Reprinted by permission of the author.

Page 57: Rinpoche, Sogyal. *The Tibetan Book of Living and Dying*. New York: HarperCollins, 1992.

Page 59: Suzuki, Daisetz Teitaro. *What Is Zen?* New York: Harper & Row, 1972.

Page 61: Shikibu, Izumi. "Watching the Moon" from *The Ink Dark Moon: Love Poems*, trans. Jane Hirschfield with Mariko Aratani. New York: Vintage Books, 1990. Copyright © 1990 by Jane Hirschfield and Mariko Aratani. Reprinted by permission of Vintage Books, a division of Random House, Inc.

Page 63: Kornfield, Jack. *A Path With Heart.* New York: Bantam Books, 1993.

Page 64: Lusseyran, Jacques. *And There Was Light.* Boston: Little, Brown & Co., 1963.

Page 79: Hanh, Thich Nhat. *Peace Is Every Step.* New York: Bantam Books, 1991.

Page 86: Mascaro, Juan, trans. *Dhammapada.* London: Penguin Books, 1973.

Page 90: Mar, Laureen. "My Mother, Who Came From China, Where She Never Saw Snow" from *The Third Woman: Minority Women Poets of the United States,* Dexter Fisher, ed. Boston: Houghton Mifflin Co., 1980. Copyright © 1977 by Laureen Mar. Used by permission of the author.

Page 97: Williams, Terry Tempest. *Pieces of White Shell.* New York: Charles Scribner's Sons, 1984. Copyright © 1983, 1984 by Terry Tempest Williams. Reprinted with the permission of Scribner, a division of Simon & Schuster.

Page 100: Easwaran, Eknath, ed. *God Makes the Rivers to Flow.* Petaluma, Calif.: Nilgiri Press, 1982. Copyright © 1982 by Nilgiri Press. Reprinted by permission of Nilgiri Press, Tomales, Calif. 94971.

Page 108: Rumi, Mathnawi I. Cited in *Living Presence,* Kabir Edmund Helminski. New York: Jeremy P. Tarcher, 1992.

Page 109: Dillard, Annie. *Pilgrim at Tinker Creek.* New York: Harper & Row, 1974.

Page 117: Roshi, Shunryu Suzuki. *Zen Mind, Beginner's Mind.* New York: Weatherhill, 1983.

Page 118: Easwaran, Eknath. *The Unstruck Bell.* Tomales, Calif.: Nilgiri Press, 1982. Copyright © 1982 by Nilgiri Press, Tomales, Calif. 94971.

Page 121: Nomura, Yushi. *Desert Wisdom.* New York: Image, 1984.

Page 122: Mechtild of Magdeburg. "Of all that God has shown me" from *Women in Praise of the Soul,* Jane Hirschfield, trans. New York: HarperCollins, 1994.

Page 125: Moeller, Eileen. "ten years ago." First appeared in *Cries of the Spirit,* Marilyn Sewell, ed. Boston: Beacon Press, 1991. Used by permission of the author.

Page 131: Oliver, Mary. "Wild Geese" from *Dream Work.* New York: Atlantic Monthly Press, 1986. Copyright © 1986 by Mary Oliver. Used by permission of Grove/Atlantic, Inc.

Page 136: Griffin, Susan. *Made From This Earth.* New York: Harper & Row, 1982.

Page 141: Shange, Ntozake. FOR COLORED GIRLS WHO HAVE CONSIDERED SUICIDE/WHEN THE RAINBOW IS ENUF. Copyright © 1975, 1976, 1977 by Ntozake Shange. Reprinted with the permission of Simon & Schuster.

Page 145: Oliver, Mary. "The Summer Day" from *House of Light.* Boston: Beacon Press, 1990. Copyright © 1990 by Mary Oliver. Reprinted by permission of Beacon Press.

Page 154: Chodron, Pema. *The Wisdom of No Escape.* Boston: Shambhala, 1991.

Page 156: Hanh, Thich Nhat. "The Art of Mindful Living." Boulder, Colo.: Soundstrue Productions, 1991.

Page 161: Ackerman, Diane. *A Natural History of the Senses.* New York: Vintage, 1991.

Page 163: Olds, Sharon. "35/10" from *The Dead and the Living.* New York: Alfred A. Knopf, Inc., 1989. Copyright © 1983 by Sharon Olds. Reprinted by permission of Alfred A. Knopf, Inc.

Page 165: Frankl, Victor. *Man's Search for Meaning.* New York: Washington Square Press, 1984.

Page 172: Goldstein, Joseph. *Insight Meditation.* Boston: Shambhala, 1993.

Page 174: Hillesum, Ette. *An Interrupted Life: The Diaries of Ette Hillesum.* New York: Pantheon, 1983.

Page 180: Merton, Thomas, trans. "Cutting Up an Ox" from *The Way of Chuang Tzu.* Boston: Shambhala, 1992. Copyright © 1965 by The Abbey of Gethsemani. Reprinted by permission of New Directions Publishing Corp.

Page 189: Dillard, Annie. *Pilgrim at Tinker Creek.* New York: Harper & Row, 1974.

Page 191: Romero, Levi. "It is the 14th of May, already the days for planting are just about over." Copyright © 1994 by Levi Romero. Reprinted by permission of *THE Magazine.*

Page 196: Gates, Barbara. "A Mama Raccoon in the Net of Indra." *Inquiring Mind,* Fall 1994.

Page 198: Snyder, Gary. "Just One Breath." *Tricycle,* vol. 1, no. 1, Fall 1991.

Page 199: Hanh, Thich Nhat. *Peace Is Every Step.* New York: Bantam Books, 1991.

Page 203: Thoreau, Henry David. *Walden.* New York: Signet/New American Library, 1960.

Page 206: Jung, C. G. "Commentary" from *The Secret of the Golden Flower: A Chinese Book of Life,* Richard Wilhelm and C. G. Jung, eds. Translated by Carl F. Baynes. New York: Harcourt Brace Jovanovich, 1962.

Page 208: Willard, Nancy. "How to Stuff a Pepper" from *Carpenter of the Sun.* New York: Liveright Publishing Corp., 1974. Copyright © 1974 by Nancy Willard. Reprinted by permission of Liveright Publishing Company.

Page 216: Lindbergh, Anne Morrow. *Gift From the Sea.* New York: Vintage Books, 1991.

Page 217: Rukeyser, Muriel. "A Little Stone in the Middle of the Road, in Florida" from *Out of Silence.* Evanston, Ill.: TriQuarterly Books, 1992. Copyright © William L. Rukeyser. Used by permission.

Page 221: Chodron, Pema. *The Wisdom of No Escape.* Boston: Shambhala, 1991.

Page 223: cummings, e. e. "i thank You God for most this amazing." Copyright © 1950, 1978, 1991 by the Trustees for the e. e. cummings Trust. Copyright © 1979 by George James Firmage, from COMPLETE POEMS: 1904-1962 by e. e. cummings, edited by George J. Firmage. Reprinted by permission of Liveright Publishing Corporation.

Page 227: Barks, Coleman, trans. *Feeling the Shoulder of the Lion*. Putney, Vt.: Threshold Books, 1991.

Page 227: Hanh, Thich Nhat. *Peace Is Every Step*. New York: Bantam Books, 1991.

Page 229: Price, Reynolds. *A Whole New Life*. New York: Atheneum, 1994.

Page 230: Sexton, Anne. "Welcome Morning" from *The Awful Rowing Toward God*. Copyright © 1975 by Loring Conant, Jr., executor of the estate. Reprinted by permission of Houghton Mifflin Co. All rights reserved.

Page 240: Walker, Alice. "Medicine" from *Once*. Orlando, Fla.: Harcourt Brace Jovanovich, 1968. Copyright © 1968 by Alice Walker. Reprinted by permission of Harcourt Brace & Company.

Page 244: Easwaran, Eknath. *The Little Lamp*. Tomales, Calif.: Nilgiri Press, 1982. Copyright © 1982 by Nilgiri Press. Reprinted by permission.

Page 245: Dillard, Annie. *The Writing Life*. New York: HarperCollins Publishers, 1989.

Page 246: Vanier, Jean. *Community and Growth*. New York: Paulist Press, 1979.

Page 250: Gilbert, Jack. "Finding Something" from *The Great Fires*. New York: Alfred A. Knopf, Inc., 1994. Copyright © 1994 by Jack Gilbert. Reprinted by permission of Alfred A. Knopf, Inc.

Page 256: Steindl-Rast, David. *Gratefulness, the Heart of Prayer*. New York: Paulist Press, 1984.

Page 257: Salzberg, Sharon. *Loving-Kindness: The Revolutionary Art of Happiness*. Boston: Shambhala, 1995.

Page 258: Coles, Robert. *The Call of Service*. New York: Houghton Mifflin Co., 1994. Copyright © 1993 by Robert Coles. Reprinted by permission of Houghton Mifflin Co. All rights reserved.

Page 265: Salzberg, Sharon. *Loving-Kindness: The Revolutionary Art of Happiness*. Boston: Shambhala, 1995.

Page 267: Uhlein, Gabrielle, ed. *Meditations with Hildegard of Bingen*. Santa Fe, N. Mex.: Bear & Co., 1983.

Page 271: Goldstein, Joseph. *The Experience of Insight*. Boston: Shambhala, 1976.

Page 275: Levine, Stephen and Ondrea. *Embracing the Beloved*. New York: Doubleday, 1995. Copyright © 1995 by Stephen and Ondrea Levine. Used by permission of Doubleday Books, a division of Bantam Doubleday Dell Publishing Group, Inc.

Page 278: Williams, David. "Privacy" from *Traveling Mercies* by David Williams. Farmington, Maine: Alice James Books, 1993. Copyright © 1993 by Alice James Books. First published in *The Atlantic Monthly*, copyright © 1985. Used by permission of the author.

Page 283: Glatstein, Joseph. "Praying the Sunset Prayer" from *The Selected Poems of Joseph Glatstein*, Ruth Whitman, trans. New York: October House, 1972. Copyright © 1972 by Ruth Whitman. Used by permission.

About the Author

❖

WAYNE MULLER is an ordained minister and therapist and founder of Bread for the Journey. A graduate of Harvard Divinity School, he is Senior Scholar at the Fetzer Institute and a fellow of the Institute of Noetic Sciences. He also runs the Institute for Engaged Spirituality and gives lectures and retreats nationwide. He is the author of *Legacy of the Heart,* a *New York Times* bestseller, and *Sabbath: Finding Rest, Renewal, and Delight in Our Busy Lives.* He lives with his family in northern California.

A portion of the proceeds from this book will go to Bread for the Journey, which supports the efforts of local people serving the poor, hungry, and others in need.

There are now more than twelve chapters of Bread for the Journey nationwide. For locations and for information about starting a Bread for the Journey chapter in your community, please write or call us:

Bread for the Journey
267 Miller Avenue
Mill Valley, CA 94941
Phone: (415)383-4600
E-mail: bread@slip.net
Hyperlink: http://www.breadforthejourney.org

You can also contact us for a list of Wayne Muller's retreats, workshops, books, and tapes.

Praise for
Sabbath: Finding Rest, Renewal, and Delight in Our Busy Lives

"This is a book that may save your life. In a culture where few question that more is better, *Sabbath* offers a surprising direction for healing to anyone who has ever glimpsed emptiness at the heart of a busy and productive life."
—Rachel Naomi Remen, author of *Kitchen Table Wisdom* and *My Grandfather's Blessings*

"Wayne Muller's call to remember the Sabbath is not only rich, wise, and poetic, it may well be the only salvation for body and soul in a world gone crazy with busyness and stress." —Joan Borysenko, author of *Minding the Body, Mending the Mind* and *A Woman's Book of Life*

"Muller's insights are applicable within a broad spectrum of faiths and will appeal to a wide range of readers."
—*Publishers Weekly*

"One of the best spiritual books of the year."
—*Spirituality and Health*

"This is a superb book—but more than superb, it is a necessary one. Wayne Muller's message is one of the wisest treatments of stress that I have ever come across."
—Caroline Myss, Ph.D., author of *Anatomy of the Spirit*